Robert Louis Stevenson
Reconsidered

Also by William B. Jones, Jr.

Classics Illustrated: A Cultural History, with Illustrations
(McFarland, 2002)

Robert Louis Stevenson Reconsidered

New Critical Perspectives

Edited by
WILLIAM B. JONES, JR.

McFarland & Company, Inc., Publishers
Jefferson, North Carolina, and London

Library of Congress Cataloguing-in-Publication Data

Robert Louis Stevenson reconsidered : new critical perspectives /
    edited by William B. Jones, Jr.
        p.   cm.
    Includes bibliographical references and index.

    ISBN 0-7864-1399-9 (softcover : 50# alkaline paper) ∞

    1. Stevenson, Robert Louis, 1850–1894—Criticism and
interpretation.   2. Scotland—In literature.   3. Oceania—
In literature.   I. Jones, William B., 1950–
PR5496 .R59 2003
828'.809—dc21

                                        2002014547

British Library cataloguing data are available

On the cover: Woodcut portrait of Robert Louis Stevenson, *The
Bookman* (1913).

Manufactured in the United States of America

*McFarland & Company, Inc., Publishers
    Box 611, Jefferson, North Carolina 28640
    www.mcfarlandpub.com*

For David Daiches

Contents

BIOGRAPHY, POPULAR CULTURE, AND PERSONAL RESPONSE

Preface

Critical interest in Robert Louis Stevenson has never been greater. New editions of the author's works, from the poems to the travel writing, from the Scottish novels to the South Seas tales, now appear under the imprints of Penguin Classics, Oxford World's Classics, Canongate Classics, and Modern Library Classics. Scottish scholars are busy reclaiming Stevenson as a major figure in their national literature. An American specialist seeks to recover the author's original intent and establish textual integrity. Stevenson's relation to the origins of anthropology and his impact on popular culture are topics of current interest. French and Italian studies have been published in recent years, attesting to the writer's transnational appeal. RLS is not only fashionable again—he's positively threatening to become academically respectable.

Since his death in 1894, the critical fortunes and misfortunes of Robert Louis Stevenson have become part of the author's legend. From the heights of near idolatry in the last decade of the nineteenth century, his reputation sank almost irretrievably after the First World War. The romance of his life and his untimely end came to overshadow his works, which were relegated to the nursery, no distinction apparently being drawn between "The Swing" and *The Beach of Falesá*. Stevenson actually never lost his popularity with readers, as the countless editions and numerous film versions of *Treasure Island* and *Dr. Jekyll and Mr. Hyde* attest. But such between-the-wars arbiters of taste as Virginia Woolf no longer considered him a serious writer. A profound cultural irony resulted—this herald of literary modernism in the guise of a romantic fabulist, this most conscious of literary artists, this most anti–Victorian of Victorian writers was deemed too unsophisticated for mature consideration.

David Daiches, to whom this volume is dedicated, helped to change all that. In his groundbreaking postwar study, *Robert Louis Stevenson*

(1947), a slender volume numbering fewer than 200 pages, the Scottish critic and man of letters recast the terms of critical discourse. Daiches argued that the Scottish identity of the author was central to an understanding of the character of his work. He asserted, in the face of received modernist dogma, that Stevenson's "greatest achievement was to use nostalgia dramatically, to suppress all personal emotion while utilizing that emotion in serious (sometimes tragic) fiction."[1] A critical vocabulary had been lacking in Stevenson studies, which had been dominated by either anecdotal memoir or iconoclastic assault—neither mode had much to do with the writer's writings. Thanks to David Daiches, new approaches were possible.

Four years later, J.C. Furnas produced one of the greatest of literary lives, *Voyage to Windward*, bringing the same spirit of open-minded inquiry to Stevensonian biography that had graced Daiches's critical study. Over the next few decades, several outstanding biographies appeared, chief among them *Robert Louis Stevenson: A Life Study* (1980)[2] by David Daiches's daughter Jenni Calder, renowned in her own right as an interpreter of Scottish history and culture. But, except for a couple of books that appeared in the 1960s and a major study and restoration of Stevenson's *Beach of Falesá* by Barry Menikoff (1984), scant attention was paid to the writer as writer.

As the 100th anniversary of the author's death approached, several biographies, a seven-volume edition of letters (and a one-volume selection), and other works appeared. Richard Dury of the University of Bergamo, Italy, established the Robert Louis Stevenson Web Site. And the worldwide community of Stevenson scholars began to realize that they were much larger than anyone had believed.

During the year 2000, the sesquicentennial of Stevenson's birth, three conferences were held in honor of the occasion: the first at the University of Stirling in Scotland, the second in Normandy, France, and the third in Little Rock, Arkansas. An international audience attended each program. This book grew out of the third event, *RLS 2000: A Celebration of 150 Years of Robert Louis Stevenson in Literature and Popular Culture*. Sponsored by the Central Arkansas Library System and held at the Main Library's Darragh Center for Intellectual Freedom, the four-day festival (9–12 November 2000) featured the presentation of academic papers by six Stevenson scholars; the screening of the 1931 Rouben Mamoulian film of *Dr. Jekyll and Mr. Hyde*; and the staging of a readers' theatre production based on a broad sampling of Stevenson's writings and dramatic adaptations of *Dr. Jekyll and Mr. Hyde*, *The Bottle Imp*, and *The Beach of Falesá*.

Five of the essays in this volume were delivered at the Little Rock symposium. Those papers are by keynote speaker Jenni Calder, author of *Robert Louis Stevenson: A Life Study*; Eric Massie of the University of Stirling, organizer of the Stirling conference; Katherine Linehan of Oberlin College, editor of the Norton Critical Edition of *Dr. Jekyll and Mr. Hyde*; Richard Ambrosini of the University of Milan, author of an Italian-language study of Stevenson; and Jason Pierce of Mars Hill College, a perceptive young Stevenson expert. A sixth participant, Barry Menikoff of the University of Hawaii, editor of original-text editions of *Kidnapped* and *The Beach of Falesá*, chose to contribute a different paper. The present editor, who served as chair of the Little Rock conference, solicited essays from two scholars who wished to attend but were unable because of academic schedule conflicts: Richard Dury, creator of the Robert Louis Stevenson Web Site, and Gillian Cookson of the University of Durham, biographer of Stevenson's mentor, Fleeming Jenkin. Additional essays were sought from Olena M. Turnbull of the University of Tulsa on Stevenson's friendship with an English admirer and from Karen Steele, a Stevenson editor who lectured on her travels at "RLS 2000" and who offers an enthusiast's perspective. And the editor contributed a piece reflecting the impact of Stevenson on popular culture in the form of comic-book adaptations.

Scholars in Australia and New Zealand, wishing to honor David Daiches, responded to a call for papers. Alan Sandison, who has taught at universities in Scotland and Australia, has provided a witty and illuminating study of *The Dynamiter* as a modernist—or even postmodernist—assault upon the citadel of realism. Another Australian contributor, Graham Tulloch of Flinders University, examines Stevenson's use of both Scottish and South Seas islands in his fiction. New Zealander John Cairney surveys Stevenson's unsuccessful theatrical collaborations with William Ernest Henley.

Impressed with two recently published articles, the editor received permission from the authors and the journals in which the pieces first appeared to include the essays in this collection. Oliver S. Buckton of Florida Atlantic University examines the coded significance of burial and reanimation in Stevenson's *Wrong Box* and other works, while Ann C. Colley of Buffalo State University explores the landscape of nostalgia in *A Child's Garden of Verses*.

The first group of essays in this volume consists of contemporary critical overviews, beginning with an assessment of the Stevensonian imagination by Jenni Calder and the author's literary theory by Richard Ambrosini. In the second section, three scholars examine the many-faceted *Strange Case of Dr. Jekyll and Mr. Hyde*, unquestionably the focal point of academic interest in the author's work. Other works—*An Inland Voyage*

(Stevenson's first published book and an example of his travel writing), *A Child's Garden of Verses* (his best-known poetry), *The Dynamiter* (a neglected but extraordinary performance), *The Master of Ballantrae* (perhaps his finest novel), and *Prayers Written at Vailima* (a devotional work from the years in Samoa)—are the subjects of essays in the third section. Views through the lenses of biography, popular culture, and personal response fill the fourth section.

It is hoped that the essays presented here will reflect something of the scope of Robert Louis Stevenson's achievement and the range of current critical response. It is also hoped that this volume will carry forward into a new century the good work begun more than fifty years ago by David Daiches.

— *William B. Jones, Jr.*

NOTES

1. David Daiches, *Robert Louis Stevenson: A Revaluation* (Norfolk, Conn.: New Directions Books, 1947), p. 187.
2. Jenni Calder, *Robert Louis Stevenson: A Life Study* (New York: Oxford University Press, 1980).

Acknowledgment: The editor wishes to thank Robyn D. Rektor for her assistance in proofreading the text.—WBJ

CRITICAL OVERVIEWS

The Eyeball of the Dawn: Can We Trust Stevenson's Imagination?

Jenni Calder

I slept that night, as was my somewhat dangerous practice, on deck upon the cockpit bench. A stir at last awoke me, to see all the eastern heaven dyed with a faint orange, the binnacle lamp already dulled against the brightness of the day, and the steersman leaning eagerly across the wheel. "There it is, sir!" he cried, and pointed in the very eyeball of the dawn.[1]

This is Robert Louis Stevenson in the South Pacific. In these few sentences he is conveying danger, wonder, excitement. What lies ahead? What does the steersman see? Even without context we can guess it is land, but why such eagerness? Is it just the first sight of land after many days at sea, or is there something more? The sun is rising—light, promise. From one sentence to the next the "faint orange" of the eastern sky becomes first "the brightness of the day" and then is concentrated into "the eyeball of the dawn." Anticipation intensified, and at the same time blinded. The eye of the sun looking into the eye of the beholder.

Some years before, Stevenson had been writing about the art of fiction. Fiction, he argued in his essay "A Humble Remonstrance," requires that "you half shut your eyes against the dazzle and confusion of reality."[2] Art can't appropriately express the real world—life is too complex, too confused. It has to select, to contain. Experience is reduced to a painting or a paragraph, an approximation. So what makes literature worthwhile? Why do we need it? And I believe, and Stevenson certainly believed, that we do need it. There are a lot of answers to that question, but I'm going to suggest just two. The first is that we need that containment. Literature may not be able to accommodate the full ambiguity and discombobulation of reality but it can give it a shape and a sequence that help us to deal with life. The second is that that shape and sequence need the transforming power of the imagination. You can't be a good storyteller without it.

The paragraph I quoted isn't fiction. It's Stevenson writing about his experience of sailing in the Pacific—he produced a series of articles which he later revised for his *In the South Seas*. But the imagination is already at work. It is the imagination that gives us metaphor—"the eyeball of the dawn." And notice that Stevenson writes here "pointed *in* the eyeball of the dawn" not "*to* the eyeball of the dawn." That little preposition makes all the difference. It makes the scene fragile, subsumed by the rising sun, the dull light of the binnacle lamp ineffectual against the dazzle of reality. The yacht *Casco*, which has survived storms and avoided reefs, and the two men on deck, are revealed in all their isolation and vulnerability.

The South Seas were of course providing material for fiction, too. Arising directly from what Stevenson encountered and observed in his voyagings came his novel *The Ebb-Tide* (1893). Here is the first sight of an island that has no existence in the charts: "a greenish, filmy iridescence could be discerned floating like smoke on the pale heavens." With thoughts of pearls, or at the very least of "fish, and cocoanuts, and native stuff," the trio of dubious characters who have taken charge of a quarantined schooner make for the island. "And the schooner's head was laid for that elusive glimmer in the sky, which began already to pale in lustre and diminish in size, as the stain of breath vanishes from a window pane."[3]

The following morning the island gradually takes on substance, but first Stevenson lets us watch the sunrise:

> A brightening came in the east; then a wash of some ineffable, faint, nameless hue between crimson and silver; and then coals of fire. These glimmered a while on the sea line, and seemed to brighten and darken and spread out, and still the night and the stars reigned undisturbed; it was as though a spark should catch and glow and creep along the foot of some heavy and almost incombustible wall-hanging, and the room itself be scarce menaced. Yet a little after, and the whole east glowed with gold and scarlet, and the hollow of heaven was filled with the daylight.
>   The isle—the undiscovered, the scarce-believed in—now lay before them and close aboard: and Herrick thought that never in

his dreams had he beheld anything more strange and delicate ...
so slender it seemed amidst the outrageous breakers, so frail and
pretty, he would scarce have wondered to see it sink and disappear without a sound, and the waves close smoothly over its
descent.[4]

This is the prelude to the second part of the novel, which explores layers
of illusion and reality—visual, psychological, moral. You can tell, I think,
even if you haven't read the novel and know what Herrick and his two
confederates encounter, that the reader is being prepared for something
elusive, something baffling, even sinister. I would almost say beyond
description, except Stevenson describes it for us so precisely, with such
stunning clarity. And, as in the earlier quote, land, delicate and frail, is
overwhelmed by the combined power of the ocean and the dawn.

But what I want to draw attention to here is the blend of penetrating observation and the imagination, of meticulous articulation and
metaphor—those precise colors, "crimson and silver," and then "coals of
fire"; the care with which Stevenson details the way a wall-hanging might
burn in order to provide just the right analogy to help the reader visualize what Herrick sees. This is at the core of Stevenson's writing: he wants
the reader to see exactly what he sees, and imagination is the route through
which our visual and cognitive horizons are opened up. It is a bridge
between writer, reader and the players on the page. "Herrick thought that
never in his dreams had he beheld anything more strange and delicate...."
This tells us something important about Herrick; it reinforces our perception of him as more aware, more sensitive, more imaginative, than his
two companions. We already know that he is familiar with Beethoven and
Virgil; in other words, he is middle-class and educated. By suggesting that
he dreams of what is strange and delicate, Stevenson lends his character
something of himself, and reinforces the reader's understanding of him
as the story's pivotal character.

We know that Stevenson himself had dreamt of voyaging in the South
Seas long before he found himself on the edge of the Pacific Ocean. A
quick glance at *A Child's Garden of Verses* reveals a preoccupation with
voyages and journeys—"Where go the boats?" "I would like to rise and
go/Where the golden apples grow"[5]—which reflects his childhood play.
Familiar as he was as a youngster with the North Sea and Scotland's rugged
coasts and formidable islands, skerries and tidal races, it was dreams, in
other words, imagination, which led him to create Treasure Island. Just
as in *The Ebb-Tide*, Stevenson's descriptions of the island are extremely
precise, which has led many people to believe that he is describing a real
rather than an invented place. The configuration of the hills, the rivers,

the trees are detailed and identified. What is interesting is that little of it conforms to a stereotypical picture of a romantic tropical island.

The *Hispaniola* is becalmed and Jim is gazing out at the island:

> Grey-coloured woods covered a large part of the surface. This even tint was indeed broken up by streaks of yellow sandbreak in the lower lands, and by many tall trees of the pine family, out-topping the others—some singly, some in clumps; but the general colouring was uniform and sad. The hills ran up clear above the vegetation in spires of naked rock. All were strangely shaped, and the Spy-glass, which was by three or four hundred feet the tallest on the island, was likewise the strangest in configuration, running up sheer from almost every side, then suddenly cut off at the top like a pedestal to put a statue on.[6]

At this time Stevenson's knowledge of islands was confined to Scotland, and although he goes on to describe pounding surf, cliffs, fog, all of which he knew well from accompanying his father on lighthouse inspection trips, this is very different from, for example, Erraid off Mull, which he describes in "Memoirs of an Islet":

> ...the rude disorder of the boulders, the inimitable seaside brightness of the air, the brine and the iodine, the lap of the billows among the weedy reefs, the sudden springing up of a great run of dashing surf....[7]

Even if taken totally out of context the description of Treasure Island would soon have been identified as exotic by Scottish readers. The sun is "bright and hot," the vegetation is denser and "the foliage ... had a kind of poisonous brightness," there is a "peculiar stagnant smell." When Jim goes ashore the foreign-ness of the island unfolds. The "grey, melancholy woods" are ominous, the plants are strange, there are rattlesnakes, a marsh is "steaming in the strong sun."[8] Stevenson is blending first-hand experience and second-hand knowledge, the latter from the adventure stories he devoured as a boy. Acting on all this, like a weaver's shuttle creating a pattern out of warp and weft, is the imagination.

Treasure Island is anonymous and unlocated, but in many ways it is more tangible than Attwood's island in *The Ebb-Tide*. They are both sinister places. *Treasure Island* subverts the adventure story, because Jim's appetite for the escapade has been shattered by his newly acquired knowledge of the true nature of Long John Silver: "From that first look onward, I hated the very thought of Treasure Island."[9] The enterprise has gone sour. Very soon, we move from the sinister to the malevolent:

> Far away out in the marsh there arose, all of a sudden, a sound like a cry of anger, then another on the back of it; and then one horrid, long-drawn scream. The rocks of the Spy-glass re-echoed it a score of times; the whole troop of marsh-birds rose again, darkening heaven, with a simultaneous whirr; and long after that death yell was still ringing in my brain, silence had re-established its empire, and only the rustle of the redescending birds and the boom of the distant surges disturbed the languour of the afternoon.[10]

Again, Stevenson wants the reader to see and hear what he sees and hears. He succeeds. He imprints that sequence of sounds in the reader's mind — a cry of anger, then another; a scream; the echo "a score of times"; the whirr of the birds; the sound of the scream ringing in Jim's brain; the rustle of the descending birds; the boom of the surf. Do we trust what Stevenson's imagination offers us here? How can we not, when he presents it with such meticulous authority. If Jim had been a news reporter providing an eyewitness account we would trust it less, because we would sense how the witness was being affected by danger, fear, the heat of the moment. At the same time, the storyteller of *Treasure Island* is showing us how Jim, in the process of losing his innocence, is beginning to understand danger and fear. "I do not know what it rightly is to faint, but I do know that for the next little while the whole world swam away from before me in a whirling mist."[11] The world Jim thought he knew has vanished. He is in a moral as well as a physical environment that he does not recognize.

The storyteller's sleight of hand convinces us of authenticity, within the territory of the narrative, that is both pragmatic and psychological. Stevenson came to fiction relatively late, in that he had already published several volumes of non-fiction before he began to turn his hand increasingly to fiction. He himself tells us how he served his apprenticeship as a writer, imitating the styles of writers he admired, "playing the sedulous ape," as he practiced his skills.[12] We can see books such as *Travels with a Donkey* and *Edinburgh, Picturesque Notes*, and perhaps particularly *The Amateur Emigrant* and *Across the Plains*, as the first stages on the road to becoming a great novelist. By 1877 Stevenson was writing short stories, and the following year Leslie Stephen, then editor of the *Cornhill Magazine*, had identified his potential, which he expressed in a rather remarkable letter to Stevenson himself:

> It has occurred to me lately that you might be able to help me in an ever recurring difficulty. I am constantly looking out ... for a new novelist. I should like to find a Walter Scott or Dickens or

even a Miss Bronte or G. Eliot. Somehow the coming man or
woman has not yet been revealed. Meanwhile I cannot help thinking that, if you would seriously put your hand to such a piece of
work you would be able—I will not say to rival the success of
Waverley or Pickwick but—to write something really good &
able....[13]

At this time Stevenson had published only *An Inland Voyage* and a few
essays and stories. It would be five years before he embarked on a long
piece of fiction, and that was *Treasure Island*, ostensibly for boys. But the
direction in which his writing was taking him was clear long before. Here
he is on Calton Hill in Edinburgh, looking out towards Leith and the Firth
of Forth:

Leith camps on the seaside with her forest of masts; Leith roads
are full of ships at anchor; the sun picks out the white pharos
upon Inchkeith Island; the Firth extends on either hand from the
Ferry to the May; the towns of Fifeshire sit, each in its bank of bil-
lowing smoke, along the opposite coast; and the hills inclose the
view, except to the farthest east, where the haze of the horizon rests
upon the open sea.[14]

It is the same trademark blend of precise observation and metaphor that
we find in *Treasure Island* and *The Ebb-Tide*. I'm not saying that only writers of fiction adopt this tactic. I am suggesting that it is evidence of the
imagination at work, and the imagination tends to lead the writer to make
things up—which is of course precisely why we have to ask ourselves
whether we can trust it.

The spurs to Stevenson's movement into fiction were France and
America. Stevenson grew up in Edinburgh and in many respects felt himself to be captive there. Escape from the city of his birth was a theme that
played throughout his childhood and youth. The exercise that this gave
his imagination was crucial to his development and aspirations as a writer
but there were huge inhibitions. There was the physical containment of
his ill health, the relentless grip of history, and the heavy hand of Victorian and Presbyterian moral containment. When he began to go to France
as a young man, he escaped the latter at least. When he went to America
in 1879, to join if he possibly could the woman with whom he had
embarked on an affair in France, he was breaking free in a more unorthodox way, and it had a striking effect on his writing.

What Stevenson experienced and witnessed in the long journey from
the Clyde to California was a rawness of human relationship and activity

with little to disguise or mollify it. There is an edge to the writing in *The Amateur Emigrant* and *Across the Plains,* an absence of metaphor, as if in recognition that it is inappropriate or inadequate. Although he began work on a novel called *A Vendetta in the West,* soon abandoned, there is little sense in *Across the Plains* that Stevenson is inspired by his journey. True, he is exhausted and uncomfortable most of the time, and ill some of the time, but as the train rolls through the territory of the adventurous American West he is depressed by the landscape, the racism, the rudeness. Only the romance of the railroad itself relieves the emptiness.

> [W]hen the day came, it was to shine upon the same broken and unsightly quarter of the world. Mile upon mile, and not a tree, a bird or a river. Only down the long, sterile canyons, the train shot hooting and awoke the resting echo. That train was the one piece of life in all the deadly land; it was the one actor; the one spectacle fit to be observed in this paralysis of man and nature.

He goes on to describe the "roaring, impromptu cities, full of gold and lust and death," "Chinese pirates" working alongside "border ruffians and broken men from Europe," and what he calls the "epical turmoil" of the invasion of the West, and adds:

> [I]t seems to me ... as if this railway were the one typical achievement of the age in which we live, as if it brought together into one plot all the ends of the world and all the degrees of social rank, and offered to some great writer the busiest, the most extended and the most varied subject for an enduring literary work. If it be romance, if it be contrast, if it be heroism that we require, what was Troy town to this?[15]

It was a romance that Stevenson did not write, and perhaps he abandoned *A Vendetta in the West* because he was not quite ready for the blend of reality and imagination that it required. But that would come. (It is interesting, incidentally, that Stevenson enthusiasts can hire a donkey and retrace Stevenson's footsteps in the Cevennes, but no one, so far as I know, has tried to replicate the experience of crossing the Plains.)

Landlocked desert was not a source of inspiration for Stevenson: he needed mountains and oceans. But the experience of America, the experience of sharing the condition of a displaced underclass, embedded itself deeply. It expanded his frame of reference; it gave a new rigor to his style, as several have noted; it also began the process of liberating his imagination. It wasn't just distance that helped him engage with his native land in fictional terms, it was also experience of a world that was without the weight of history and tradition that he could not escape from in Scotland.

Scotland was a hard taskmaster. Its geography and landscape, the relentlessness of its history, the moral rigor of the Calvinism which distrusted the imagination side by side with a rich tradition of storytelling: there were contradictions that were as likely to dam as to release the flow of narrative. As a child Stevenson embarked on imaginary voyages, as a young man he saw the steam locomotive as an emblem of escape. Going to America altered his perspective on sea voyages and railroad journeys but it did not kill the dream.

What that first trip to the United States highlighted was the need for Stevenson, as a writer, to match the imagination with experience. He had always been aware of it—why else did he lurk with his notebook in the dark corners of Edinburgh's underworld establishments? Those needs, as much as the search for health, drew him eventually to the Pacific. Here is the beach at Monterey:

> The waves which lap so quietly about the jetties of Monterey grow louder and larger in the distance; you can see the breakers leaping high and white by day; and at night, the outline of the shore is traced in transparent silver by the moonlight and the flying foam; and from all round, even in quiet weather, the low, distant, thrilling roar of the Pacific hangs over the coast and the adjacent country like smoke above a battle.[16]

Everywhere he goes around Monterey he is aware of "the haunting presence of the ocean" and hears "the voice of the Pacific." Nine years later he was getting to know that ocean rather more intimately.

By that time, 1888, Stevenson was well known as a writer of fiction. He had put his imagination to the test, perhaps most strikingly and provocatively in *Strange Case of Dr. Jekyll and Mr. Hyde*. It was a best seller, but there were those who were disturbed by the book. His friend John Addington Symonds was one. "I am trembling under the magician's wand of your fancy," he wrote to Stevenson, "and rebelling against it with the scorn of a soul that hates to be contaminated with the mere picture of victorious evil." Symonds did not want to trust Stevenson's imagination, because he could not accept the view that evil was inevitably the consequence of released constraint. "Our only chance seems to me to be to maintain, against all appearances, that evil can never in no way be victorious."[17] Symonds felt that Stevenson had imagined this scenario, almost willfully it is implied. Well, of course he did. But it represented an interpretation of human nature, an interpretation that was a continuing process throughout Stevenson's fiction. In the South Seas, the process led into deeper, murkier, and more ambivalent waters.

Stevenson had a particular talent for imagining life before living it. Several of the passages I have already quoted show how this talent alerts his senses in a particularly receptive way. It is an essential part of his creativity. This alertness in turn informed the imagination and results in a symbiosis between the observed and the invented which I believe is particularly evident in the writing of Stevenson's last years.

It is tempting to see the Pacific Ocean itself as a metaphor of liberation. Here is the schooner in *The Ebb-Tide* carrying her trio of deadbeats away from the ignominy of being "on the beach" in Tahiti: "[T]he schooner meanwhile slipt like a racer through the pass, and met the long sea of the open ocean with a souse of spray." "No more Tahiti for me," says the captain. He and Herrick look astern:

> The fair island was unfolding mountain top on mountain top;
> Eimeo, on the port board, lifted her splintered pinnacles; and still
> the schooner raced to the open sea.
>   "Think!" cried the captain with a gesture, "yesterday morn-
> ing I danced for my breakfast like a poodle dog."[18]

Freedom: freedom from the need to conform, and freedom from rejection. But at sea you need discipline and direction. Shortly afterwards the captain is poring over the chart plotting a course through the Dangerous Archipelago. He has to think about currents, tides, weather, submerged threats. And the only way he can test direction is by landfall. In *The Ebb-Tide* that landfall is on an island that should not exist. Is the chart wrong? Have measurement and calculation let them down? Are they wrong? Has their lack of discipline led them astray? And the layers of metaphor are exposed. The concepts of direction and of both inner and externally imposed discipline are at the heart of this story.

Stevenson never detached himself from the hold of Victorian Scotland and the great weight of its past—he did not wish to. His travels if anything strengthened his identity as a Scot—he wrote in his essay "A Scot Abroad" of how distance and foreign places etched more sharply both his own Scottishness and a positive perception of that of others,[19] and it is in the Pacific that he completes *The Master of Ballantrae*, begins *Weir of Hermiston*, and writes his most evocative poetry about his native land. But the Pacific was nevertheless a liberation and a source of new forms of creative tension. There is an engagement with experience and the environment, an immediacy, an awareness of issues. He becomes involved; he is no longer the observer making notes.

This engagement is reflected in his concern for an expropriated Polynesia, and also in his fascination with the effects in the expropriators. All around him were examples of what had already commanded the attention of his fiction: individuals transplanted from their customary environment and cut off from the social and ethical framework that normally sustained them: Jim in *Treasure Island*, David Balfour in *Kidnapped*. Out of his Pacific voyages came two of his best pieces of fiction which brought a new complexity to these explorations: *The Beach of Falesá* and *The Ebb-Tide*. They both enabled Stevenson to explore the territory that most strongly attracted him, the territory of human behavior with all masks and disguises stripped away—Mr. Hyde territory. The hero of *The Beach of Falesá* works out his own moral salvation, imperfectly but at least reasonably honest. Herrick in *The Ebb-Tide* is left with no choice but to face himself and recognize weakness, his own and that of his companions. In the process he acknowledges the appeal of anything that shields him from the unpalatable truth that he controls his own life. In the context of Stevenson's own Calvinist upbringing, this examination of personal responsibility is particularly resonant.

Herrick finds on Attwood's island an abandoned heap of cables, windlasses, anchors, "a whole curiosity shop of sea curios," fragments of ships and voyages and lives.

> Two wrecks at least must have contributed to this random heap
> of lumber; and as Herrick looked upon it, it seemed to him as if
> the two ships' companies were there on guard, and he heard the
> tread of feet and whisperings, and saw with the tail of his eye the
> commonplace ghosts of sailormen.[20]

Not treasure, but wreckage—but perhaps *Treasure Island's* treasure is also wreckage? A metaphor here for moral as well as physical disintegration—for this is the detritus of an illegal pearl fishery, of exploitation, the destruction of a traditional way of life, and the destruction by disease and violence of the people themselves—a destruction which Stevenson commented on consistently in his writing on the South Seas, drawing analogies with the demolition of Highland tradition and the Gaelic language in Scotland. What Herrick is looking at, augmented by what his imagination is furnishing, are the relics of the expropriators. They are telling him that the values and traditions of the expropriators as well as of the expropriated are damaged.

As Herrick gazes on these relics, a voice behind him says, "Junk ... only old junk."[21] Similarly, the cast-offs of civilization, like Herrick himself, are junk. Yet a romance attaches to it and them. Like objects in a museum, they have a tantalizing reality, cut off from their origins, displaced, yet with the ghosts of some other function, some other life, clinging to them. They are wreckage, but perhaps also salvage.

The erosions of traditional island life also produced wreckage, as Stevenson's Polynesian stories *The Isle of Voices* and *The Bottle Imp* illustrate. In both, the protagonists are caught between the power of tradition and the fragmenting grip of imperialist advance and the corruption that came in its wake. Stevenson's sensitivity to this was part of his inheritance. Scotland helped him to see and understand the Pacific, just as the Pacific sharpened his way of looking at Scotland. At Tautira on Tahiti, he swapped stories with his host Ori a Ori: "[T]he black bull's head of Stirling (a signal at a royal banquet for the annihilation of two challengers to the throne) procured me the legend of Rahero; and what I knew of the Cluny Macphersons, or of the Appin Stewarts enabled me to learn, and helped me to understand, about the Tevas of Tahiti."[22] He goes on to say that a sense of kinship is essential to mutual trust and understanding; it takes imagination to recognize kinship below the surfaces of things that look very different.

In Scotland, Stevenson had found it difficult to confront the fragmentations of what he called "the commercial age" in his writing. Except in *Jekyll and Hyde*, he looked to the past to enable him to deal with the confusions of the present. In the Pacific, he cannot do this, or only to a limited to extent. The present forces itself upon him with an urgency that he cannot escape, indeed, that he welcomes. But without the groundwork of his earlier fiction it is unlikely that he could have handled the seductive, insistent environment of the Pacific. The dynamic juxtapositions of *Kidnapped* and *Jekyll and Hyde*, political, psychological, cultural, enabled him to tackle much more complex and less definable probings of moral positioning. *The Master of Ballantrae*, begun in New York State and finished in Hawaii, founded on that quintessential split of Scotland's historic personality, the 1745 Jacobite Rising, initiates the process of throwing all easy definitions into doubt. Stevenson's explorations of morality as subjective and personal are a profound challenge to both religious and political establishments.

In the Pacific, Stevenson was experiencing an environment where he confronted the present without being burdened by the past. Europe wasn't far enough away from Scotland; nor was the USA. The perspective 10,000 miles distance gave him on Scotland is marked. He tackled head on issues that had played such a powerful part in the shaping of his own consciousness. In *Weir of Hermiston* the examination of a father-son relationship, of the clash between the authority of experience and raw idealism, of dark traditions of violence embodied in folklore and echoed in landscape, has a quality almost of urgency. I would argue that the Pacific contributed to this. Distance and the new-found ability to write with immediacy of direct, living incident were crucial. He was no longer dependent on landscape and imagination. He had access to layers of experience which had previously existed only in his head. And being no longer dependent on the imagination gave it freedom to travel much further.

The needs of the writer and the needs of the adventurer both involved the urge to match the imagination with experience. I have suggested that from the outset of Stevenson's literary career he was reaching for metaphor, and that the need to find and express resemblances set him on the road to fiction. The road took him a very long way.

I want to go back to one of the passages with which I started, where Herrick in *The Ebb-Tide* is trying to take in the "scarce-believed in" island. This time, I'll include what I left out earlier.

> The isle—the undiscovered, the scarce-believed in—now lay before them and close aboard: and Herrick thought that never in his dreams had he beheld anything more strange and delicate. The beach was excellently white, the continuous barrier of trees inimitably green; the land, perhaps ten feet high, the trees thirty more. Every here and there, as the schooner coasted northward, the wood was intermitted; and he could see clear over the inconsiderable strip of land (as a man looks over a wall) to the lagoon within—and clear over that again to where the far side of the atoll prolonged its pencillings of trees against the morning sky. He tortured himself to find analogies. The isle was like the rim of a great vessel sunken in the waters; it was like the embankment of an annular railway grown upon with wood: so slender it seemed amidst the outrageous breakers, so frail and pretty, he would scarce have wondered to see it sink and disappear without a sound, and the waves close smoothly over its descent.[23]

What Stevenson achieves in this passage is a description that is both precise and resonant; tangible and elusive; distinct and sinuous. He is saying, this place has a reality, but it is the reality of observation, conveyed through the eyes of an individual, through manipulated language and moulded sentences, as is all reality represented in words. To fix it, we need analogies. We understand the whole of experience, the whole of life, through metaphors. It is the only way we can get a grip on things. Stevenson was fully aware of the challenge of Darwin and Spencer to the conventional Judaeo-Christian interpretation of the world. If the metaphors offered by religion are rejected or fragmented, our need for the intervention of the imagination is all the greater. Storytelling has always been at the heart of religious belief. It is no accident that in the course of the nineteenth century the novel strengthened and grew more complex, as it reached out to reside in spaces less confidently occupied by faith. (And no accident that fiction continues to flourish, in spite of predictions to the contrary.)

The articulation of analogies is, I think, what Stevenson is about. He searches for and finds metaphors for experience, and experience brought him the opportunities for both the search—the voyages of exploration—and the discovery—landfalls on psychological and emotional as well as physical territory. The South Pacific, especially, challenged his creativity and dared his capacity for response. "This climate; these voyagings; these landfalls at dawn; new passing alarms of squalls and surf—the whole tale of my life is better to me than any poem," he wrote in a letter of June 1889.[24] Here is experience to outstrip the imagination, but in Stevenson's case the imagination keeps pace. It is there, absorbing and transforming, ensuring that the tale, the story, the metaphor, has meaning. And that is the way that he ensures that we do, indeed, trust his imagination, for it is precisely the imagination that allows him to look "in the eyeball of the dawn" and tell us what he sees.

NOTES

1. *In the South Seas* (1890), London, 1986, 143.

2. "A Humble Remonstrance," in *Memories and Portraits* (1887), (Glasgow, 1990), 196.

3. *The Ebb-Tide* (1893), in *Dr. Jekyll and Mr. Hyde and Other Stories*, (Harmondsworth, 1979), 234–35.

4. Ibid., 236–37.

5. *A Child's Garden of Verses* (1887), (London, 1976), 24, 17.

6. *Treasure Island* (1883), (Oxford, 1985), 68.

7. "Memoirs of an Islet," *Memories and Portraits*, 91.

8. *Treasure Island*, 68–70.

9. Ibid., 69.

10. Ibid., 75.

11. Ibid., 76.

12. "A College Magazine," in *Memories and Portraits*, 42–3.

13. Leslie Stephen to RLS, Beinecke Collection, Beinecke Library, Yale University.

14. *Edinburgh: Picturesque Notes* (1879), (Edinburgh, 1983), 72–3.

15. *The Amateur Emigrant* (*Across the Plains*, 1892), (London, 1984), 122.

16. "Monterey" (*Across the Plains*, 1892), in *From the Clyde to California*, ed. Andrew Noble, 161.

17. J. A. Symonds to RLS, *John Addington Symonds, Letters and Papers*, ed. Horatio F. Brown (London, 1923), 405.

18. *The Ebb-Tide*, 207.

19. "A Scot Abroad," in *The Silverado Squatters* (1883).

20. *The Ebb-Tide*, 250.

21. Ibid.

22. *In the South Seas*, 13.

23. *The Ebb-Tide*, 236–37.

24. RLS to James Payn, 13 June 1889, *The Letters of Robert Louis Stevenson*, ed. Booth and Mehew, vol. 6, 316.

The Art of Writing and the Pleasure of Reading: R.L. Stevenson as Theorist and Popular Author

Richard Ambrosini

Robert Louis Stevenson owes his enduring popularity to *Treasure Island* and *Dr. Jekyll and Mr. Hyde*. Reprinted over and over again, and adapted for the cinema or the television, these two works have ended up subsuming within the categories of children's literature or the horror-story *de auteur* a literary output which fills over thirty volumes. The bracing adventure tale and the tortured investigation into the double in man, moreover, have proved too difficult to reconcile within one single artistic project. As a result, the existence itself of such a project has been denied altogether—and the many questions raised by the pleasure Stevenson's fiction continues to induce, over one hundred years after they were written, left unanswered.

The view that a writer who purports to entertain his readers must by definition be oblivious of any theoretical concerns is a legacy of the twentieth century.[1] The critical status of authors such as Virginia Woolf, Joseph Conrad, or James Joyce remains undisputed precisely because they are credited with having contributed to transforming the novel into a theoretically informed artistic artifact. Nobody would even dream of claiming today that they are "popular"—an adjective which comes natural instead, when we think of Stevenson.[2] And yet, it is interesting that Con-

21

rad himself once wrote: "When it comes to popularity I stand much nearer the public mind than Stevenson, who was super-literary; a conscious virtuoso of style."[3] He is right. Absolutely nothing in Stevenson's upbringing and early career suggests that he could ever seek popularity. Scion of a distinguished Edinburgh dynasty of engineers, throughout his life he remained a true-blood Tory, and when in his mid-twenties he "came into his fantastic critical and popular prominence,"[4] the celebrity he attained was marked by definite class connotations. His first travel book, *An Inland Voyage* (1878), was adopted at Eton for translations from English into Latin, and a society at Oxford chose the same slim volume as "the 'best specimen of the writing of English of this century.'"[5] This success, however, left him dissatisfied. And this because he "longed to be something more than the darling of a literary set," what he called being "a literary cherub—a head and a pair of wings, with nothing to sit down upon."[6] *Treasure Island* seemed to give him the chance to break free from this artificial position, but the story appealed only to an élite of readers, among whom was the Prime Minister, William Gladstone. When American painter John Singer Sargent wrote to Stevenson to tell him that Gladstone "[talked] all the time about *Treasure Island*," he was almost annoyed, and replied: "he would do better to attend the imperial affairs of England" (*Letters* V, 49). And when another of his friends passed on the same piece of literary gossip to him, he commented: "As for respecting … that fatuous rabble of burgesses called 'the public,' God save us from such irreligion; that way lies disgrace and dishonour. There must be something wrong in me, or I would not be popular" (*Letters* V, 171). Little did he know at the time what it meant to be popular: one week later, *Dr. Jekyll and Mr. Hyde* appeared, and sold 40,000 copies in the first few months—a huge number, for him, but nothing for a truly popular author. Propelled by this success, the following year he arrived in the United States, where he was lionized by the popular press. He fled to a log cabin in upstate New York, close to the Canadian border, and was naive enough to torture himself over what he felt were the "princely sums" he was being offered by American publishers. In fact, his American agent later confessed in his memoirs that for any established American author those sums would have been nothing but "peanuts."[7]

Obviously, we need to clarify what we mean by "popular" before applying it to Stevenson, and a good way to start is to look up the word in the *Oxford English Dictionary*. Here are the main definitions: "Plebeian; Adapted to the understanding, tastes, or means of ordinary people; Designed to gain the favour of the common people; favourite, acceptable, pleasing." Leaving aside the horribly condescending tone of these dictionary entries, we find in them terms which can contribute to an understanding of Stevenson's life and works: "pleasing," of course, but also "designed to gain the favour of the common people." His artistic project evolved from an investigation into the correlation between the pleasure he himself derived from creating a work of art, and the pleasure he could induce in the reader. When he became a novelist, it was the aesthetic and ethical implications of the creation of pleasure which motivated his search for a fiction of universal effectiveness. And we do not need to check the *Oxford Dictionary* to know that "universal" includes, in addition to the British Prime Minister, the "common people"—and children.

In Stevenson's numerous collections of essays, as well as in the eight volumes of his collected letters, we find a plurality of statements on art and literature, which reflects the variety of his narrative production. One particular definition of "theory" can be found in a letter to Henry James written from Samoa in which Stevenson informs his friend about his difficulties in giving a representation of the South Seas. Imagine, he tells him, writing a book, while continually revising one's opinions. Very soon, he fears,

> I shall have no opinions left. And without an opinion, how to string artistically vast accumulations of fact? Darwin said no one could observe without a theory; I suppose he was right, 'tis a fine point of metaphysic; but I will take my oath, no man can write without one—at least the way he would like to [*Letters VII*, 65–66].

After a century in which so many artists have invoked every sort of dogma, political creed, or intellectual fashion to justify their works, it is refreshing to find an author who claims that theory is needed to write "the way he would like to." But more importantly, this formulation captures the key note of a life characterized by a search for an ever greater freedom of expression, in France, America and the Pacific. Let's forget the romantic myth built around Stevenson's travels. His first long stay in France coincided with the first exhibition of the Impressionist painters; he lived for long periods in the United States at the beginning and the end of the 1880s, at a time when mass circulation newspapers—at the peak of their power to define public reality—were creating the new structure of celebrity and fame which made possible the forty-year love affair between America and that other master stylist cum popular author, Mark Twain.[8] In the South Seas, Stevenson witnessed the effects of European colonization, and reacted by taking considerable personal risks to defend the Islanders' rights—something few other white men did, let alone literary purveyors of exotic stories. Stevenson lived through all these experiences, always searching, always testing and extending his art. And in doing so, rather than building one theory, he reformulated over and over again concepts he had developed early on, during his literary apprenticeship.

The continuity underlying Stevenson's whole corpus can be viewed only by setting the few of his narrative works which are still read today within the context of his entire fictional and non-fictional production. His essays and letters, in particular, can help set up a perspective on his entire literary career—which covered a span of twenty-one years, even though only the second half, after *Treasure Island*, is usually taken into consideration. He himself was the first to complain about this elision, but he knew that there was nothing to do about it, because, as he wrote, "I am well aware that my paymaster, the great public, regards what else I have written with indifference, if not aversion"; just the same, he felt the need to remind his readers that *Treasure Island*, "was far, indeed, from being my first book, for I am not a novelist alone."[9] The question to be asked, then, is what were the dynamics which led Stevenson from being a cele-brated essayist to becoming not simply a "novelist," but a manipulator of sub-genres derived from popular literature—and later the creator of fictional and non-fictional works impossible to classify? Once these dynamics are uncovered, a certain set of theories emerge, which guided the essay-writing of the first half of his career and were reformulated once new experiences forced him to question the social composition of his ideal readership.

The first intimations of the artistic project which guided Stevenson's entire work can be found in the letters to his cousin, Bob, a promising young painter. Starting around 1868, when he was eighteen years old, Stevenson developed his early theories on writing, understandably out of comparisons between painting and literature. The theoretical premises of this particular view of writing found an ideal audience in the summer of 1873, when he met Sidney Colvin, one of the best known art critics of his time, Professor of Fine Arts at Cambridge, and a friend of John Ruskin, Sir Edward Burne-Jones, and Dante Gabriel Rossetti. Colvin was instru-mental in launching Stevenson on a literary career, introducing him into the London literary set, and helping him publish his first essay, "Roads." A few weeks later, Stevenson was "ordered South" to recover from a ner-vous breakdown and various physical ailments, and left for Menton, at the time, "the capital of the Riviera ... for English invalids."[10] Colvin joined him there, for two long stays, between December 1873 and March 1874. We do not know what the twenty-three year old Scottish youth and the Cambridge Professor of Fine Arts talked about. What is certain, is that starting from that period we find in Stevenson's letters references to a new and very personal theory of literature.

The most illuminating document from this period is a letter in which Stevenson tells his mentor about the difficulties he is encountering in trying to apply to a short story the abstract principles of "the realistic movement of the age." The convention adopted, he explains, is so difficult that "I have to put out much that pleases me ... without producing commensurate power of giving pleasure in the accomplished work." There was however an alternative to "realism"—and as a matter of fact he himself had hit upon it years before, when with his cousin Bob they had discussed about how to recreate a certain scene, through different media, words or colors. He then gives three examples of how he would use the interplay of lights and shadows, or describe stairs and doors only when someone is descending or passing through them: every detail, he writes, must be functional to keeping the reader's attention focused on "the essential interest of the situation."[11] His apprenticeship over, on the brink of his chosen profession, we find that his aim is to clearly capture a scene with a painter's eye, without having to conform to any dogmatic notion of realism—and at the same time bearing in mind that the pleasure felt by an artist in the act of creation must be transmuted into the pleasure of its receptor.

He is confident enough to end the letter by declaring: "That is the best example of my theory that I can give" (*Letters I*, 476–7). But as is often the case with Stevenson, his "theory" was also influenced by stimuli he found in the culture he lived in at the time. In reacting to new ideas, he transformed them into principles which then guided his writing. After leaving the Riviera, on his way back to Scotland, he stopped in Paris in the very same days when the first Impressionist exhibition was inaugurated. He did not visit it, but he most probably heard about it from Bob, who was living there at the time. At any rate, a few months later he used the adjective "impressional" to describe a natural scene, which he compares to "a clever French landscape," as well as to "a Japanese picture" ("An Autumn Effect," *XXII*, 112).

A first indication of the direction in which his "theory" developed—guiding his metamorphosis from essayist to novelist—emerged in an essay, "Notes on the Movements of Young Children," in which he argues that children's play exemplifies a beauty that turns "upon consideration not really aesthetic," as well as "an impulsive truth ... that shows throughout all imperfection" (*XXII*: 98). (The same, of course, could be said about Impressionist paintings.) On July 15, 1874, in a letter to Colvin he explained that "Notes"—together with his first essay, "Roads"—marked the beginning of a project "which dates from early at Mentone," when he envisaged a series of essays whose purpose was to stimulate "a friendlier and more thoughtful way of looking about one," without necessarily feeling "bound to drag about Art every time to make it suitable" (*Letters II*, 32). The outline of this project becomes clearer in a third essay, "On the Enjoyment of Unpleasant Places," which six weeks later he described as a sequel to the other two, conceived as "a word in season as to aesthetic contentment and a hint to the careless to look around them for disregarded pleasures." These three essays already made an interesting start to a personal aesthetic theory, and he announced that he would soon have ready "a little budget of little papers all with this intention before them, call it ethical or aesthetic as you will.... Twelve or twenty such Essays ... put together in a little book ... ESSAYS ON THE ENJOYMENT OF THE WORLD: BY ROBERT LOUIS STEVENSON" (*Letters II*, 43). The "little book" never materialized. But the young writer's ethically founded refusal of all aesthetic conventions inspired him to create a literary prose both elegant and free of any explicit moral burden, through which he portrayed his reaction to nature and human life in his essays and travel books of the 1870s.

Later in his career, while he was revising *Treasure Island*, Stevenson was consulted by a young painter who had sought his advice on how to become an artist. He replied: "For any art think less of what pays, first of what pleases.... Progress in art is made by learning to enjoy" (*Letters III*, 333). He knew what he was talking about. His own "progress in art" had evolved through continuous reformulations of the aesthetic and ethical implications of his wanting to instruct his readers in new ways to "enjoy the world." These reformulations had eventually become a theory about how to create pleasure through reading—and it was according to this theory that he was revising his pirate story for an adult readership. This "progress" involved a number of risks for an upper-class writer like Stevenson, who had to adopt psychological strategies and narrative techniques derived from the sub-genres of popular literature in order to induce in the readers of his own class the pleasure-creating effect he aimed at. If he went ahead, and combined his artistic prose with sensational plots, it was in response to moral imperatives, implicit in a second reference to a personal "theory" that we find one month after the announcement of the twelve-essay project. One day in London, he wrote to a friend, after leaving her,

> I found an organ grinder in Russell Square playing to a child; and the simple fact that there was a child listening to him, that he was giving this pleasure, entitled him according to my theory, as you know, to some money; so I put some coppers on the ledge of his organ, without so much as looking at him [*Letters II*, 59–60].

What is striking about this scene is that it contains all the evidence repeatedly invoked to build a case against Stevenson, the author who betrayed his artistic vocation writing stories for boys, only to make money. How different the scene appears, however, once the elements of a theory of pleasure begin to emerge. What has been mistaken for a commodification of Stevenson's art was in fact the result of his ethically motivated openness toward the challenges posed by the publishing market. Never in fact did he allow the market to dictate his ideals in writing. Though he may have been influenced by the desire to entertain, this does not mean that he compromised the artistic and moral integrity which guided his attempts to reach out to a wider public.

It was a shift in his notion of an author's responsibility towards his readers that prompted him to invest with a new significance his notion of "creating pleasure." This happened as a consequence of the most formative experience of his life: his trip to the United States in the summer of 1879, when he left Edinburgh to rescue Fanny, the American woman he had met in France, who had been forced by her husband to return to California. It was not going to be a holiday on the French Riviera. He could not count on his father's money, and had to travel in the steerage of an emigrant ship. (He never recovered from this voyage and the continental crossing aboard an emigrant train: his tuberculosis was diagnosed for the first time in San Francisco, and ever after he led the life of a chronic invalid.)

This voyage marked for Stevenson an exit from his previous social sphere. In *The Amateur Emigrant*, the book he wrote about this experience, he recorded his discovery of the "Labouring mankind," of their misery and their nobility, which, he wrote, "I had never represented ... livingly to my imagination" (*XV*, 11–2). One episode, in particular, reveals how the transatlantic crossing marked a turning point in the implications of "creating pleasure." One day, as he entered the steerage, he saw that a

> white-faced Orpheus was cheerily playing to an audience of white-faced women. It was as much as he could do to play, and some of his hearers were scarce able to sit; yet they had crawled from their bunks at the first experimental flourish, and found better than medicine in the music.... Humanly speaking, it is a more important matter to play the fiddle, even badly, than to write huge works upon recondite subjects. What could Mr. Darwin have done for these sick women? But this fellow scraped away; and the world was positively a better place for all who heard him [*XV*, 20–1].

Colvin and his other London friends were scandalized by the "lurking subversive classlessness"[12] of *Amateur Emigrant*, and tried in every way to discourage him from writing it. But he not only went ahead, he also claimed, to his friends William Ernest Henley, that after writing on contemporary life, "all [my] past work is nothing to me.... I am only beginning to see my method" (*Letters III*, 55–6). And to Colvin, he announced that once *The Emigrant* was finished, "I'll stick to stories.... I know I shall do better work than ever I have done before.... My sympathies and interests are changed. There shall be no more books of travel for me. I care for nothing but the moral and the dramatic, not a jot for the picturesque or the beautiful, other than about people" (*Letters III*, 59–60). What he meant by "caring about people" becomes clear in a letter written a few days later to a Scottish Professor of Education:

> When I suffer in mind, stories are my refuge; I take them like opium; and I consider one who writes them as a sort of doctor of the mind. And frankly ... it is not Shakespeare we take to, when we are in a hot corner; nor, certainly, George Eliot—no, nor even Balzac. It is ... Old Dumas, or the *Arabian Nights*, or the best of Walter Scott. It is stories we want, not the high poetic function which represents the world.... We want incident, interest, action [*Letters III*, 61–2].

Rather than writing to show to the reader how to *look* at the world to extract pleasure from it, from now on he would have struggled to *create* fictional worlds which would give pleasure to flesh and blood human beings whom he respects, and with whom he shares both sufferings and pleasures.

It is no coincidence that Stevenson began his first novel only after living in America. (He returned to Europe on August 17, 1880, and by August 25, 1881, he was already working on *Treasure Island*.) This breakthrough was not only a consequence of his discovering that the "Unknown Public"[13] of the consumers of popular literature were not an anonymous mass, but individuals with common needs and aspirations. It was his having witnessed in the U.S. the growing power of the nascent mass media that made it impossible for him to return to a condition in which, as he wrote in a letter, "We all live in a clique, buy each other's books and like each other's books; and the great, gaunt, gray, gaping public snaps its big fingers and reads Talmage and Tupper" (*Letters III*, 297).[14] The American lesson prompted him, early in 1881, to write an essay—"The Morality of the Profession of Letters"—in which we find a moral urgency unknown up to that moment in his public voice. In these days of daily papers, he writes, "The total of a nation's reading ... greatly modifies the total of the nation's speech; and the speech and reading, taken together, form the efficient educational medium of youth." Whether we seek to please or to instruct, he adds, it is a moral duty for all practitioners of "the art of words" to contrast the "incalculable influence for ill" and the "public falsehood" represented by journalism. The "American reporter or the Parisian *chroniquer*" are not for him "so much baser" than English journalists, but are much more dangerous: it is because they are "so much more readable," that "their evil is done more effectively, in America for the masses, in [France] for the few that care to read." The remedy he has to offer is contained in his injunction to choose, for one's stories, only facts which are "eternally more necessary than others [and] more interesting to the natural mind of man" (*XXII*, 278–81)—endowed, that is, with an effectiveness which transcends class and age.

Four months later, in August 1881, while spending the summer in a cottage in the Highlands, Stevenson wrote to Henley to announce that he was working on the story which then became *Treasure Island*. This must certainly have been a "progress in art," since he declares: "It's awful fun boy's stories, you just indulge the pleasure of your heart, that's all." The story—we learn from this letter—was not addressed to boys: he had a particular publisher in mind, ideally suited for the project, and provokes his friend, by asking, "Would you be surprised to hear, in this connection, the name of *Routledge*?" (*Letters II*, 244–5)—at the time a by-word for literary mass-production, following the great success of their "Railway Library," a series of cheap reprints aimed at commuters.

The story of how the pirate story intended for Routledge was first conceived has often been told but is worth recalling in this context. One morning, in the cottage, to entertain his bored twelve-year-old stepson, Stevenson drew the map of an island in watercolors. The painted image ignited his own fancy, and he started adding names to mountains, beaches and coves. There is no need to invoke comparisons between painting and writing to describe what was happening: in watching an ideal locus for adventure taking shape, he was transforming the game into an experiment in how to communicate, to an audience, "the pleasure of your heart." The otherwise fastidious author started writing a chapter a day, using his stepson as a guinea pig (it was the kid who decreed: "No women in the story!" [*Letters III*, 225]). In the evening, the entire family met around the fireplace, and his father, a redoubtable sixty-three-year-old engineer, was "caught at once with all the romance and childishness of his original nature" (*II*, xv). The result of this experiment was a tale in which the author, resorting to his own experience as a reader—and drawing on the lessons of his American experience—tried to reach out to a mass readership, after the immediate enthusiastic participatory response of the flesh-and-blood audience he had available in the cottage in the Highlands.

(Unfortunately, a few weeks later the circle of readers was joined by a flesh-and-blood critic, the first of a long series who classified *Treasure Island* as a "boys' tale." If the pirate story was sent to *Young Folks*—and not to Routledge—it was because this critic heard the writer reading a chapter to the congregated family, and—transforming the game into reality—offered to bring the fifteen chapters written so far to the juvenile paper's editor, who was a friend of his.)

Whatever intention the author had when he began the story in August 1881, the text as we know it today was published in book form two years later, on November 14, 1883, after a long revision. Fortunately, we can retrace what the author had in mind in preparing the version intended for an adult readership. In the very same days in which he committed himself to proceed with the revision of *Treasure Island*, he was asked to write an essay (*Letters III*, 276–9); thus, he had an opportunity to explain to the public of his essays, travel books, and first short stories why he had adopted a particular sub-genre for his first novel. In this essay, "A Gossip on Romance," we find many of the themes and ideas formulated in the 1870s. And, significantly, in underlining the continuity between his earlier works and his first experiment with the novel-form, Stevenson gave particular emphasis to the way in which his former theory of pleasure had become in the meanwhile a reading-model.

"Gossip" opens with a description of what the act of reading should be like:

> In anything fit to be called by the name of reading the process itself should be absorbing and voluptuous; we should gloat over a book, be rapt clean out of ourselves, and rise from the perusal, our mind filled with the busiest, kaleidoscopic dances of images, incapable of sleep or continuous thought. The words, if the book be eloquent, should run thenceforward in our ears like the noise of breakers, and the story, if it be a story, repeat itself in a thousand coloured pictures to the eye. It was for this last pleasure that we read so closely, and loved our books so dearly, in the bright, troubled period of boyhood [*XIII*, 327].

The kaleidoscopic dances of images, the thousand colored pictures: this description of the act of reading constitutes an historical document of the creative tension felt by an artist who could not count on special effects, computer-created images. He only had words available, and to allow the reader to escape from reality, and travel in fantasy, identifying with a projected image of oneself, indeed they had to resonate in the ear like the noise of breakers.

Starting from this description of the reading process, Stevenson unravels a complex argument which leads him to postulate a reader-response psychology built around mechanisms based on the pleasure of reading. The great creative writers, he claims, are those who show us "the realisation and the apotheosis of the day-dreams of common men" (*XIII*, 332). These day-dreams have nothing to do with the "self-fulfilling stories of the pulp magazines"; rather, they are "bridges between experience and desire."[15] The difference lies, as usual in Stevenson, in the quality of the writing, which he describes—characteristically—as the "pictorial or picture-making romance [which is] not only the highest art possible in words, but the highest art of all, since it combines the greatest mass and diversity of the elements of truth and pleasure" (*XIII*, 335). But he is not thinking of the Impressionist writing of his essays. He is invoking what is for him the fundamental premise for creating a universal effect through words: the creation of "epoch-making scenes"—such as, "Crusoe recoiling from the footprint, Achilles shouting over against the Trojans, Ulysses bending the great bow." Each one of these scenes "has been printed on the mind's eye forever," because it has "put the last mark of truth upon a story [filling] up, at one blow, our capacity for sympathetic pleasure." Time, he adds, cannot "efface or weaken the impression" (*XIII*, 332). This, he concludes, is "the highest and hardest thing to do in words," but once accomplished it "equally delights the schoolboy and the sage, and makes, in its own right, the quality of epics" (*XIII*, 333). This is the word he was driving at.

"A Gossip on Romance" is crucial to an understanding of both Stevenson the theorist and the "popular author." Critics who have tried to assess his ideas on literature have recognized its importance, along with that of another essay, "A Humble Remonstrance," which he wrote after *Treasure Island* was published to defend his use of a sub-genre associated with juvenile fiction. Since Stevenson's name is most readily associated with adventures for boys, however, these two essays have been construed as being the sum total of Stevenson's theoretical thinking—and as profound as the psychology of a pasteboard pirate. We ought to reject this view, which has become a caricature when one particular phrase from "Gossip" has been cited to put a seal on Stevenson's reputation as a children's writer: "Fiction is to the grown man what play is to the child." As a matter of fact, this comparison is only the beginning of a sentence which then proceeds to explain that only in fiction the grown man "changes the atmosphere and tenor of his life; and when the game so chimes with his fancy that he can join in it with all his heart, when it pleases him with every turn, when he loves to recall it and dwells upon the recollection with entire delight, fiction is called romance" (*XIII*, 340). Once set in the context of an argument culminating in the invocation of "epics," the fiction-play comparison means in fact that fiction can express all its evocative power only if it touches something ancestral, common to all humanity. The reading-model set forth in "Gossip" was founded on a pleasure which was "infantile" only in the sense of primordial.

The repeated qualifications he offers in "Gossip" of what he means by "romance" constitute a vindication of how successful he had been in applying to a narrative in prose the theories which up to that point had guided his essay-writing. The pride he could feel in having accomplished this transition can be fully understood if we return to the winter of 1874, when in Menton Stevenson conceived the project of twelve essays on "the Enjoyment of the World." In those very same months, he was also articulating the rudiments of ideas which would later become his theory of fiction. It is a striking confirmation of the continuity underlying his artistic project to find that in a book review written in those months, he argued that the short-story form was in fact nothing else than a post–Darwinian version of classical fable. Even more importantly, in his essay on "the movements of young children," the children's play is not only offered as an example of a beauty free from conventions but is also described as a "reminiscence of primitive festivals and the Golden Ages" (*XXII*, 98). If child psychology was instrumental in advancing a model for an adult reader's response to literature, it was because it could explain how to bring new life to myths, by reaching down to the deepest, atavistic components of narrative.

These may appear to be hints and elliptical suggestions, but in fact they are indications of Stevenson's view of the potentialities implicit in narrative fiction. He gave to this view definite theoretical connotations when while staying in Menton he was offered an opportunity to address, for the first time, a public of intellectuals and literati. Victor Hugo's latest novel, *Ninety-Three*, had just appeared, and Stevenson was asked to review it for the prestigious *Cornhill Magazine*. As it turned out, however, only eleven out of the twenty-eight pages of the essay he wrote, "Victor Hugo's Romances," deal with the French master's works. The others are devoted instead to suggesting possible further developments for the nineteenth-century novel—developments which happen to coincide with what Stevenson proposed to realize himself. (The extent to which he hijacked the review to voice his own ideas is revealed when he makes quite clear that if it was up to him, he would have chosen an American champion of the romance, Nathaniel Hawthorne.) The essay begins, by outlining a transnational history of the novel, alternative to the English line linking

Henry Fielding to the Victorian "novel with a purpose." The purpose of this personal genealogy is to demonstrate that romance had progressed from Scott to Hugo following an ever-increasing artistic self-awareness; and as to what the next step may be, this Stevenson makes clear by choosing for the essay's epigraph a passage in which Victor Hugo envisages a future where, "After the picturesque but prosaic novel of Walter Scott, another kind of novel remains to be created ... picturesque but poetic, real but ideal, true but grandiose, which will set Walter Scott alongside Homer."[16]

Having announced, in his first literary essay, that he is the ideal candidate as Sir Walter Scott's successor, the twenty-three-year-old who had so far published only one essay switches to the first person to address directly his readers. He begins by suggesting that literary criticism has until then found great difficulties in defining the "artistic result of a romance, what is left upon the memory by any really powerful and artistic novel." And—of course—he invokes a comparison between painting and writing to overcome these difficulties, describing this artistic result as an "impression." He then declares: "in the present study ... I propose chiefly ... to throw in relief ... this idea which underlies and issues from a romance, this something which it is the function of that form of art to create, this epical value" (*XIV*, 25–6). In reading "Victor Hugo's Romances," one understands why in "A Gossip on Romance" Stevenson argued that the "impression" created through "epoch-making scenes" can contribute to fiction "the quality of epics." And when we think that in the earlier essay he had also specified that "epical value is not to be found ... in every so-called novel," we find an explanation for the crucial choice which marked his entire career: he wrote adventurous romances, rather than realistic psychological novels, because he was convinced this was the most elevated path toward artistic expression in prose narrative.[17] If Stevenson became a "popular author," it was because—given the cultural and historical conditions of his times—this was the only way open to him to reach the universal source of every literary form, and develop the myth-making potentials of fiction.

This is why we should not become defensive when we are told that Stevenson does not belong among the "great English novelists." He was the first to feel he was not only a "novelist": he was more than that, he was a polygraphic craftsman of words; and even less did he consider himself "English," having adopted as forefathers a Scotsman (Scott), a Frenchman (Hugo), and an American (Hawthorne); and finally, he did all he could to avoid becoming "great," experimenting with the sub-genres of popular literature, contaminating his pure prose with sensational plots—

and thus contradicting that hierarchy of literary forms which later critics have taught us to consider as "natural."

One year before he died, Stevenson started writing an essay in which he went back to when, in his childhood, he first discovered the power of words—which dawned on him, in listening to his nurse recite aloud, in her strong Scottish accent, the Bible and the Psalms. The pleasure he derived from words, however, was unconscious: he followed whatever was read to him, listening for "news of the great vacant world upon whose edge [he] stood," eager, he recalls, "for delightful plots that I might re-enact in play" (*XXII*, 440). As it is already obvious, Stevenson is retracing here the steps which led him to construct his own artistic identity. The next step came when he passed "from hearing literature to reading it"—for him, "a kind of second weaning." He is thinking of a particular spot in time: an evening, when alone in the woods he pulled out a book of fairy tales. "The shock of that pleasure," he writes, "I have never since forgot, and if my mind serves me to the last, I never shall; for it was then that I knew I loved reading" (*XXII*, 441).

The essay remained unfinished, and we do not know what conclusion Stevenson would have reached, given his stated intention to investigate, "by what hints and premonitions, the consciousness of the man's art dawns first upon the child" (*XXII*, 436). A possible indication is provided however by the verse from a short poem by Horace contained in title—"Random Memories: Rosa Quo Locorum." It is a revealing choice. In the poem, the Latin poet imagines he is sitting under a bower in a vineyard. He orders only some wine and enjoins the youth who is serving him not to embellish the table, in the fashion of the Persians, with wreaths of intertwined lime tree boughs: there is no use, he adds, to go in search for the places where the tardy rose blossoms—the "*rosa quo locorum / Sera moretur*" [*Odes*, I.xxxviii. 3–4]). Set at the end of his first book of *Odes*, this scene signals Horace's leave-taking from his readers, in which he reaffirms his love for simple things as well as his fidelity to the Muse who has inspired him to sing not of weighty matters but of convivial banquets and fleeting passions.

It was not a Muse who inspired Stevenson to treat apparently "simple" matters: it was a personal poetics of fiction that led him to test the universality of his own pleasure of reading by drawing on his experience as a sickly child whose longing for life could find an outlet only in reading Scott, *The Arabian Nights* and Dumas. In doing so, he who was the most elegant stylist of his times broke every conventional notion of literary decorum. But it was worth doing, because the modern myths he thus created have endured, as popular and resonant of meanings as ever. Indeed, simple epics.

Horace's "simple" poetry was cherished by Caesar Augustus, who in any case could count on Virgil to have his family's origin traced back to Homer. Nineteen centuries later, William Gladstone carried upon his shoulders the weight of an even larger dominion and had enough writers more than willing to praise him. And yet, he was happy to take one night away from the cares of the British Empire, and enjoy *Treasure Island*. Two thousand years have been enough to get rid of senseless comparisons between Horace and Virgil. Let's hope that Robert Louis Stevenson will not have to wait so long.

NOTES

1. See Jeremy Hawthorn, *A Concise Glossary of Contemporary Literary Theory* (London: Arnold, 1998), 3rd ed., p. 175: "The attitude of literary critics towards pleasure can perhaps be compared to that of [Marxists] towards sartorial fashion: during the present century they seem never to have been quite sure whether or not they approve of it, but on the balance they do not. Freud's *pleasure principle* dominated the new-born infant, but in the maturing or mature individual was placed under the sway of the *reality principle*, regaining its sway only in fantasy or day-dreaming."

2. The *MLA Bibliography* lists, for the years 1963–2000, 384 entries on R.L.S, 6552 on Joyce, 3193 on Conrad, and 2747 on Woolf. How crucial for a writer's status is the perception of his or her being also a theoretician is amply illustrated by the number of essays dedicated to Umberto Eco since the publication of *Il nome della rosa* [*The Name of the Rose*] (1980): 430, that is, fifty more than those written on Stevenson in forty years.

3. Frederick Karl and Laurence Davies (eds.), *The Collected Letters of Joseph Conrad*, vol. V (Cambridge: Cambridge University Press, 1986*), p. 257.

4. Travis R. Merritt, "Taste, Opinion, and Theory in the Rise of Victorian Prose Stylism," in George Levine and William Madden (eds.), *The Art of Victorian Prose* (New York: Oxford University Press, 1968), p. 27.

5. Paul Maixner (ed.), *Robert Louis Stevenson: The Critical Heritage* (London: Routledge and Kegan Paul, 1981), p. 8.

6. Quoted in Bradford A. Booth and Ernest Mehew (eds.), *The Letters of Robert Louis Stevenson* (New Haven and London: Yale University Press, 1995), vol. III, p. 278, note 11.

7. Frank McLynn, *Robert Louis Stevenson: A Biography* (London: Hutchinson, 1993), p. 281.

8. Emory Elliott (general editor), *Columbia Literary History of the United States* (New York: Columbia University Press), p. 633.

9. Robert Louis Stevenson, "My First Book—'Treasure Island,'" in *The Thistle Edition of the Works of Robert Louis Stevenson* (New York: Charles Scribner's Sons, 1924), vol. II, p. ix. All quotations from Stevenson's works are from this edition.

10. William Pemble, *The Mediterranean Passion: Victorian and Edwardians in the South* (Oxford: Oxford University Press, 1987), pp. 86–7.

11. Valerie Shaw, in *The Short Story: A Critical Introduction* (London: Longman, 1983), p. 35, points out how Stevenson employed these three principles in his first short story, "A Lodging for the Night."

12. McLynn, p. 165.

13. Wilkie Collins, "The Unknown Public," *Household Words*, XVIII (August 21, 1858), p. 222. Cf. Peter Keating, *The Haunted Study: A Social History of the English Novel 1875–1914* (London: Fontana, 1989), pp. 401–2.

14. The compiler of a book of commonplaces entitled *Proverbial Philosophy* (1838–42) and a popular American preacher.

15. David Daiches, *Robert Louis Stevenson: A Revaluation* (Norfolk, Conn.: New Directions Books, 1947), p. 26.

16. "*Après le roman pittoresque mais prosaïque de Walter Scott il restera un autre roman à créer, plus beau et plus complet encore selon nous. C'est le roman, à la fois drame et epopée, pittoresque mais poétique, réel mais idéal, vrai mais grand, qui enchâssera Walter Scott dans Homère*" (*XIV*, 17).

17. Once in the South Seas, when he adopted a realistic mode of writing to portray the colonial scene of the Pacific, Stevenson found new motivations for defining his work as "epic." On December 5, 1892, Stevenson wrote to Henry James—his one-time opponent in the 1884 romance-realism *querelle*—that "You don't know what news is, nor what politics, nor what the life of man, till you see it on so small a scale and with your own liberty on the board for stake. I would not have missed it for much. And anxious friends beg me to stay at home and study human nature in Brompton drawing-rooms! And anyway you know that such is not my talent. I could never be induced to take the faintest interest in Brompton *qua* Brompton or a drawing-room *qua* a drawing-room. I am an Epick Writer with a k to it, but without the necessary genius" (*Letters VII*, 449).

Reanimating Stevenson's Corpus

Oliver S. Buckton

The 1994 centenary of Robert Louis Stevenson's death was the occasion for a major reevaluation of the life and career of this important late–Victorian writer. Indeed, given the recrudescence of scholarly and critical attention to Stevenson—including two major biographies, a critical study of the entire oeuvre, and the superb multi-volume edition of his letters published by Yale University Press under the editorship of Ernest Mehew—one might justifiably speak of the reanimated corpus of a writer whose extraordinary popularity during his own lifetime was followed by decades of critical neglect and dismissal.[1] Robert Kiely wrote, in his groundbreaking 1964 study, of "the pedestal upon which Stevenson's contemporaries had set him being used as the ram to batter him with" and Stevenson's reputation has undergone several deaths and rebirths during the twentieth century.[2] Yet the significance of a vital source of narrative energy and interest in Stevenson's fiction has remained buried in obscurity: that of the reanimated corpse, a figure that plays a central role in Stevenson's comic masterpiece of 1889, *The Wrong Box*, and surfaces in many other of his fictions of adventure, including *Treasure Island* (1883), *The Master of Ballantrae* (1889), and *The Ebb-Tide* (1893–94). This figure is of central importance to the forms of narrative desire in Stevenson's late fiction, and by attending to the narrative energies associated with the corpse, I shall argue, we are better able to grasp an important technique of "romance" fiction by which Stevenson and other writers, such as Oscar Wilde and H. Rider Haggard, sought to reanimate the corpse of Victorian realism through a revitalized use of Gothic and sensational motifs.[3]

The desire brought into play by the narrative of reanimation is, I argue, problematic: at once secret and homoerotic in nature, such desire emerges in a context of physical intimacy between men who seek to dissociate themselves from the contaminating effects of the corpse by burying it, by passing it on to another unsuspecting recipient, or by treating it as a joke. What one reviewer of *The Wrong Box* called "a kind of ghastly game at hide and seek with a dead man's body" becomes imbued with homoerotic import as the game enters into ever more promiscuous forms of exchange.[4] What is at stake in this game is the representation of the corpse as a reminder both of the mortality—the potential for decay—of the body and of "unspeakable" sexual practices between men. Such practices, which claimed a prominent place in public discourse following the Labouchère Amendment of 1885 and the Cleveland Street scandal of 1889, were ripe for fictional treatment, but only in cryptic or displaced form. Yet, as Wayne Koestenbaum has argued, Stevenson was aware of the significance of this anti-homosexual legislation, and sought to give representation to illicit forms of masculine desire in *Strange Case of Dr. Jekyll and Mr. Hyde*, published a few months after the Labouchère Amendment was passed.[5] Pointing out that the original readers of the story would not have known of Jekyll and Hyde's shared identity, Koestenbaum argues that "the novel's opening pages suggest ... a socially transgressive story about a Dr. Jekyll and a Mr. Hyde, two men from different social classes, who are involved in a shadowy, illicit relationship that is probably sexual, or at least involves the blackmail which was, by 1885, a sign for homosexuality" (p. 52).

The "horror" of Stevenson's story, in this reading, derives significantly from its representation of desires that were at once repugnant and fascinating to Victorians, and which the legislation of the period made increasingly visible and problematic. Similarly, the "horror" at the presence of the corpse—expressed both by characters in the fiction, and by reviewers of it—indicates the presence of somatic desires that are unmentionable and disturbing, and which the corpse promotes by engendering dangerous intimacies and comic confusions. Specifically, the contaminating effects of the corpse on the agents of narrative closure in Stevenson's fiction—including the narrators themselves—eventually require the deployment of various "strategies of containment" by which the disruptive effects of the corpse may be managed and the narrative desires it has produced be terminated.[6] This tension between narrative desire and containment is, I argue, embodied by the reanimation of the corpse that suggests the impossibility of finally stifling the desire that it has brought into play. Hence, the reanimated corpse is illustrative of a broader pattern of erotic disavowal in which, as Joseph Bristow writes, "The more Western culture devise[s] methods for speaking about the unspeakability of sex, the more sex itself [becomes] a type of open secret, ushering into the public domain a scandal that ha[s] to be masked."[7]

The erratic—and erotic—movements of the animated corpse serve to draw attention to the radical emptiness—in realist terms, the "lifelessness"—of character within the plot-centered narrative typical of the late–Victorian romance. In his 1882 essay, "A Gossip on Romance," Stevenson explains the necessary focus of romance on the extrinsic action—or "incident"—of the story, at the expense of the intrinsic experience or traits of character: "The interest turns, not upon what a man shall choose to do, but on how he manages to do it; not on the passionate slips and hesitations of the conscience, but on the problems of the body and of the practical intelligence, in clean, open-air adventure."[8] In *The Wrong Box* the "problems of the body" are of a specific and unusual kind (involving the need to dispose of an unwanted corpse), while the "practical intelligence" is thoroughly absorbed in devising convoluted strategies for disposing, transmitting, or concealing the taboo object. And yet, while certainly not a realist novel, *The Wrong Box* cannot satisfactorily be characterized as a "romance," as several of Stevenson's earlier narratives can. It is, in a word, unclassifiable: a hybrid work in which romance elements combine with comic misadventure to produce a narrative that refuses to conform to established generic conventions and cannot be contained within any narrative "box." Stevenson's novel presents similar generic problems to James Hogg's 1824 Gothic novel, *Confessions of a Justified Sinner*, which Magdalene Redekop describes as "characterized by numerous false starts, false endings, and digressions."[9] Hogg's refusal to conform to generic expectations is itself designed to disorient the reader, "a plot to trap us in our own rigid expectations of the laws of genre," by refusing to provide satisfying "closure" to the narrative (Redekop, p. 160). Hogg's and Stevenson's disruptions and derailings of plot undermine the narrative agenda of nineteenth-century realism, refusing to take seriously the demand for "lifelike" characters and plausible plots. Moreover, the very centrality of the corpse to the economy of desire in both the *Justified Sinner* and *The Wrong Box* mocks the realist novel's emphasis on heterosexual desire, marriage, and class as the passports to subjectivity.

While critics have aligned Stevenson with "romance" as opposed to "realism," his position is best understood less as a refutation of realism as such than as a rejection of the system of classifications itself. Ultimately

Stevenson disputes both the entombment of narrative art into such theoretical "boxes," and the subsequent disavowal of romance as a secondary, inferior or decadent aesthetic form. In "A Note on Realism" (1883) he writes: "This question of realism, let it be then clearly understood, regards not in the least degree the fundamental truth, but only the technical method, of a work of art."[10] By focusing on "style" and "method," Stevenson shifts the ground of the debate about realism from the ontological status of mimetic representation to the material techniques and effects of narrative composition. Whereas the skilled artist is concerned primarily with "what to put in and what to leave out" ("Realism" p. 69) the realist author—in an impossible quest to reproduce reality—risks burying his audience with words: "The immediate danger of the realist is to sacrifice the beauty and significance of the whole to local dexterity, or, in the insane pursuit of completion, to immolate his readers under facts" (p. 74).

For Stevenson, therefore, the romance novel is energizing precisely for its failure to be either inclusive or conclusive. As M.M. Bakhtin would later argue, the novel (or novelistic discourse) is less a genre in itself than a reanimating influence on other genres: "The novel inserts into these other genres an indeterminacy, a certain semantic open-endedness, a living contact with unfinished, still-evolving contemporary reality." As "the only developing genre," the novel "sparks the renovation of all other genres, it infects them with its spirit of process and inconclusiveness."[11] This insight brings into focus *The Wrong Box*'s realization of the subversive, anticanonical energies of the novel as theorized by Bakhtin, embodying "whatever force is at work within a given literary system to reveal the limits, the artificial constraints of that system."[12]

Stevenson's errant and inconclusive narrative practice in *The Wrong Box*, therefore, raises a number of interesting and important questions, both concerning the relationship between character and incident in late–Victorian fiction, and the tension between subversive desire and strategies of containment that seek to produce narrative closure. In its transgressions of literary propriety, the novel's greatest sin—at least in the eyes of Victorian critics—was to set the nameless body adrift indefinitely until, carried off by an unsuspecting carter, the corpse further defers its own burial. In part this uneasiness with the fiction is the manifestation of cultural taboos about death: as Christine Quigley observes, "Fear of the dead may stem from the fear that their bodies are contagious."[13] The fear of "contagion" by the corpse—manifested in *The Wrong Box* as the desire of each recipient of the body to get rid of it as soon as possible—is also linked to the novel's secret figuration of homoeroticism, a discourse of "unspeakable" desire that is hastily dissolved into comic scenarios of dispersal or exchange. Sodomy, and its metonymic displacement as burial in a secret site, is the source of the "jokes" in *The Wrong Box* (the corpse as a "stiff" misdirected to the wrong orifice) and of specific scenes of male intimacy in which the corpse figures as an unspeakable secret that must be "buried." As Guy Hocquenghem writes, "The anus is so well hidden that it forms the subsoil of the individual, his 'fundamental' core ... Your anus is so totally yours that you must not use it: keep it to yourself."[14] This paradox of secrecy—that which is most "hidden" is also most "fundamental," both to text and to body—will resurface time and again in Stevenson's fictions of reanimation. Like the "cloak of silence" that, Koestenbaum argues, "veils Jekyll's bachelor community" (p. 48), the "unspeakability" of the corpse in fact articulates a buried significance in Stevenson's narrative practices, and so puts in reverse the intended effects of legislation of the period: "When the Labouchère Amendment focused its eye on the homosexual, it articulated practices it had meant to silence" (Koestenbaum, p. 48). We should not be surprised to find such articulations in other texts by Stevenson; perhaps especially in those written collaboratively with other men—such as his stepson Lloyd Osbourne, with whom Stevenson shared the "excitement" of "the metaphorically sexual conception of a 'romance'" (Koestenbaum, pp. 39, 41).

Burying Desire in The Wrong Box

When it first appeared in June 1889, *The Wrong Box*—published under the joint authorship of Robert Louis Stevenson and Lloyd Osbourne—was almost unanimously dismissed by the critics as a kind of tasteless practical joke or as a mistaken attempt on Stevenson's part to boost the credibility of his amateurish collaborator. As Paul Maixner observes, this novel "provoked more adverse reviews than any book [Stevenson] would publish."[15] The discomfort aroused by the work was initially due to the uncertainty concerning the respective contributions of Stevenson and his collaborator: as one critic expressed it, with discernible anxiety, "What Mr. Osbourne's share in the story may be it is hard to determine."[16]

As Stevenson's correspondence of the period makes clear, Lloyd had written the original draft of the novel which Stevenson was so impressed with that he had "taken it in hand" and developed it.[17] Stevenson wrote Henry James on 6 October 1887, that "from the next room the bell of Lloyd's type-writer makes an agreeable music, as it patters off (at a rate which astonishes this experienced novelist) the early chapters of a humorous romance"

(*Letters*, VI, 15). Asserting that "if it is not funny, I'm sure I don't know what is," Stevenson informed Charles Baxter that "I have split over writing it" (*Letters*, VI, 263). He expressed no embarrassment in publishing the novel under their joint authorship; rather, he viewed the writing of it as an amusing pastime.[18] For Stevenson the book allowed an escape from the laborious process of completing *The Master of Ballantrae*—of which he wrote to Charles Baxter in March 1889, as though anticipating his own reanimation, "When that's done I shall breathe" (*Letters*, VI, 264). Hence, we can see the composition of *The Wrong Box* as itself an act of reanimation, in which the experienced author takes in hand the embryonic effort of an enthusiastic amateur and injects it with life and comic vitality. According to Bernard Darwin, "Lloyd Osbourne was little more than a boy at the time and was Stevenson's stepson to whom he would be glad to give a helping hand"; Darwin also cites Osbourne's own comment that Stevenson "breathed into it, of course, his own incomparable power, humour and vivacity and forced the thing to live as it had never lived before."[19] At the same time, as his letters reveal, Stevenson's own creative energies are reanimated by this collaboration with the youthful novice.

Yet the critics were unwilling to applaud either Stevenson's generosity to his protegé, or the new lease of life he gained from working on the "humorous romance." For example, Stevenson's fellow Scot, Margaret Oliphant, objected that he "had deluded us by the loan of his name into that undignified and unworthy exhibition,"[20] a comment that reflects the Victorian anxiety about the unique identity of the author, and the value of the literary commodity-text as determined by the seal of the author's signature. The (literally) decadent subject matter of the novel was itself offensive to Victorian sensibilities; the *Pall Mall Gazette* reviewer angrily asserting that Stevenson "ought to be ashamed of himself" for "the choice of so repellant a subject," and added: "we must ... enter our forcible protest against the funereal fun of a story which has as the pivot on which the whole plot turns the buffeting from pillar to post of a corpse" ("Mr. R.L. Stevenson," p. 3). The indecency of making a corpse the basis for a prolonged joke—even though the story moved fast enough "to prevent the olfactory nerve discovering the whereabouts of the concealed carcase"—earned the contempt of the *Pall Mall* reviewer, despite its similarity to "a weird story under the title of 'The Body Snatcher'" which Stevenson had published in 1884 ("Mr. R.L. Stevenson," p. 3). The plot of *The Wrong Box* is no less byzantine than that of a sensation novel, and it shares with that popular genre of the 1860s a feature that Patrick Brantlinger identifies as "the subordination of character to plot."[21] Consequently, the "box"—or plot—of this novel must be carefully measured in its various dimensions if we are to grasp its capacity to both shock and entertain the Victorian reader.

Stevenson took Osbourne's initial idea of an unwieldy, economically-motivated "box" involving the two elderly survivors of a "tontine fund"—an agreement by which a group of parents contribute to a fund on behalf of their children, the last surviving member of the original group of children receiving the entire accumulated figure—and injected the grotesque "game" involving a misidentified corpse. The two surviving members of the original group are brothers, Joseph and Masterman Finsbury, and are jealously guarded by their youthful relatives—Joseph's nephews Morris and John, and Masterman's son Michael. Due to a prior episode in which they have been defrauded by their Uncle Joseph of an inheritance, Morris and John consider themselves entitled to the proceeds of the tontine fund, and anxiously protect Joseph so that he will outlive his rival: the narrative describes how, in Morris's view, "His uncle was rather gambling stock in which he had invested heavily; and he spared no pains in nursing the security" (p. 6).

The course of this "inheritance" plot of sorts, however, is disrupted when a train transporting Joseph, Morris, and John Finsbury from Bournemouth to London is wrecked in a collision with another train.[22] In the ensuing carnage and confusion, Morris and John mistakenly identify the dead body of another passenger—dressed identically to Joseph, in "the uniform of Sir Faraday Bond" (*Wrong Box*, p. 15)—as the corpse of their uncle. Another reason for their misidentification of the corpse is that in the train wreck "the face had suffered severely, and it was unrecognisable" (pp. 19–20). The two brothers temporarily bury the body until they can find some means of moving it to their London address—their chief concern is to prevent discovery of their uncle's death, as then they would lose the tontine. They eventually pack the body into a water-butt and place it on a train to London, directing it to their address in Bloomsbury. On the journey, however, a prankster—coincidentally, a friend of Michael Finsbury—switches the address label with that of a crate containing a statue, which is supposed "'to lie at Waterloo till called for,' and [is] addressed to one 'William Dent Pitman'" (p. 39). Meanwhile the real Joseph, who has survived the crash, has been wandering around the countryside, and ends up on the same London-bound train as the packing-cases. Pitman unwittingly receives the water-butt containing the corpse, and is assisted by his lawyer—who happens to be Michael Finsbury—in disposing of it. They deposit the body in a Broadwood Piano owned by a young man-about-town, Gideon Forsyth.

Morris, meanwhile, is appalled to discover that he has received a packing-crate containing a statue of Hercules, rather than the barrel con-taining the corpse of his uncle. The crate has in fact been opened by Gideon and Julia Hazeltine, a young woman who lives at Joseph's home. In a rage at the mistake, Morris attacks the statue with a hammer and destroys it. Gideon, having discovered the corpse concealed in his Broad-wood piano, takes a houseboat under the false name of Jimson (suppos-edly a frustrated composer), and plans to drop the body into the canal, feigning the suicide of his alter-ego. But the cart carrying the piano—inside which the corpse remains hidden—is stolen, and is last seen dri-ving away into the distance. As Gideon says of the cart-driver, "The man has been ass enough to steal the cart and the dead body; what he hopes to do with it I neither know nor care" (p. 144). The real Joseph Finsbury is finally restored to his relatives.

As this summary indicates, *The Wrong Box* is a story about error, mistaken identity, and misadventure. Though several calamities have already occurred as the narrative commences—in particular, the loss of Morris's and John's fortune in their Uncle's declining leather business—the central disaster determining the plot occurs with the train wreck. The narrator draws attention to the link between the fiction and the railway journey in the opening paragraph, by lamenting the labor, on the part of the author, necessary "to while away an hour for him [the reader] in a railway train" (p. 1). The railway carriage is here posited as the presumed locale in which the narrative is consumed: a fact borne out by John Suther-land's observation that "The great Victorian railway expansion (or 'mania') took place in the late 1830s and early 1840s, creating a distinct new market for portable, entertaining books."[23] In constructing the reader as a railway traveler, the narrator may be referring not only to the casual relationship between text and reader common to such consumers, but also to the tolerance they had for sensational or shocking subject matter: "The railway boom created a new lease of life for the authors who were favourites with the traveling public, who tended to be broader in their tastes than circulating library subscribers" (Sutherland, p. 519). Yet the train wreck effectively derails the story Stevenson has begun to construct around the tontine, precipitating the characters into a wholly new and unexpected sequence of events. This first violently interrupted journey inaugurates a series of failed or incomplete expeditions: just as the train fails to deliver Joseph's body—by this time a very valuable commodity—to its destination, the corpse which results from the wreck will never be properly delivered or, indeed, identified.

The motif of the random, aimless, or interrupted journey is an impor-tant feature not only of Stevenson's fiction but also of the travel writings with which he began his career. In the Preface to his first published book, *An Inland Voyage* (1878), Stevenson warns the reader that "Caleb and Joshua brought back from Palestine a formidable bunch of grapes; alas! my little book produces naught so nourishing," yet then expresses the hope that "the eccentricity may please in frivolous circles."[24] This address to the "frivolous" reader identifies the journey as a quaintly unproductive, dilettante exercise, in describing which Stevenson refers to himself and his traveling companion frequently as "pedlars." Framing the journey as a gentle rebellion against Victorian bourgeois work practices and efficiency, Stevenson describes his travels as "the most leisurely of progresses" characterized by delay and disruption, "now waiting horses for days together on some inconsiderable junction" (p. 45). Yet the narrative takes on a serious purpose as the journey down the river becomes a metaphor for the vagaries of life and the deferral of death:

> we may look upon our little private war with death somewhat in this light. If a man knows he will sooner or later be robbed upon a journey, he will have a bottle of the best in every inn and look upon all his extravagances as so much gained upon the thieves.... So every bit of brisk living, and above all when it is healthful, is just so much gained upon the wholesale filcher, death [p. 50].

Yet death returns to haunt the traveler-author, as even the shape of his canoe becomes a *memento mori*: "There are people who call out to me that it is like a coffin" (p. 57). Stevenson warns the reader that "There is no coming back ... on the impetuous stream of life.... And we must all set our pocket watches by the clock of fate. There is a headlong, forthright tide, that bears away man with his fancies like straw, and runs fast in time and space" (pp. 68–69). Anticipating the metaphorical language of *The Ebb-Tide*, in *An Inland Voyage* Stevenson depicts the journey as a futile struggle against death, and yet affirms its random quality with the claim that "the most beautiful adventures are not those we go to seek" (*Inland Voyage*, p. 111).

The Wrong Box ends with the jarring image of the corpse going astray on the stolen cart, emblematic of the narrative as a risky journey on which things never go according to plan, characters fail to arrive at their proper destinations, and the narrative itself fails to reach a satisfactory conclusion. The railway, like the novel itself, came of age in a century of increasing speed, population growth, and travel, and was designed to accelerate the transportation of bodies from one location to another. In his study of the dynamics of desire in narrative fiction, Peter Brooks has compared the plot of the nineteenth-century novel to an engine or motor which moves the reader forward in time and space. Representing the "fascination with engines and forces" characteristic of the period, the presence of machines in fiction indicates that "Life in the text of the modern is a nearly thermodynamic process; plot is, most aptly, a steam engine."[25] In Stevenson's novel, the "engine" that moves the comic plot forward is, in fact, a steam engine: yet its progress is brutally halted by a more powerful engine, "the down express" (p. 17) which might represent the dominant "engine" of narrative realism, with which Stevenson's "railway novel" collides. In the resulting crash, the narrative is fragmented and the plot is transformed into utter chaos which will require the utmost ingenuity to restore to order. The corpse, then, emerges from the wreckage as an embodiment of the contingency and disorder produced by the derailing of realist narrative. As the doctor says at the scene of accident, while "the vomit of steam ... still spouted from the broken engines": "there's terrible work before us" (pp. 18–19).

Of course, Stevenson has skillfully engineered this wreckage of his plot to allow the emergence of a different kind of narrative desire; one that eschews the logic of narrative order for something more open-ended. What Brooks terms the "totalizing" movement of narrative desire, in which the "ultimate determinants of meaning lie at the end," embraces "a system of potentially unlimited energetic transformations and exchanges" (*Reading for the Plot* pp. 52, 43). Paradoxically, the chief figure for this reanimation of the narrative from the wreckage of its own plot is the mutilated corpse: an object described, with a telling reference to the loss of lifelike characteristics, as "something that had once been human" (*Wrong Box* p. 19). The mistaken identification of this corpse by Morris and John as the body of their uncle can occur only because—as has been made clear in fascinating self-reflexive passage—the followers of Sir Faraday Bond are already so interchangeable that even at the moment of his first appearance, this "character" has already ceased to exist: "Many passengers put their heads to the window, and among the rest an old gentleman on whom I willingly dwell, for I am nearly done with him now.... His name is immaterial" (p. 16). This refusal to provide an identity for a character who is so eminently dispensable rejects the sheer pleasure of creating and elaborating a character that typifies a Dickens novel, for example, and shirks the obligation to narrate the precise details of character and location that are the hallmark of the realist novel.

This gesture of dismissal is a far more effective death than the one that follows in the train wreck. Indeed, the narrator makes clear that the modern age makes individual members of society highly dispensable: "If the whole of this wandering cohort were to disappear tomorrow, their absence would be wholly unremarked. How much more, if only one—say this one in the ventilating cloth—should vanish!" (p. 17). The only trace of interiority attributed to this anonymous man is his sadness as he contemplates his own obsolescence: "Perhaps the old gentleman thought something of the sort, for he looked melancholy enough" (p. 17). Yet another significant dynamic here is, precisely, the narrative desire to destroy the "old gentleman," one of several substitutes in the novel for the father with whom Stevenson himself had such a conflicted relationship. The desired death of the father—which, in Thomas Stevenson's case had occurred two years earlier in 1887, leaving Louis financially independent—here anticipates the ending of the novel leaving the narrative with no goal to pursue.[26] Yet this premature "death" leads to a crucial error—perhaps a wish-fulfillment—as John and Morris hastily identify the deceased as their uncle and go on to engage in a series of new "games" and "fictions," beginning with the brothers' decision to hide the body and their realization that "we must take assumed names" (*Wrong Box* p. 23). Morris Finsbury, in fact, takes advantage of the wrecked plot to appropriate the role of author in determining the fates of characters, saying of his uncle, "He's not dead, unless I choose" (p. 21). Morris decides that the "fiction" of his uncle's being alive has, unlike the life itself, no need for closure: "There's no sort of limit to the game that I propose" (p. 22).

The "wrongness" evoked by the novel's title, then, alludes not only to the destruction of the train that redirects the plot and the ensuing series of ill-chosen containers in which the corpse is deposited, but also to the novel's "repellant" subject matter, in which death and the deceased body are treated as prolonged jokes. Additionally, Margaret Oliphant's critique of Stevenson's text identifies another construction of "wrongness," as when she refers to the novel itself as "a very wrong box indeed."[27] Here an element apparently belonging to the plot—the confusion between packing-cases or boxes that leads to the misdirection of the corpse—is appropriated within a critique of the "errors" of the narrative as a work by a recognized author, especially its failure to conform to conventions of genre and authorial responsibility. What is "wrong" about *The Wrong Box*, from Oliphant's point of view, is that Stevenson never should have written it and, having done so, he should never have published it, because it deals with subject matter not suitable for fictional treatment and does not belong to any particular "box" used to classify narrative fiction.

But Oliphant's comment also reveals a slippage—a pun—in the title of the novel itself. If the "wrong box" refers at the level of plot to the confusion between the packing case and the water-barrel, it also implicitly alludes to the failures of the "box"—the novel or the plot itself—to adequately contain the desires it so impermissibly represents. As an illicit object of desire, the corpse can only be safely removed by burying it in a coffin, which would thereby be the "right box." None of the "boxes" in the novel, however, achieve the status of what D.A. Miller terms the "ultimate mortifying box" in which the corpse may finally, and with propriety, be laid to rest.[28] Consequently, the coffinless corpse is allowed—like Stevenson's body in the coffin-shaped canoe—to wander aimlessly, functioning as a contaminated object of desire that eludes societal control. Far from being privatized in the novel, this "box" escapes its rightful owner and is passed from one unwilling host to another, so that by the novel's end all characters are implicated in, and contaminated by, the transgressive desire of/for the body.

This desire inevitably surfaces in displaced forms, for the corpse can only be represented in terms of its movements or its coverings, all of which imbue the body with a kind of unruly animation that the artifice of narrative plot manifestly fails to contain. Following the discovery of the body in a water-barrel by Pitman and Michael Finsbury, it is described in terms that allude to its inhuman and inscrutable form: "In the midst of these [fragments of water-barrel] a certain dismal something, swathed in blankets, remained for an instant upright, and then toppled to one side and heavily collapsed before the fire. Even as the thing subsided, an eye-glass tingled to the floor and rolled toward the screaming Pitman" (*Wrong Box*, p. 75). This scene explicitly renders the corpse—as an object of dehumanized materiality and mortality—a source of disgust and horror. Yet this adverse reaction is itself productive of a screening discourse that transposes the response of sheer terror at the inanimate body into a sequence of ingenious jokes and puns tending to generate amusement at the appalling lifelessness of the object. Returning to his darkened apartment, Gideon first bumps into the Broadwood piano which has been placed in the center of the room, or as the narrative playfully states, "dashed himself against a heavy body; where … no heavy body should have been" (p. 115). Attempting to play the piano, he is shocked to find the keyboard will produce no sound: "He gave the Broadwood two great bangs with his clenched fist. All was still as the grave" (p. 115). The inactive, silent bulk of the piano—its "heavy body"—metonymically represents the corpse it contains, while the powers of expression previously possessed by Gideon and his instrument are paralyzed by the corpse's mortifying presence.

Stevenson's comic manipulation of novelistic discourse in *The Wrong Box*—a violation of propriety against which Victorian critics protested stridently—derives from the reliance of the plot on a presence that threatens to implode the "artifice" of novelistic character. The narrative mischievously generates a sequence of metonymic and euphemistic displacements for the corpse which substitute for the "inner life" of character, and endow the inanimate corpse with the illusion of substance and vitality. The self-reflexive status of the characters' speech when in the vicinity of the corpse suggests the extent to which discourse has ceased to be transparent, and has become a problem of selective represention, best expressed by the words of one of the characters in this scene: "What language am I to find?" (p. 77). A typical exchange occurs when Michael Finsbury and Pitman decide to "get him out of sight," by means of hiding the body in a closet, in the course of which the corpse is referred to evasively as "it," as "you know what" (p. 78), "that horror in my studio" (p. 79) and once, most bizarrely, as "Cleopatra" (p. 78).

Following its concealment, the corpse's anonymity is preserved by referring to it as the "party in the closet" (p. 77), at which point it becomes a dangerous yet unmentionable secret between the two men. Pitman's fear that his "eminently respectable" life, which he deems hitherto "entirely fit for publication" (p. 76), will be fatally compromised by the presence of the corpse seems to mock authorial anxiety at the hostile reception in store for the novel itself, which was deemed as being entirely unfit for publication under Stevenson's imprimatur. Additionally, however, the scene invokes the specifically male secret as a site of "horror" with sexual connotations and scandalous consequences. Indeed, the morbid "game" of hide-and-seek played between characters in *The Wrong Box* invokes, with its fixation on the materiality of the male body, a context of homoeroticism. In the course of this "game," the proximity of the corpse becomes part of a transgressive scene of male intimacy that leads to what might be termed the novel's primal scene, as Michael Finsbury suggests that he and Pitman bury the body: "We should look devilish romantic shoveling out the sod by the moon's pale ray" (*Wrong Box* p. 76). This in turn is supplanted by another plan, eventually adopted, of passing the corpse onto someone else: "If you won't take the short cut and bury this in your back garden, we must find some one who will bury it in his" (p. 77). The "sod" is, of course, an abbreviated term for "sodomite." "Shoveling out the sod," then, or indeed "bury[ing] in your back garden," may be read as a coded representation of sodomy.[29] This scenario is linked to the imminent threat of invasion by the police, whom Michael describes, to a terrified Pitman, "digging up your back garden" (p. 78). The sodomitic encryption of the secret burial suggests the threat that the corpse poses to the sanctity of masculine character as possessing an inviolable "inner life." Leo Bersani has carefully traced the discursive association between sodomy and the death of subjectivity, whereby the "rectum" becomes rhetorically configured as a "grave" for the masculine subject.[30] Bersani's account is useful in this context, because it examines the association between anal pleasure and the evacuation of subjectivity that is viewed, in Western culture, as the self-destructive abdication of masculine power and privilege.

What is at stake for Bersani's analysis is less the pleasures and problems of a specific sexual practice than the production of male sexual passivity as the abandonment of the Western masculine ideal of autonomy and selfhood. According to Bersani the specter of anal penetration invokes the loss of a culturally privileged identity, and it is this "death" that is figured by the disturbing receptivity of the "rectum" and helps to account for the astonishing persistence of homophobic prejudice. Though Bersani examines this "frenzied epic of displacements" (p. 220) in the context of AIDS discourse, his argument goes on to embrace the "suicidal" implications of male sexual passivity. Pointing to "the heterosexual association of anal sex with a self-annihilation originally and primarily identified with the fantasmatic mystery of an insatiable, unstoppable female sexuality," Bersani celebrates the notion that "the rectum is the grave in which the masculine ideal ... of proud subjectivity is buried" and encourages the assault on, or fragmentation of, "the sacrosanct value of selfhood that sexual *jouissance* achieves" (p. 222).

The notion of "selfhood" that Bersani invokes precisely to discard is one that the nineteenth-century realist novel establishes as the ideological basis for its fiction, and reproduces through its strategies of containment. In *The Wrong Box* Stevenson carries out his attack on this notion of the novelistic plot, specifically as one based on the individual life story, through the comic possibilities of the corpse. Despite Stevenson's repeated attempts to control and "box in" its contaminating influence, the corpse successfully evades the containment strategies of the novel brought into play by the prospect of the burial. As Jameson argues in *The Political Unconscious*, such containment seeks to "manage" impulses that represent the "unthinkable," in order "to defuse them, to prepare substitute gratifications for them" (p. 266).[31] In the scene I have cited from *The Wrong Box*, the "grave" is imagined as being the final and proper container of the erotically charged corpse, and yet the intention of "shoveling out the sod" must be abandoned in favor of a strategy of containment that, by passing the corpse onto someone else, only produces further chaos and failures of closure. The fact that the scene of burial is a doubly imaginary one—it is fantasized by a character in a novel, and never actually "occurs" even in the plot of a fiction—emphasizes the relation of this episode to the manipulation of narrative techniques.

The homoeroticism of the scene, however, becomes a new narrative "engine" that drives the plot forward and keeps the body in circulation. Here, Stevenson defers a closural strategy of "burial"—initially attempted when the Finsbury brothers dig a shallow grave only then to set the corpse on its course again—in favor of a new displacement, by which it enters a new economy of desire. The dead body cannot remain lifeless: it must be reanimated by a series of competing intentions that take the form of the various containers—the "boxes"—in which the corpse is strategically deposited and transported. These "boxes" serve at once as the metonymic displacements of the body, by means of which its disruptive influence is disseminated through the narrative, and the futile strategies of containment generated by the plot to contain the errant desires it has aroused. The Broadwood piano in which Michael and Pitman transfer the body to the unsuspecting Gideon's apartment is, perhaps the most absurd of the "wrong boxes" in which the corpse is deposited. Indeed, the very "wrongness" of this box draws attention to the fact that the narrative produces no "right box" with which finally to govern and close off the generative effects of the corpse.

There is "no sort of limit to the game" in which the body participates, no termination of the discursive transformations it might undergo. With no clear limit to the number of "wrong boxes" that might be invented, the plot itself becomes a limitless "box," a space that cannot be measured because it is without boundaries. Even when it has outlived its usefulness in the plot—when the body is eventually discovered not to be that of Joseph Finsbury, it loses its economic or narrative significance—the corpse continues to dominate the discourse. Gideon's final "qualms of conscience" (*Wrong Box* p. 179) concerning the unidentified dead body being carried away in a cart indicate the narrative's bypassing of the problematic question that it had posed earlier: "How does a gentleman dispose of a dead body, honestly come by?" (p. 119). The situation is embarrassing, of course, because a "gentleman" ought not to be in the possession of a "dead body" in the first place: to desire, let alone to possess, such an object, as my discussion of the earlier scene argues, is to enter an unstable discourse of uncontrolled desire, sodomy, and secrecy, and to risk the contaminating influence of the incriminating object. In a telling exchange between Gideon and Morris over the whereabouts of the corpse, a dangerous desire is at once foregrounded and disavowed by its very interrogation and repetition:

> "Where is the body? This is very strange," mused Gideon. "Do you want the body?"

> "Want it?" cried Morris. "My whole fortune depends upon it!
> I lost it. Where is it? Take me to it!"
>   "O, you want it, do you? And the other man, Dickson—does
> he want it?" enquired Gideon [p. 167].

If the corpse can never be decisively claimed or named during the novel—if it remains to the end an object in limbo, without a proper owner—this does not prevent it from becoming an object of improper desire. The silence surrounding its decease is attributable to the scandalous associations that have accrued to the concept of possession and desiring the body, even—or especially—the desire to bury it: to "bury in the back garden" is now to commit buggery, and the body must be kept in motion if only indefinitely to defer the perpetration of this unspeakable act.

Consequently, the fate of the corpse—and hence of the narrative itself—is left unresolved, by delivering it up to a new destination that will never be represented in the text or mastered by the plot. Concerning the ignominious fate of the corpse—"the man in the cart" (p. 179)—these flagrantly fictional figures can, with an insouciance which betrays their own relieved liberation from the corpse's scandalous presence, do "nothing but sympathize" (p. 179). Though the body has not been buried, it has at least been (temporarily) banished. If, as D.A. Miller argues in *The Novel and the Police*, the Dickensian character is "frequently coupled with boxes: bags, parcels, luggage" (p. 200), then the ending of *The Wrong Box* develops that coupling to a promiscuous extreme: the character has *become* a box, a parcel presumably to be packed off to the next unsuspecting host, perhaps to initiate another series of connected events, another "plot." The *Pall Mall* reviewer's protests against the "funereal fun" and "Churchyard humours" (p. 3) of *The Wrong Box* register, among other things, a cultural uneasiness with a narrative in which the rhetorical and comic productivity of the corpse is the central feature. Yet this disgust at the fictional corpse is also symptomatic of a deeper unease with the production of desire that cannot be contained by the familiar boxes of character and narrative closure. Among the most disturbing features of *The Wrong Box* is its power to suggest, without naming them, the presence of unspeakable desires that surface in other works by Stevenson, only then to reappropriate them for a comic purpose. In fact, the reanimated corpse appears in many of Stevenson's works, including highly praised novels such as *Treasure Island*, *Kidnapped*, and *The Master of Ballantrae* on which his literary reputation was chiefly based. This double function of the reanimated corpse—both driving narrative desire and disrupting its progress towards closure—emerges as a central element of Stevenson's narrative achievement.

Excavating the "Unburied"

It was, of course, the centrality of the corpse as protagonist that critics found most distasteful in *The Wrong Box*. Yet from his earliest success as a writer, Stevenson had displayed a keen interest in the reanimation of dead bodies. The story that most resembles *The Wrong Box* in its macabre humor and its treatment of the corpse as a gruesome secret is "The Suicide Club," first published in 1882 as part of the *New Arabian Nights*. The three sections of this story are loosely connected by the "suicide club," an organization in London that offers a quick and easy death to men who are tired of life. In "The Story of the Physician and the Saratoga Trunk," Silas, a young American in Paris, is unwittingly lured into a murder plot, and returns from an assignation with a mysterious woman to find the corpse of a young man in his room. Like Pitman in *The Wrong Box*, Silas is induced to conceal the unwanted corpse by a stronger-willed, more worldly man, Dr. Noel. The body becomes a homoerotic secret between the two men, as Noel asks pointedly, "Do you think this piece of dead flesh on your pillow can alter in any degree the sympathy with which you have inspired me?"[32] Having noticed Silas's saratoga trunk in the room, Noel concludes that "the object of such a box is to contain a human body" (p. 46). Together they pack the corpse into the trunk: "Silas taking the heels and the Doctor supporting the shoulders—the body of the murdered man was carried from the bed, and, after some difficulty, doubled up and inserted whole into the empty box. With an effort on the part of both, the lid was forced down upon this unusual baggage" (p. 46).

Silas's evident uneasiness at the unorthodox burial of the body suggests the guilt of the sinner and the fear of discovery: it is significant that the dead body is discovered in Silas' bed, and the Doctor's initial question, "how came this body in your room?" (p. 43) seems to invite a confession of a sexual motive for its presence (earlier the dead man had been described as "a very handsome young fellow of small stature" [p. 35]). Hence, the corpse becomes associated in the narrative with a stifled, unacknowledged sexuality, bringing into the open inclinations Silas has not recognized. Silas becomes increasingly obsessed with the secret contents of his box, fearing that "a single false step ... and the box might go over the banisters and land its fatal contents, plainly discovered, on the pavement of the hall" (p. 52). The same fear of discovery leads Silas to check the concealed corpse for signs of decay: "As soon as he was alone the unfortunate New Englander nosed all the cracks and openings with the most passionate attention. But the weather was cool, and the trunk still managed to contain his shocking secret" (p. 53). As in *The Wrong Box*, the container is metonymically substituted for the corpse it contains, the "cracks and openings" of the trunk substituting for the prohibited orifices of the body. In this early story, the corpse is incriminating not only because it implicates Silas in murder, but also because it suggests the "unspeakable" vice of sodomy elicited by the presence of what Silas terms "this object in my bed, not to be explained, not to be disposed of, not to be regarded without horror" (p. 45).

The figure of the reanimated corpse makes several appearances in *Treasure Island*—Stevenson's first important literary success, published in volume form in 1883—in which several of the more memorable scenes involve pirates who are presumed dead but come back to life. A turning point in the narrative occurs when Jim Hawkins, having set the *Hispaniola* adrift, finds the apparently dead bodies of Israel Hands and the "red cap" O'Brien: "I observed, around both of them, splashes of dark blood upon the planks, and began to feel sure that they had killed each other in their drunken wrath."[33] Hands's death proves to be illusory, as Jim writes that "in a calm moment, when the ship was still, Israel Hands turned partly round, and, with a low moan, writhed himself back to the position in which I had seen him first" (p. 155). The horror of the ensuing scene, in which the reanimated Hands makes a villainous attempt on Jim's life before plunging to his own death, has as a prelude Hands's interrogation of Jim on the question of reanimation: "There was this here O'Brien, now—he's dead, ain't he? Well, now, I'm no scholar, and you're a lad as can read and figure; and, to put it straight, do you take it as a dead man is dead for good, or do he come alive again?" On being informed that the body may die but the spirit lives on, Hands succinctly replies "that's unfort'nate—appears as if killing parties was a waste of time" (p. 159). The life-and-death struggle between Hands and Jim unfolds in the grim company of O'Brien's corpse, which at one point is itself reanimated: "the dead red-cap with his arms still spread out, tumbling stiffly after us.... Blow and all, I was the first afoot again; for Hands had got involved with the dead body" (p. 165). Threatening Hands with a pistol, Jim warns him that "Dead men don't bite, you know" (p. 165) and, after Hands's thrown knife narrowly misses him, shoots him dead. Yet even after he hits the water, Hands threatens to return to life: "He rose once to the surface in a lather of foam and blood, and then sank again for good.... Sometimes, by the quivering of the water, he appeared to move a little as if he were trying to rise. But he was dead enough, for all that, being both shot and drowned" (p. 167).

David Balfour, the narrator and hero in Stevenson's most famous adventure narrative, *Kidnapped*, is also reanimated, making two dramatic returns from presumed death. On first seeking the help of his uncle Ebenezer after his father's death, David is treacherously sent up a tower by his uncle, to retrieve "the chest that's at the top."[34] While climbing the staircase, David turns a corner in the dark, and "feeling forward as usual, my hand slipped upon an edge and found nothing but emptiness beyond it. The stair had been carried no higher: to set a stranger mounting it in the darkness was to send him straight to his death" (p. 25). Upon David's return to his uncle's house, Ebenezer "flung up his arms, and tumbled to the floor like a dead man" (p. 26) and then returned to consciousness apparently believing that David had returned from the dead: "'Are you alive?' he sobbed. 'O man, are ye alive?'" (p. 27). Though David physically survives this episode, it effectively leads to the elimination of his identity as, following his kidnapping, David has frequent difficulty in proving who he is. On returning to Edinburgh at the end of the narrative, for example, he realizes that "I had no grounds to stand upon; and no clear proof of my rights, nor so much as of my own identity" (p. 197). David has in fact returned from presumed death a second time; for as the lawyer explains, following David's disappearance Captain Hoseason appeared "with the story of [David's] drowning; whereupon all fell through" (p. 202).

With his body restored to safety, and again clothed in civilized fashion, the hero's reanimation is complete, "and David Balfour [came] to life again" (p. 205). The restoration of his identity—his "coming back to life"—is the necessary precursor of the restoration of his property, which occurs after a final encounter with his conniving uncle. David's reanimation, however, is immediately followed by the sudden loss of animation of his uncle, who David says "stared upon us like a man turned to stone," paralyzed by the return of the dead (p. 218). Finally, David's new life as "a man of means" is also compromised by a loss of his own, as he remarks, "This good change in my case unmanned me more than any of the former evil ones" (p. 219). In particular, the parting from Alan Breck—who has acted as David's unofficial, surrogate father and tutored him in the skills of manhood and survival—produces a mourning for the lost self he had cultivated in physical intimacy with Alan, "a cold knawing in my inside like a remorse for something wrong" (p. 223). Even as David comes back to life and gains a fortune, his return to Edinburgh interpellates him—like Stevenson himself—as a guilty, fatherless son.

The narrative force of reanimation again emerges in a context of familial conflict in *The Master of Ballantrae* (1889), a work that, like *Kidnapped*, uses the Jacobite rebellion of 1745 as a historical background. While the corpse is itself an object of desire and competition between relatives in *The Wrong Box*, and David's "death" is the result of fraternal hatred in *Kidnapped*, *The Master of Ballantrae* features an animated corpse that returns to exacerbate an already-existing sibling rivalry. Although the laudatory critical reception enjoyed by *The Master of Ballantrae* could hardly have contrasted more with the cries of derision and outrage that greeted *The Wrong Box* earlier the same year, the historical romance was also criticized for the confusion of narrative modes that resulted from the improper reanimation of a corpse. Indeed, *The Master of Ballantrae* blends together narrative techniques from several of Stevenson's earlier works, including the pirate story (*Treasure Island*), the historical romance (*Kidnapped*) and the tale of reanimation (*The Wrong Box*).[35] This blurring of narrative categories reflects the disruptions of Stevenson's unsettled life during this period, the frequent journeying between the Adirondacks, California, and the South Seas in search of a climate that suited his failing health. In January 1888 Stevenson wrote to Henry James of his concern about the latter chapters of *The Master of Ballantrae*: "I regret to say are not so soundly designed ... they are fantastic, they shame, perhaps degrade, the beginning." He also acknowledged the influence of location on the bizarre conclusion to the narrative in stating that "the devil and Saranac suggested this *dénouement*" (*Letters*, VI, 105).[36] But the *dénouement* also suggested his resistance to being "boxed in" by narrative categories and generic conventions: even as he struggled to construct a coffin for *The Master of Ballantrae*, Stevenson recognized that his hero could not be contained.

The venerable Mrs. Oliphant, in her *Blackwood's* review of *The Master of Ballantrae*, dismissed Stevenson's collaboration with Osbourne on *The Wrong Box* as an "unworthy exhibition," and then wrote of *Ballantrae* that the critic is "proportionately grateful and joyful now to find him [Stevenson] in his right mind, in a piece of work which would do credit to any name" (p. 696). The implication that Stevenson had "lost his mind"—was alienated from himself (in a manner at least implicitly comparable to the self-division of Henry Jekyll)—and was now restored to his "right mind" is attributable less to Oliphant's admiration of the aesthetic merits of the novel than to her relief that the proper role of the author as the unique creator of his work has been reestablished, and the true (literary and economic) value of his commodity-text reaffirmed. The confusions and disturbances over identity, desire, and authorship that had been generated by *The Wrong Box* and its errant corpse were, it seemed, reassuringly laid to rest by the appearance of *The Master of Ballantrae*.

And yet, in another reviewer's apparently positive verdict that "in 'The Master of Ballantrae' [Stevenson] has produced something very like a classic," we may detect a lingering reservation about the literary value of Stevenson's art: for a work that is "very like" a classic is still not quite a classic. The same critic would single out the very passages that had given Stevenson the most trouble as he completed the novel—the burial, resurrection, and ultimate death of the Master—for rebuke as "an inadmissible plunge into the supernatural."[37] As its concluding drama suggests, *The Master of Ballantrae* brings into sharp focus the violently homoerotic nature of this proximity of bodies—of corpses—in its narrative of prolonged and violent fraternal conflict. The final disinterral is in fact the third of the Master's reanimations: the first occurs when he returns to Durisdeer after being presumed killed fighting for the rebels' side in the Jacobite uprising of 1745. The second follows his apparent death in the duel between the brothers, a scene described by one critic as "one of the most powerful and touching in the annals of romance."[38] The duel takes place after Henry, jealous of his brother's relationship with Alison, "struck the Master in the mouth," at which point Mackellar comments, "I had never seen the man so beautiful."[39] The ambiguity here—which "man" is he referring to?—registers the arousing and disorienting power of violence on a male spectator, and continues with Mackellar's witnessing of the duel itself: "I cannot say I followed it, my untrained eye was never quick enough to seize details, but it appears he [James] caught his brother's blade with his left hand, a practice not permitted. Certainly Mr. Henry only saved himself by leaping on one side; as certainly the Master, lunging in the air, stumbled on his knee, and before he could move the sword was through his body" (p. 97).

Mackellar's uncertainty over exactly what happens suggests he may be mistaken in his judgment that the Master has received a fatal wound— "the heart was quite still, it gave not a flutter" (p. 97)—and thus prepares the reader for the return of the Master from the dead. At the same time, it raises the possibility that the Master is possessed of some supernatural agency, as his disappearance from the scene of his death seems magical: "There was the blood-stain in the midst; and a little farther off Mr. Henry's sword, the pommel of which was of silver, but of the body, not a trace" (p. 105). Mackellar depends for the incident of his narrative on the Master's supernatural ability to return from the dead, yet these repeated resurrections threaten to disrupt the narrative's progress towards closure, by invoking the unstable dynamic of repetition and circularity.[40] Even as the reanimation of the Master drives the narrative forward, it also indicates its failure to survive without the demonic hero's disruptive, vitalizing influence.[41]

Exploring the violent ambivalence of this fraternal and filial conflict, Stevenson's narrative passes through a series of "false" conclusions—the

Master's alleged death in the '45, his apparent end in the duel—to reach
its culmination in the "double funeral" (p. 233), where the brothers'
corpses are reunited and laid to rest in a long-resisted intimacy. The desire
to be "rid of the Master" and the disturbing energies he represents suggests a longing for purification, by dismissing the contaminated corpse
and terminating the narrative. In relating his failure to destroy the Master, Henry Durie reenacts his violent encounter with his brother:

> "He's not of this world" whispered my lord, "neither him nor the
> black deil [devil] that serves him. I have struck my sword through-
> out his vitals," he cried; "I have felt the hilt dirl [ring] on his
> breastbone, and the hot blood spirt in my very face, time and
> again, time and again!" he repeated, with a gesture indescribable.
> "But he was never dead for that," said he and sighed aloud. "Why
> should I think he was dead now? No, not till I see him rotting,"
> says he [p. 223].

We again confront the limits of Mackellar's narrative powers—Henry's
gesture can only be represented as "indescribable"—as the passage strongly
represents the duel as a gruesome enaction of sexual penetration and ejac-
ulation, issuing in a reanimated corpse. Henry's desire to bury his brother
surfaces as he mis-remembers the outcome of the duel, claiming that
Mackellar had "buried him with his own hands" (p. 233). This mistake
reveals a frustrated wish that he had, in fact, achieved this complete
removal of his brother's demonic body and, thus, the termination of the
story it dominates. But the wish to "bury the master" is at the same time
a return in displaced form of the desire to bury his weapon in the master's body, to penetrate him. This is a wish which is first realized in Mackellar's description "the sword was through his body"—and then obsessively
repeated in Henry's discourse: "I have struck my sword throughout his
vitals ... time and again." As in *The Wrong Box*, the desire for burial takes
on a prohibited, displaced association with the "indescribable" act—"a
practice not permitted"—of buggery.

The Master's end, finally, brings to a climax the uneasy hybridity
between literary genres and foregrounds the feature of the narrative perceived as "inadmissible"—the improper animation of a dead body. This
transgression, however, is precisely what links *The Master of Ballantrae* to
the narrative practices that had disturbed critics of *The Wrong Box*.[42] The
key episode—in which the Master, James Durie, after being buried alive
in the Adirondacks by his Indian servant, Secundra Dass, is brought back
to life—is recounted by the Durie family's retainer and the story's chief
narrator, Mackellar:

I thought I could myself perceive a change upon that icy countenance of the unburied. The next moment I beheld his eyelids
flutter; the next they rose entirely, and the week-old corpse looked
me for a moment in the face. So much display of life I can myself
swear to. I have heard from others that he visibly strove to speak,
that his teeth showed in his beard, and that his brow was contorted
as with an agony of pain and effort. And this may have been; I
know not, I was otherwise engaged. For at that first disclosure of
the dead man's eyes my Lord Durisdeer fell to the ground, and
when I raised him up he was a corpse [p. 232].

Paradoxically, the exhumation scene's most powerful effect is on Henry
Durie, who dies of the shock of seeing his "dead" brother return to life.
This is perhaps the most traumatic instance in Stevenson's fiction of the
contaminating influence of the corpse on a living body. The younger
brother falls, as it were, into the grave created for the elder—as he has previously stepped into his position as Lord Durisdeer and intended husband of Alison—and they are subsequently buried side by side. Hence, one
might say that the Master's reanimation produces an *excess* of closure—
both brothers die at once, the noble life is erased along with the demonic
one, the end of *The Master* represents the death of the novel's "official values," as embodied by Henry. And yet, Mackellar's conclusion discloses a
perhaps unconscious preference for the Master over his less animated
brother: there is a note of regret in the servant's account of "the earth
heaped for ever on his once so active limbs" (p. 227). Moreover, the epitaph "with a copy of which I may fitly bring my narrative to a close" (p.
233) contains an encomium of the "Master of the arts and graces" that
dims the light of his brother's "Life of unmerited distress" (pp. 233–34).
Thus this double grave and its epitaph uncovers the plot of the novel's
official values as being where, perhaps, they have always been buried: in
Mackellar's unreliable and inconsistent narrative.

Stevenson also expresses this fantasy of "burying the Master" in a
May 1889 letter to Will H. Low, as he describes his relief at finishing the
novel that he feared he would never finish: "*The Master* has been a sore
cross to me; but now he is buried, his body's under hatches,—his soul, if
there is any hell to go to, gone to Hell" (*Letters*, VI, 302). Dependent on
the highly narratable potency of the Master's subversive speech, inventive plotting, and erotically charged body, Stevenson's narrative must
nonetheless strive ineluctably towards the conclusive event of the Master's burial. Yet, what the narrative finally, perhaps perversely, renounces
is precisely this satisfying equation of burial with (narrative) closure. By
inserting the highly gothic scene of exhumation, following which the

Master returns to life, the narrative once more defers its closural strategy and reveals instead its investment in a circuit of repetition, powered by an inadmissible erotic fascination with the dead body. Hence, the grimly prophetic paradox uttered by Secundra—"He bury, he not dead" (p. 231)—indicates the disruption of the narrative's desire for "burial" as the final resting-place, both of the Master's body and of the text it names.

Stevenson's Ebb

In the year following the publication of *The Wrong Box* and *The Master of Ballantrae*, Stevenson moved permanently to the island of Samoa in the South Seas. Here he became deeply involved in Samoan politics and scathingly critical of the interference of colonial powers, including Britain and the United States, in the affairs of the Polynesian South Pacific. Stevenson's late fictions of the South Sea islands, especially "The Beach of Falesá" (1892) and *The Ebb-Tide*, reflect his initial optimism and ultimate disillusionment concerning the political stability and social progress of his chosen home.[43] *The Ebb-Tide*, the final work that Stevenson published during his lifetime, transports the trope of reanimation to the South Seas in order to develop a critique of colonial power, amoral materialism, and religious fanaticism. Lacking the humorous and macabre treatment of the corpse in *The Wrong Box* and "The Suicide Club," *The Ebb-Tide* is closer to *The Master of Ballantrae* in its view of reanimation as a sinister, perhaps inhuman power of evil, adding a new dimension in the character of the English colonialist, Attwater, a religious fanatic who justifies his plundering of the Pacific island's wealth by appealing to God: "I was a man of the world before I was a Christian; I'm a man of the world still, and I made my mission pay."[44] Attwater is not a missionary in any conventional sense: indeed, he criticizes them for being "too parsonish, too much of the old wife" (203) and describes his religion as "a savage thing" (p. 89).

Through Attwater's discourse, the narrative links the reanimation of the dead to the resurrection of Christ in what becomes, from one perspective, a religious parable of redemption. The degenerate trio of beach-comber-adventurers—Herrick, Captain Davis, and Huish—begin the story as human refuse stranded on the beach in Tahiti before being reanimated by the chance of a new "mission" when Davis is offered a ship, *The Farallone*. This "forbidden ship" (p. 31), however, turns out to be a floating coffin, the previous crew of which died of smallpox: the imagined presence of a "disfigured corpse" (p. 33) haunts the men as they pursue their illicit journey, and Herrick in particular is tormented by "the horror of that grave that we've escaped from" (p. 40). The purpose of this doomed voyage, to steal the cargo of champagne and sell the ship, is abandoned when the cargo is discovered to consist mainly of water in champagne bottles. Arriving at Attwater's island in search of a new source of wealth, the men soon penetrate the facade of peace and civilization, as Attwater's island proves to be not an escape from but an intensification of the link between colonialism and deadly disease. The ominous "silence of death" (p. 72) and "sense of desertion" (p. 74) are soon explained by Attwater's announcement that the island has been infested with smallpox: "That is why the house is empty and the graveyard is full" (p. 78). In answer to Herrick's immediate question, how they disposed of all the bodies ("when it came to burying—or did you bother burying?") Attwater haltingly confesses that, with people dying all around him, he "took the ... empty bottles ... into the lagoon, and ... buried them" (p. 78). The description of the natives' corpses as "empty bottles" inevitably links them with the fraudulent cargo of champagne, epitomizing the European view of the native islander as a commodity to be exploited and then discarded when its "content"—its labor—is used up.

Significantly, given Herrick's interest in death and burial, the crucial encounter between he and Attwater takes place in "the cemetery of the island," where "nothing but the number of the mounds, and their disquieting shape, indicated the presence of the dead" (pp. 89–90). Attwater, godlike, reanimates the spirits of the dead islanders, calling into being their living characters: "'Here was one I liked though,' and he set his foot upon a mound. 'He was a fine savage fellow; he had a dark soul; yes, I liked this one'" (p. 90). As Vanessa Smith observes, by this strategy "the populace of his island, decimated by disease, are resurrected as the subjects of story."[45] Curiously, it is in the cemetery that the relationship between the two Oxbridge men reaches a new intimacy, as Attwater tells Herrick, "You are attractive, very attractive" (p. 91). This statement leads Herrick to an erotic fascination with his host, and a desire to save him from the "two wolves": he experiences "an immense temptation to go up, to touch him on the arm and breathe a word in his ear: 'Beware, they are going to murder you'" (p. 93).

Perhaps the most intriguing symbol of reanimation in *The Ebb-Tide* is that of the diving-suit, which is transformed by Attwater into a metaphor for "God's grace" and by Herrick into a slogan of human "self-conceit" (p. 88). The practical function of the diving-suits is to assist in Attwater's hoarding of pearls (the original title of the story was "The Pearl Fisher"),[46] but Attwater describes the effects of the suits in a striking scene of reanimation: "It ... was a queer sight when they were at it, and these marine monsters … kept appearing and reappearing in the midst of the lagoon" (p. 88). This reappearance of the divers suggests the reanimation of the corpses that Attwater has "buried" in the lagoon, perhaps returning to rebuke the colonialist for their exploited lives and ignominious grave. The connection between the resurfacing divers and reanimation of the dead is strengthened when Attwater links the diving-suit to the resurrected Christ, "He who died for you, He who upholds you, He whom you daily crucify afresh" (p. 88). Offering a "parable" for the suits, Attwater says, "I saw these machines come up dripping and go down again, and come up dripping and go down again … and I thought we all wanted a dress to go down into the world in, and come up scatheless" (pp. 87–88). The body inside the "diving suit" of faith has become a resurrected corpse, an animated "machine": the body as machine appears again when Attwater tries to convert Herrick, who is shocked "to find the whole machine thus glow with the reverberation of religious zeal" (p. 88).

Stevenson's readers were no less appalled to find the "machine" of his anti-colonial narrative fuelled by religious zeal, especially embodied in such a debased incarnation. Reviewers—and to some extent Stevenson himself—saw *The Ebb-Tide* as a kind of barely animated literary corpse, "bringing together parts that failed to cohere, producing waste material, rather than a useful new object" (Smith, p. 156). In *The Speaker* a reviewer wrote: "Of grace, virtue, beauty, we get no glimpse. All we have in exchange is a picture of the fag-ends of certain useless and degraded lives."[47] Signaling the end of the collaboration between Stevenson and his stepson, *The Ebb-Tide* was taken by its critics as the symptom of Stevenson's literary ebb and creative demise, as in fact the "fag-end" of his career. As one critic expressed it, "This is not the Stevenson we love."[48] When the time came to evaluate Stevenson's career after his death in 1894, the South Sea tales were quietly buried by neglect, "as if this body of work did not exist" (Jolly, p. xxx).

Stevenson's animated corpses both vitalize and disrupt the narratives in which they appear, at once driving the engine of the plot and introducing a disorderly dynamic of circularity and bodily intimacy. By intruding its presence in narrative—by refusing to be contained or "boxed" in—the corpse in Stevenson's corpus blatantly violates the cultural convention of secrecy, whereby "the dead are shielded from view to protect them and us from our natural curiosity" (Quigley, p. 12). But, further undermining the unity of character and plot, these uncontained bodies circulate freely through their narratives, blurring the lines between Gothic romance, domestic tragedy, and macabre humor. Stevenson develops the animation of the corpse in *The Wrong Box* within a discourse of morbid

humor and homoerotic desire, thus elaborating his earlier comic treatment of the corpse in "The Suicide Club." Reanimation takes on much
darker significance in the adventure romances and South Sea tales, however, in which evil—in its most extreme case, demonic possession—is
associated with the reanimation of an abject, colonized body. Attwater's
fatalism and powers of reanimation in *The Ebb-Tide* link him to James
Durie in *The Master of Ballantrae*, while the three degenerate beach-
combers, traveling under assumed names, join the anonymous railway
victim of *The Wrong Box* as animated corpses whose restless journeying
betrays a submission to narrative contingency, moral futility, and abdication of will. Provocatively burying an unstable body of desire—a
"romance"—at the heart of Stevenson's corpus, the corpse's errant, unpre-
dictable progress might finally be characterized as a narrative journey that
ends up where it began.

NOTES

This essay has benefited from the careful readings and generous comments
of several colleagues. I would like in particular to thank Joseph Bristow and the
anonymous reader at *Nineteenth-Century Literature* for their scrupulous and
insightful criticisms to the manuscript. I am grateful also to Catherine Gallagher
for her insightful and constructive criticisms of an earlier version of this essay. I
would like, finally, to thank Hayden White and the members of his seminar on
"The Theory of the Text" at the 1998 School of Criticism and Theory, Cornell University, for creating a stimulating environment in which to think further about
the argument developed and the issues explored in this essay.

1. Recent publications include the multi-volume edition of the letters (*The
Letters of Robert Louis Stevenson*, ed. Bradford A. Booth and Ernest Mehew, 8 vols.
[New Haven: Yale Univ. Press, 1994–95]; hereafter referred to as *Letters*), as well
as two major biographies: Ian Bell, *Dreams of Exile: Robert Louis Stevenson: A
Biography* (New York: Henry Holt and Co., 1992), and Frank McLynn, *Robert
Louis Stevenson: A Biography* (New York: Random House, 1993), In addition, Alan
Sandison's recent study of Stevenson is the most extensive and important criti-
cal discussion to have appeared in many years (see *Robert Louis Stevenson and the
Appearance of Modernism* [New York: St Martin's, 1996]).

2. *Robert Louis Stevenson and the Fiction of Adventure* (Cambridge, Mass:
Harvard Univ. Press, 1964), p. 11.

3. The concept of reanimation is central to the fictional masterpieces of both
Wilde (*The Picture of Dorian Gray* [1891]) and Haggard (*She* [1887]). Dorian's
painting is animated by the wish that Dorian himself should be able to indulge
his desires without penalty, and the aesthetic object thereafter takes on the degenerative aspects of the corpse. In Haggard's romance, Ayesha, or She-Who-Must-
Be-Obeyed, preserves the corpse of her ancient lover, Kallikrates, while awaiting
his reincarnation. The character of Leo is, of course, just such a reanimated version

of Kallikrates, while Ayesha herself is a reanimated corpse, endlessly renewed by the "pillar of life." Moreover, Stevenson's narrative representation of the reanimated corpse participates in a Scottish Gothic tradition in fiction originating with James Hogg's *Confessions of a Justified Sinner* (1824), which uses the corpse to dramatize a concern with the continuing vitality of an oral tradition and expose the deathly powers of narrative itself. At the conclusion of Hogg's novel, the "editor"—who first narrates the series of events that are retold in Robert Wringhim's narrative—descends into the grave in a search for the corpse that will also disclose the origin of the narrative of Wringhim. This descent produces a dizzying circularity in the narrative, characteristic of the Gothic mode in which, as Fiona Robertson argues, "Narrative and historical processes are repeatedly figured as tortuous approaches through hidden subterranean passageways to a secret which may finally be revealed, but which can never be an adequate recompense for the terrors of the quest" (*Legitimate Histories: Scott, Gothic, and the Authorities of Fiction* [Oxford: Clarendon Press, 1994], p. 17).

    4. "Mr. R. L. Stevenson in the Wrong Box," rev. of *The Wrong Box, Pall Mall Gazette,* 19 June 1889, p. 3.

    5. See Wayne Koestenbaum, "The Shadow on the Bed: Dr Jekyll, Mr. Hyde, and the Labouchère Amendment." *Critical Matrix* Special Issue 1 (Spring 1988) 31–55. Koestenbaum argues that Stevenson's most famous "Gothic" story is an example of "bachelor" literature of the *fin-de-siecle* which, by excluding women, concentrates on the production of erotic and violent energies between men and involves "flight from wedlock and from the narrative conventions of bourgeois realism" (pp. 32–33). This focus on male desire is read by Koestenbaum as a response to the Labouchère Amendment, passed into law in 1885, and making any act of "gross indecency" between men, whether in public or private, punishable by a maximum sentence of two years imprisonment with hard labor. The effect of the Amendment, certainly apparent before the trials of Wilde in 1895, was to consolidate the association of male homosexuality with secrecy since concealment was the only effective defense against prosecution. See also Jeffrey Weeks, *Coming Out: Homosexual Politics in Britain from the Nineteenth Century to the Present,* rev. ed. (London: Quartet, 1990), pp. 14–20.

    6. For Fredric Jameson's use of this concept of "containment strategies"—which may have both ideological and formal applications—see his *The Political Unconscious: Narrative as a Socially Symbolic Act* (Ithaca: Cornell Univ. Press, 1981), pp. 53–54. For my argument, Jameson's relevant insight is that a strategy of containment "allows what can be thought to seem internally coherent in its own terms, while repressing the unthinkable ... which lies beyond its boundaries" (Jameson, p. 53).

    7. *Sexuality* (London: Routledge, 1997), p. 174.

    8. Stevenson, "A Gossip on Romance," in *Memories and Portraits,* vol. 29 of *The Works of Robert Louis Stevenson,* Tusitala Edition (London: William Heinemann, 1923), p. 121. Further references to Stevenson's works are to this edition, hereafter referred to as Works. "Incident" is perhaps the key term in Stevenson's defense of romance, and entirely eclipses the significance of character, to the extent that in the successful romance "the characters are no more than puppets.

The bony fist of the showman visibly propels them; their springs are an open secret; their faces are of wood, their bellies filled with bran; and yet we thrillingly partake of their adventures" ("Gossip," p. 126).

9. "Beyond Closure: Buried Alive with Hogg's *Justified Sinner*" *ELH* 52 (1985), 159.

10. Stevenson, "A Note on Realism," in *Essays Literary and Critical*, vol. 28 of *Works*, p. 71.

11. M. M. Bakhtin, *The Dialogic Imagination: Four Essays*, ed. Michael Holquist, trans. Caryl Emerson and Michael Holquist (Austin: Univ. of Texas Press, 1981), 7.

12. Holquist, introduction to *The Dialogic Imagination*, p. xxxi.

13. *The Corpse: A History* (Jefferson, N.C.: McFarland and Co., 1996), p. 15.

14. *Homosexual Desire*, trans. Daniella Dangoor (London: Allison and Busby, 1978), p. 86.

15. Paul Maixner, introduction to *Robert Louis Stevenson: The Critical Heritage*, ed. Maixner (London: Routledge and Kegan Paul, 1981), p. 31.

16. Rev. of *The Wrong Box*, *Scotsman* 24 June 1889, quoted in *Critical Heritage*, p. 337. This assessment continues today, as Frank McLynn in his recent biography of Stevenson dismisses *The Wrong Box* as "a truly calamitous apology for a novel" that "should never have seen the light of day" (p. 284).

17. See Stevenson, letter to Elizabeth Anne Ferrier, 23 March 1888, in *Letters*, VI, 138.

18. In their short preface Stevenson and Osbourne quote a character in the novel: "'Nothing like a little judicious levity,' says Michael Finsbury in the text: nor can any better excuse be found for the volume in the reader's hand" (Robert Louis Stevenson [and Lloyd Osbourne], *The Wrong Box*, vol. 11 of *Works*, p. xiv).

19. Bernard Darwin, introduction to Stevenson and Osbourne, *The Wrong Box* (London: Oxford Univ. Press, 1954), pp. xi, xii.

20. Oliphant, "The Old Saloon," rev. of *The Master of Ballantrae*, *Blackwood's Edinburgh Magazine*, 146 (1889), 696.

21. "What is 'Sensational' About the Sensation Novel?" *Nineteenth-Century Fiction*, 37 (1982), 12.

22. The point of origin of the train is itself significant, in that Stevenson, his wife Fanny, and Lloyd had lived in Bournemouth for three years, between 1884 and 1887: Stevenson, like the fragile Joseph Finsbury, was staying at this seaside resort in an attempt to restore his health.

23. *The Stanford Companion to Victorian Fiction* (Stanford: Stanford Univ. Press, 1989), p. 519.

24. Robert Louis Stevenson, *An Inland Voyage and Travels with a Donkey in the Cevennes*, vol. 17 of *Works*, pp. xvii–xviii..

25. *Reading for the Plot: Design and Intention in Narrative* (New York: Alfred A. Knopf, 1984), pp. 45, 44. Brooks's focus on the plot of the novel as an engine—"these emblematic motors and engines invented by novelists"—motivates his critique of the rigid formalism that examines narrative as a structure rather than a dynamic process. Brooks seeks to develop a reading strategy "that would be more adequate to our experience of reading narrative as a dynamic

operation—what makes plot move us forward to the end, to put it in simplest terms" (p. 47).

26. Stevenson related his ambivalent response to his father's death in a letter to Sidney Colvin: "I ... can but say that I am glad. If we could have had my father, that would have been a different thing. But to keep that changeling—suffering changeling—any longer, could better none and nothing. Now he rests: it is more significant, it is more like himself" (*Letters*, V, 411).

27. Oliphant, "The Old Saloon," p. 255.

28. See *The Novel and the Police* (Berkeley and Los Angeles: Univ. of California Press, 1988) p. 214 n.

29. Christopher Craft, in his insightful reading of the sodomitical significance of "Bunburying" in Wilde's *The Importance of Being Earnest*, traces in the play's deployment of the "alias" of Bunbury a displaced desire for anal penetration—"to bury in the bun" (see *Another Kind of Love: Male Homosexual Desire in English Discourse, 1850–1920* [Berkeley and Los Angeles: Univ. of California Press, 1994], p. 118).

30. See "Is the Rectum a Grave?" *October*, no. 43 [1987], 197–222.

31. Jameson identifies the novel as a repressive discourse that organizes "the rewriting of a narrative whose dynamics might otherwise elude categories of the ethical and of the individual subject" (p. 266).

32. Robert Louis Stevenson, "The Suicide Club" in *New Arabian Nights*, vol. 1 of *Works*, p. 43.

33. Robert Louis Stevenson, *Treasure Island*, vol. 2 of *Works*, p. 155.

34. Robert Louis Stevenson, *Kidnapped, Being Memoirs of the Adventures of David Balfour in the Year MDCCLI...*, vol. 6 of *Works*, p. 23.

35. According to Penny Fielding, the generic disharmony of *The Master* has implications for gender roles, as James Durie is "associated with an irrational, female, and subversive orality which threatens the male romance." (*Writing and Orality: Nationality, Culture, and Nineteenth-Century Scottish Fiction* [Oxford: Clarendon Press, 1996], p. 165.)

36. Stevenson links the fates of the two works in a letter to Sidney Colvin of 22 August 1889: "I wonder what has befallen me too, that flimsy part of me that lives (or dwindles) in the public mind; and what has befallen *The Master*, and what kind of a Box *The Wrong Box* has been found. It is odd to know nothing of all this" (*Letters*, VI, 329).

37. "Mr. Stevenson's New Novel" [rev. of *The Master of Ballantrae*], *Pall Mall Gazette*, 24 Sept. 1889, p. 3.

38. Rev. of *The Master of Ballantrae*, *Dundee Courier*, 11 October 1889; quoted in *Critical Heritage*, p. 349.

39. Robert Louis Stevenson, *The Master of Ballantrae: A Winter's Tale*, vol. 10 of *Works*, p. 94.

40. Maggie Kilgour comments on the double effect of this technique: "By reviving the dead, recalling to life an idealized past, the gothic tries to heal the ruptures of rapid change, and preserve continuity;" yet this desire can be undermined by the spectre of repetition, when "the past comes back not to critique or reform the present, but to deform and destroy it." (*The Rise of the Gothic Novel* [New York: Routledge, 1995], pp. 30–31.)

41. Stevenson wrote to Sidney Colvin on 24 December 1887, "The Master is all I know of the devil; I have known hints of him, in the world, but always cowards; he is as bold as a lion" (*Letters* vi, 87).

42. Apparently recognizing the novel's hybridity, Stevenson himself, in a January 1888 letter to Henry James, doubted whether he had "not gone too far with the fantastic;" he warns James that "the third supposed death and the manner of the third reappearance is steep; steep, sir" while also boasting "how daring is the design" (*Letters* VI, 105).

43. For Stevenson's non-fictional accounts of his experiences in the South Seas, see in particular *A Footnote to History: Eight Years of Trouble in Samoa*, in *Vailima Papers*, vol. 21 of *Works*; and *In the South Seas*, vol. 20 of *Works*. For a fuller account of Stevenson's changing opinions and moods about Samoan society and politics, see McLynn, pp. 366–505.

44. Robert Louis Stevenson [and Lloyd Osbourne], *The Ebb-Tide: A Trio and Quartette*, vol. 14 of *Works*, p. 89.

45. *Literary Culture and the Pacific: Nineteenth-Century Textual Encounters* (Cambridge: Cambridge Univ. Press, 1998), p. 164.

46. See Roslyn Jolly, introduction to Stevenson, *South Sea Tales*, ed. Jolly (New York: Oxford Univ. Press, 1996), p. xxv.

47. Rev. of *The Ebb-Tide*, *Speaker*, 19 (1894): quoted in *Critical Heritage*, p. 458. Koestenbaum offers an interesting discussion of the potentially homosexual associations of "fag" in the late–Victorian period, which he terms "the fag-end of the nineteenth century, when fears of degeneration abounded" ("The Shadow on the Bed," p. 54).

48. Quoted in *Critical Heritage*, p. 459. The situation with respect to the two writers is thus a curiously inverted one as compared to *The Wrong Box*. Smith writes of the collaboration on *The Ebb-Tide* that "adverse reviews lead Stevenson to consider deleting Osbourne's name from the book's cover: erasure, rather than signature of authorship seemed in this instance more likely to serve Osbourne's literary reputation" (*Literary Culture* p. 156).

Stevenson and Islands: Scotland and the South Pacific

Graham Tulloch

The topic of Stevenson and islands is in many ways an obvious one.[1] After all, his best known novel remains *Treasure Island*, and few titles are quite so succinct in summing up the themes of a work as this one: it is indeed about treasure and it is indeed about an island. Moreover, if we look at Stevenson's other works we find other islands aplenty. There is, for example, the island on which David Balfour is marooned in *Kidnapped*, in many ways the most frightening episode in that novel; there is the island in the short story *The Merry Men,* the same island, in fact, as in *Kidnapped*, though given another name, and there is the Bass Rock, another island, in "The Tale of Tod Lapraik." But these are only his Scottish stories. If we turn to his South Pacific writing, we find inevitably even more islands. They could be said to be the essential subject matter *In the South Seas*, but they also figure in his fiction, most notably in *The Beach of Falesá, The Isle of Voices*, and *The Ebb-Tide*. Thus there is no shortage of material on islands in Stevenson even without looking at his letters, or indeed his poetry.

However, the topic to be examined in this paper is a little more specific than simply "islands in Stevenson." As the title implies, this paper presents some comparisons between Stevenson's Scottish islands and his South Pacific ones. This particular topic was suggested by a comment of Stevenson's from *In the South Seas* about the ways in which he was able to establish good relations with the islanders:

68

It was perhaps yet more important that I had enjoyed in my youth some knowledge of our Scots folk of the Highlands and the Islands. Not much beyond a century has passed since these were in the same convulsive and transitory state as the Marquesans of to-day. In both cases an alien authority enforced, the clans disarmed, the chiefs deposed, new customs introduced.... The grumbling, the secret ferment, the fears and resentments, the alarms and sudden councils of Marquesan chiefs, reminded me continually of the days of Lovat and Struan. Hospitality, tact, natural fine manners, and a touchy punctilio, are common to both races: common to both tongues the trick of dropping medial consonants. ... that prevalent Polynesian sound, the so-called catch, written with an apostrophe, and often or always the gravestone of a perished consonant, is to be heard in Scotland to this day. When a Scot pronounces water, better, or bottle—*waíer, beíer,* or *boíle*—the sound is precisely that of the catch.[2]

I should perhaps say that what caught my eye when I first read this passage was not the general point that Stevenson is making about similarities between Scotland and the South Pacific but the specific linguistic point about the glottal stop in Scots: I was interested in finding out when references to the glottal stop, Stevenson's "catch," first appeared with regard to Scots. As Charles Jones has noted, "Despite the fact that the glottalisation of voiceless obstruents is such a common feature of modern English in general and some varieties of Scots in particular, it is difficult to find evidence for the phenomenon in the eighteenth- or the nineteenth-century source materials."[3] In this volume, which presents so much evidence of Stevenson's achievements, it is perhaps worth mentioning that he appears to be one of the earliest people to mention this now much-discussed feature of modern Scots. He is yet again, as he so often is, ahead of his times.

But this is not my point here. Rather, in this paper I want to explore Stevenson's more general comment about some similarities between Scotland and the South Pacific. This was not the only time that Stevenson makes this sort of comment in *In the South Seas.* Take this instance:

And then I turned shoreward, and high squalls were overhead; the mountains loomed up black; and I could have fancied I had slipped ten thousand miles away and was anchored in a Highland loch; that when the day came, it would show pine, and heather, and green fern, and roofs of turf sending up the smoke of peats; and the alien speech that should next greet my ears must be Gaelic, not Kanaka.[4]

Here the similarity is in the landscape and seascape rather than the people, but it is interesting to notice that Stevenson is again moved to make a comment on language, although it is Gaelic this time rather than Scots dialect. As this paper moves on to focus specifically on Stevenson's presentation of islands, it will become apparent that language, whether familiar or alien, or, in other cases, the absence of language, is a key factor in Stevenson's picture.

Along with the people, the stories, the landscape and the language come other connections for Stevenson. Take, for example, this description of a powerful physical and emotional sensation reminding him of Scotland, which he experienced in Vailima the day after finishing *The Ebb-Tide*:

> I am exulting to do nothing. It pours with rain from the westward, very unusual kind of weather; I was standing out on the little verandah in front of my room this morning, and there went through me or over me a heave of extraordinary and apparently baseless emotion. I literally staggered. And then the explanation came, and I knew I had found a frame of mind and body that belonged to Scotland, and particularly to the neighbourhood of Callander. Very odd these identities of sensation, and the world of connotations implied; Highland huts, and peat smoke, and the brown swirling rivers, and wet clothes, and whisky, and the romance of the past, and that indescribable bite of the whole thing at a man's heart, which is—or rather lies at the bottom of—a story.[5]

In turning now to that specific focus on islands, it is necessary first of all to make an obvious but important point. For Stevenson there are two kinds of islands: the real islands that he actually encountered and the imagined islands which he read about. In terms of real islands, one in particular dominates his Scottish writing, as seen in the chapter "Memoirs of an Islet" in *Memories and Portraits*:

> There is another isle in my collection, the memory of which besieges me. I put a whole family there, in one of my tales; and later on, threw upon its shores, and condemned to several days of rain and shellfish on its tumbled boulders, the hero of another.[6]

As further reading makes clear, this island was Earraid in the Hebrides, which Stevenson first visited with his father when Thomas Stevenson was planning to use the island as a base for the building of a lighthouse fifteen miles away. This is the island that figures so graphically in *Kidnapped* and also plays a key role in *The Merry Men*. As Stevenson tells us, it was not quite an uninhabited island, but the population was very small:

> There stood upon it, in these days, a single rude house of uncemented stones, approached by a pier of wreckwood.... the house was making a sweet smoke of peats which came to me over the bay, and the bare-legged daughters of the cotter were wading by the pier.[7]

Later a small village was built there: "a pier of stone, rows of sheds, railways, travelling-cranes, a street of cottages, an iron house for the resident engineer, wooden bothies for the men."[8] But it was the first impression of a nearly uninhabited island that stuck in Stevenson's mind for imaginative recycling. In fact, in *Kidnapped* it becomes an entirely uninhabited island while in *The Merry Men* it is inhabited by only four people.

One can only speculate as to why this island was so captivating to Stevenson's imagination, but one thing is certain: for a writer, Earraid had the enormous advantage—it was at the same time an island and not an island. At the lowest tides of the month it is connected to the Isle of Mull so that it is possible to walk across. The author thus has all the advantages of an isolated island but can end the character's isolation when he wants. In *Kidnapped*, David spends several days on the island living on raw shellfish, which makes him sick, and calling out to a passing boat until he realizes that he can cross at low tide. The island becomes for a while that ultimate symbol of human isolation, a place where a single human being is cast away without a companion. It is, as David says, "the most unhappy part of [his] adventures"[9] but when Stevenson wants to end this isolation he can simply reveal that the "island" is connected to the mainland. No wonder he found it useful in his fiction.

Although, in his fiction, Stevenson clearly used, and re-used, islands he had actually visited, it is hardly necessary to point out that books reflect other books as well as reflecting life. Moreover, islands have a long history as a literary subject, as Stevenson was well aware. When he discusses that slippery term *romance* in "A Gossip on Romance" he defines it in a way that specifically associates it with literary texts and then turns to the first classic island novel, *Robinson Crusoe*, as his primary example and pays tribute to its enduring qualities by comparing it with Richardson's *Clarissa*:

> *Clarissa* is a book of a far more startling import, worked out, on a great canvas, with inimitable courage and unflagging art.... And

yet a little story of a shipwrecked sailor, with not a tenth part of
the style nor a thousandth part of the wisdom, exploring none of
the arcana of humanity and deprived of the perennial interest of
love, goes on from edition to edition, ever young, while *Clarissa*
lies upon the shelves unread.[10]

It may just be coincidence but, of the other novels mentioned in the essay
as examples of romance, two are crucially connected with islands: Dumas's
The Count of Monte Cristo (with its own treasure island) and Scott's *The
Pirate*. Furthermore he tells us that the first author he actually met was
R.M. Ballantyne, whose best known work is *The Coral Island*.[11]

Lloyd Osbourne's account of the first conception of *Treasure Island*
makes it clear that these literary images of the island were there in Stevenson's mind from the very beginning:

> … busy with a box of paints, I happened to be tinting the map of
> an island I had drawn. Stevenson came in as I was finishing it, and
> … leaned over my shoulder, and was soon elaborating the map
> and naming it. I shall never forget the thrill of Skeleton Island,
> Spy Glass Hill, nor the heart-stirring climax of the three crosses!
> And the great [*sic*] climax still when he wrote down the words
> "Treasure Island" at the top right-hand corner! And he seemed
> to know so much about it too—the pirates, the buried treasure,
> the man who had been marooned on the island.[12]

The pirates, treasure, the marooned man: these are all literary images, yet
we also notice the appearance of a Spy-Glass Hill: maybe it is more than
coincidence that Stevenson in his account of the real island of Earraid
mentions a hill on which a spy-glass is set up and also, for that matter, a
northern inlet such as Treasure Island has.

Be that as it may, it is clear enough that islands are places of the imagination as well as real places, and, as we would expect, Stevenson's islands
are influenced as much by what he has read as by what he has seen. Not
surprisingly, the characters in the novels also show themselves aware of
the both real and literary islands. David Balfour in recalling his experiences on the island notes that

> In all the books I have read of people cast away, they had either
> their pockets full of tools, or a chest of things would be thrown
> upon the beach along with them, as if on purpose. My case was
> very different. I had nothing in my pockets but money and Alan's
> silver button; and being inland bred, I was as much short of
> knowledge as of means.[13]

What David is remembering is what Stevenson singled out for special praise in *Robinson Crusoe*:

> Every single article the castaway recovers from the hulk is "a joy for ever" to the man who reads of them. They are the things that should be found, and the bare enumeration stirs the blood.[14]

But for David, cast away on the real island of Earraid, the literary expectations aroused by Crusoe fail to materialize.

The same kind of experience can be seen in a crucial passage in *Treasure Island* where Jim Hawkins, looking back, compares his expectations of what Treasure Island would bring with the reality:

> I lived on at the Hall ... full of sea-dreams and the most charming anticipations of strange islands and adventures. I brooded by the hour together over the map, ... I approached that island in my fancy, from every possible direction; I explored every acre of its surface; I climbed a thousand times to that tall hill they call the Spy-glass, and from the top enjoyed the most wonderful and changing prospects. Sometimes the isle was thick with savages, with whom we fought, sometimes full of dangerous animals that hunted us; but in all my fancies nothing occurred to me so strange and tragic as our actual adventures.[15]

Once again the imagined world fails to materialize for the hero, and he must come to terms with reality.

The reader, it would seem, goes through a similar process. The novel appears to begin as a romance, and Stevenson prefaced it with a poem which declared:

> If sailor tales to sailor tunes,
> Storm and adventure, heat and cold,
> If schooners, islands, and maroons
> And Buccaneers, and buried Gold,
> And all the old romance, retold
> Exactly in the ancient way,
> Can please, as me they pleased of old,
> The wiser youngsters of today:
> —So be it, and fall on![16]

But if *Treasure Island* presents itself initially as a romance, it steadily moves against the expectations of romance, ending in fact with Jim offering to the reader a repudiation of treasure-hunting and adventure. Yet, while Jim, like David, rejects expectations about islands that are raised by literature, those literary expectations nevertheless remain embedded in the text, offering the reader a combination of allusions to both real and literary islands.

So far, in considering real and imagined islands, this paper has been dealing only with Stevenson's Scottish islands and Treasure Island. The bracketing of these two together is deliberate. It seems to me that, despite its exotic setting at its still-secret bearings in the Caribbean and even though Stevenson himself wrote to Colvin that the scenery was "Californian in part, and in part *chic*"[17] and while it has been argued by others that some features of the island are derived from Stevenson's knowledge of the Monterey Peninsula and the country around Mount Saint Helena,[18] Treasure Island belongs to the same essential class of imagined islands as Earraid, the Scottish island which "besieged' Stevenson's imagination. It is uninhabited or nearly uninhabited and is a place on which people might find themselves alone, whether cast away after a shipwreck or deliberately marooned. David is shipwrecked alone on uninhabited Earraid in *Kidnapped*; in *The Merry Men* the same island (but there called Aros) is inhabited by a few people, and a castaway black man figures dramatically at the end; and in *Treasure Island* we have an apparently uninhabited island which turns out to have only one inhabitant, the marooned Ben Gunn. Two of the islands are also linked by the theme of treasure, Treasure Island (of course) and Aros where the treasure is one from a sunken ship of the Spanish Armada. Finally these islands are linked by the issue of language: they are either linguistically silent when uninhabited or linguistically alien when inhabited.

I would like to expand a little more on this final point. Human voices are out of place on Treasure Island, as illustrated by Jim's account of the first killing:

> Far away out in the marsh there arose, all of a sudden, a sound like the cry of anger, then another on the back of it; and then one horrid, long-drawn scream. The rocks of the Spy-glass re-echoed it a score of times; the whole troop of marsh-birds rose again, darkening heaven, with a simultaneous whirr; and long after that death yell was still ringing in my brain, silence had re-established its empire, and only the rustle of the redescending birds and the boom of the distant surges disturbed the languor of the afternoon.[19]

Even when Jim comes across language on the island in the person of the marooned Ben Gunn, Ben's first words speak not of language, but of silence: "I'm poor Ben Gunn, I am; and I haven't spoke with a Christian these three years."[20] In *Kidnapped*, we encounter not silence but alien language when David on the island is passed by two fishermen in a boat:

> I shouted out, and then fell on my knees on the rock and reached up my hands and prayed to them. They were near enough to hear—I could even see the colour of their hair; and there was no doubt but they observed me, for they cried out in the Gaelic tongue, and laughed. But the boat never turned aside, and flew on, right before my eyes, for Iona.[21]

Lastly, in *The Merry Men* the narrator, being a Lowlander, speaks English or Scots, as do his relations, but he is nevertheless surrounded by alien Gaelic place names which he needs to have explained to him.

Altogether, then, we can put together a composite picture of an island: uninhabited or nearly so, a place where people might be cast away, linguistically silent or alien and very likely the site of treasure. This island is not really a pleasant place either, although it may seem so at times. Jim's judgement on Treasure Island is typical:

> perhaps it was the look of the island, with its grey, melancholy woods, and wild stone spires, and the surf that we could both see and hear foaming and thundering on the steep beach—at least, although the sun shone bright and hot, and the shore birds were fishing and crying all around us, and you would have thought anyone would have been glad to get to land after being so long at sea, my heart sank, as the saying is, into my boots; and from the first look onward, I hated the very thought of Treasure Island.[22]

This, then, is the image of an island which seems to dominate in Stevenson's writing in the period before he went to the South Pacific in 1888. This certainly is the imagined island of *The Merry Men* and *Treasure Island* (both written in 1881) and *Kidnapped* (written in 1885–6). Its sources are clearly dual: it derives both from Stevenson's vivid memories of the real island of Earraid and from his reading about literary islands such as that of Robinson Crusoe.

Now let us consider the other location mentioned in the title of this paper, the South Pacific. Stevenson set out into the Pacific in the yacht *Casco* on the 28th of June, 1888, having been commissioned by Scribner's to write a travel book. Obviously the voyage, in taking him to a number of Pacific islands, provided a new input of knowledge of real islands to supplement and perhaps partly displace that dominant image of Earraid.

As one might therefore expect, he saw the South Pacific experience as very much an experience of new islands. As he wrote to Henry James:

> this precious deep is filled with islands, which we may still visit; and though the sea is a deathful place, I like to be there, and like squalls (when they are over); and to draw near to a new island, I cannot say how much I like.[23]

Clearly, the islands of the South Pacific, whether low flat coral atolls, or places where the land rises in mountains, were very different from the bleak and barren Earraid. Yet new experiences do not always lead to new perceptions. Stevenson did not approach the South Sea islands with a blank mind; he had already surrounded them with stories and literary images. As far back as 1875, in a letter written in Edinburgh, he reports in staccato style:

> Awfully nice man here to-night. Public servant—New Zealand. Telling us all about the South Sea Islands till I was sick with desire to go there; beautiful places, green forever; perfect climate; perfect shapes of men and women, with red flowers in their hair; nothing to do but to study oratory and etiquette, sit in the sun, and pick up the fruits as they fall. Navigator's Island is the place; absolute balm for the weary.[24]

This is hardly a realistic vision of the South Pacific, and it is already present some thirteen years before he went there. The question was whether, coming with preconceived notions, he would be see the new reality before his eyes or whether he would just reconfigure it in his mind to fit his old conceptions.

Even once he is there, he can be found writing to his friend Charles Baxter in Edinburgh in terms which are admittedly joking but which all the same present the South Pacific islands as a place where traditional literary adventures might happen:

> In these ill charted seas, it is quite on the cards we might be cast on some unvisited or very rarely visited island; that there we might lie for a long time, even years, unheard of; and yet turn up smiling at the hinder end.[25]

Here, specifically, we see the reappearance of the image of the castaway. Stevenson is interpreting his new experiences in terms of old literary images. Alternatively he might be tempted to deny, or at least weaken, the reality by calling it a dream, just as Jim expressed his sense of the unreality of his expectations by calling them "sea-dreams." As Stevenson told his cousin:

> All the time, our visits to the islands have been more like dreams than realities: the people, the life, the beachcombers, the old stories and songs I have picked up, so interesting; the climate, the scenery and (in some places) the women so beautiful.[26]

The new realities were not going to inject a new element of realism into his work if they were dismissed as dreams.

Yet for all this power of the mind to reshape reality into preconceived literary molds or relabel it as dream, I would argue that the South Pacific did indeed provide Stevenson with new and different experiences of real islands, which did indeed affect the images of islands that he now presented.

One of the key differences from the earlier islands in Stevenson's South Pacific fiction relates to the issue of language. To some extent Stevenson had come to the South Pacific expecting the same linguistic alienation that he had portrayed with Earraid/Aros and Treasure Island:

> To cross the Channel is, for a boy of twelve, to change heavens; to cross the Atlantic, for a man of twenty-four, is hardly to modify his diet. But I was now escaped out of the shadow of the Roman empire [and] had journeyed forth out of that comfortable zone of kindred languages, where the curse of Babel is so easy to be remedied; and [now] my new fellow-creatures sat before me dumb like images. Methought, in my travels, all human relation was to be excluded; and when I returned home ... I should have but dipped into a picture-book without a text.[27]

A picture book without a text: islands without language. But he soon found that this was not the case at all:

> The impediment of tongues was one that I particularly over-estimated. The languages of Polynesia are easy to smatter, though hard to speak with elegance. And they are extremely similar, so that a person who has a tincture of one or two may risk, not without hope, an attempt upon the others.[28]

Willing to make every effort himself to communicate, Stevenson found that the South Pacific, far from being a place of linguistic silence, was a place of talk. It is no accident that he came to be called "Tusitala," the Teller of Tales, because, as he informs us in *In the South Seas*, it was by telling Scottish stories that he was able to encourage the people of the South Pacific to tell their own stories:

> Michael Scott, Lord Derwentwater's head, the second-sight, the Water Kelpie, —each of these I have found to be a killing bait; the black bull's head of Stirling procured me the legend of *Rahero*; and what I knew of the Cluny Macphersons, or the Appin Stewarts, enabled me to learn, and helped me to understand, about the *Tevas* of Tahiti.[29]

Through the telling of stories he could join in the islands' culture of talk.

This new vision of islands as places of talk rather than of linguistic silence or alienation shows itself in his South Pacific fiction. This is not to say that the earlier images of the uninhabited and silent island do not recur. In his travel writing Stevenson shows a particular interest in the depopulation of the South Pacific islands, and in that curious short novel *The Ebb-Tide* the three adventurers come across an uncharted island. They sail along the outer shore of the atoll "spying for an entrance, spying for signs of tenancy. But the isle continued to unfold itself in joints, and to run out in indeterminate capes, and still there was neither house nor man, nor the smoke of fire ... it was a silent ship that approached an empty island."[30] When finally they discover an opening into the lagoon they find a settlement, but most of the people have died and only four remain. Yet it soon becomes clear that this is far from being a silent island; it is dominated by a very articulate figure who overawes the adventurers with his tongue.

However, it is not in *The Ebb-Tide* but in the masterpiece of his South Pacific writing, *The Beach of Falesá*, that Stevenson's new kind of island most clearly emerges. The Falesá of the title is the name of an island, and thus the title proclaims this to be another island story, although not quite so obviously as the title of *Treasure Island*. Falesá is full of language, the language of the whites and of the indigenous people, and one of the first things that the narrator comments on is the language of the people he meets. Given, too, the story's title, it is significant that as early as the second page a character remarks to the narrator, "You know what a place the beach is for talking."[31] Symbolically, too, a key scene takes place in the aptly named Speak House. In this setting one of the first lessons to be learnt by that unlikely hero Wiltshire is the need to talk: when he first marries Uma, he thinks he will impress her by keeping his worries to himself, but he quickly learns that she has much to tell him and that he will be much better informed if he discusses his dilemma with her. He also sets himself to learn the local language. Similarly, he finds that he can gain information and an ally by talking to the missionary, although he tells us that "This was the first time in all my years in the Pacific, I had ever exchanged two words with any missionary; let alone asked one for a favour."[32]

Clearly, an island so full of language is not an uninhabited island. There are quite a large number of characters, and the island is plentifully peopled, but there is nevertheless one part that is uninhabited, the area where the villainous Case has set up idols and an underground shrine containing a devil painted with luminous paint. He brings a selected few people here at night and controls them by frightening them. Thus the uninhabited space is again an empty space into which human evil can flow, as with Treasure Island. But Wiltshire literally opens up this uninhabited space by blowing up the underground shrine and exposing it for the local people to visit it by daylight. The inhabitants can presumably return to this part of the island, and the whole island can become inhabited.

In presenting us with Wiltshire, Stevenson has created a new kind of hero to go with his new kind of island. Wiltshire indeed is more or less the opposite of Stevenson's earlier heroes, although he is, like them, the narrator of his own tale. Whereas Charles in *The Merry Men*, Jim in *Treasure Island*, and David in *Kidnapped* approach their islands with romantic notions which they have taken from books or stories, Wiltshire simply comes to make money, to do good trade, without any illusions except perhaps a too favorable view of white men. What he finds is not at first quite what he expects, but it is not because he has romantic notions which are unfulfilled but simply because he is prevented from doing the trade he came for. Nevertheless, he soon sets things to rights and is able to trade profitably. However, in the deeper meaning of the story, his path is almost exactly the reverse of the other heroes: approaching the island with matter-of-fact expectations, he is overtaken by romance. I do not mean to use the term simply in the sense of love, although it is through falling in love that he is redeemed from his limited viewpoint. The romance that enters his life is a broader sympathy and understanding of other human beings even if he never shakes off his trader mentality. He moves from realism to romance; the others move from romance to realism.

Stevenson himself was well aware that the South Pacific had opened up new material for him. Sidney Colvin, ever cautious, had urged him to be sparing in his use of it, but Stevenson would have none of this and asked in return, "What ails you, miserable man, to talk of saving material? I have

a whole world in my head, a whole new society to work." He also believed
that he was mining a new vein of realism that other writers had not yet
discovered. Writing again to Colvin, he says of *The Beach of Falesá*:

> It is the first realistic South Sea story; I mean with real South Sea
> character and details of life; everybody else who has tried, that I
> have seen, got carried away by the romance and ended in a kind
> of sugar candy sham epic, and the whole effect was lost—there
> was no etching, no human grin, consequently no conviction. Now
> I have got the smell and look of the thing a good deal.[33]

Clearly, he felt that the lived experience of the islands had been carried
over into his writing. And from observing the language of the whites of
the South Seas he had also discovered a new voice, which he describes to
Colvin in the same letter as "trader's talk, which is a strange conglomer-
ate of literary expressions and English and American slang, and Beach de
Mar, or native English." His South Pacific writing further seems to show
a new interest in those who are culturally adrift, particularly the whites
of the South Seas. This new material and new voice was obviously very
valuable to Stevenson even if he continued to write about his old material as well and produced three Scottish novels, one complete and two
unfinished at this death, during his time in the South Pacific. It is certainly
significant that Stevenson saw this new writing as primarily realistic
whereas he presents *Treasure Island* as predominantly a romance, although
I would suggest that this is an oversimplification and that the mixing of
realism and romance or the real world and the world of books, which
characterizes his earlier islands, still goes on. All the same, Stevenson's
emphasis on the realism of his South Pacific writing pays tribute to the
powerful new inspiration that his actual experience of the South Sea
Islands brought to him and which enabled him to move in interesting
new directions in his conceptualization of islands.

     This paper has concentrated on a particular aspect of Stevenson's
work, the presentation of islands, but it is important in ending to look
again at the broader picture. Just as his voyaging in the South Pacific literally expanded Stevenson's horizons, so too did it open up new literary
opportunities for him. Critics have not been slow to recognize that Stevenson found new inspiration in the South Pacific and was able to produce
some works quite unlike what he had written before. This paper is not
intended to suggest that the new kind of island he described is necessarily the most important part of this new material. Rather, it has attempted
simply to show that Stevenson's new conceptualization of islands provides

a particularly telling example of how his South Pacific experience expanded his vision and made him rethink some of his fundamental literary concepts.

NOTES

1. I first began work on this topic for a paper at the CORAIL Colloquium held at the Université Française du Pacifique in Nouméa, New Caledonia, in November 1998.

2. *In the South Seas*, Vailima Edition, Vol. 16, pp. 26–7. Unless otherwise specified, references are to the Vailima Edition of *The Works of Robert Louis Stevenson* in 26 volumes (New York: Scribner, 1921–3).

3. Charles Jones, "Phonology" in *The Edinburgh History of the Scots Language*, ed. Charles Jones, (Edinburgh: Edinburgh University Press, 1997), p. 329.

4. *In the South Seas*, pp. 36–37.

5. *The Letters of Robert Louis Stevenson*, ed. Bradford A. Booth and Ernest Mehew, in 8 volumes (New Haven and London: Yale University Press, 1994–5), Vol. 8, p. 91.

6. *Memories and Portraits*, Vailima Edition, Vol. 12, p. 95.

7. *Memories and Portraits*, p. 96.

8. *Memories and Portraits*, p. 97.

9. *Kidnapped*, Vailima Edition, Vol. 9, p. 143.

10. *Memories and Portraits*, p. 195.

11. "Memoirs of Himself by Robert Louis Stevenson," Vailima Edition, Vol. 26, p. 226.

12. Lloyd Osbourne, "Note," *Treasure Island*, Vailima Edition, Vol. 5, p. x.

13. *Kidnapped*, p. 146.

14. *Memories and Portraits*, p. 199.

15. *Treasure Island*, ed. Wendy R. Katz, Centenary Edition (Edinburgh: Edinburgh University Press, 1998), p. 47.

16. *Treasure Island*, p. 7.

17. *Letters*, Vol 4, p. 300.

18. For a brief summary of material on this subject, see Wendy R. Katz in her Introduction to *Treasure Island* in the edition cited above, p. xxxii.

19. *Treasure Island*, p. 88.

20. *Treasure Island*, p. 92.

21. *Kidnapped*, p. 151.

22. *Treasure Island*, pp. 81–2.

23. *Letters*, Vol. 6, pp. 273–4.

24. *Letters*, Vol. 2, p. 145.

25. *Letters*, Vol. 6, p. 294.

26. *Letters*, Vol. 6, p. 256.

27. *In the South Seas*, pp. 20–21.

28. *In the South Seas*, p. 23.

29. *In the South Seas*, p. 28.

30. Robert Louis Stevenson and Lloyd Osbourne, *The Ebb-Tide: A Trio and*

Quartette, ed. Peter Hinchcliffe and Catherine Kerrigan, Centenary Edition (Edinburgh: Edinburgh University Press, 1995), p. 68.

31. *The Beach of Falesá*, in Barry Menikoff, *Robert Louis Stevenson and "The Beach of Falesá": A Study in Victorian Publishing With the Original Text* (Edinburgh: Edinburgh University Press, 1984), p. 116.

32. *The Beach of Falesá*, p. 148.

33. *Letters*, Vol. 7, p. 161.

APPROACHES TO
DR. JEKYLL AND MR. HYDE

"Closer Than a Wife": The Strange Case of Dr. Jekyll's Significant Other

Katherine Bailey Linehan

The central plot idea of Robert Louis Stevenson's 1886 novella, *Strange Case of Dr. Jekyll and Mr. Hyde*, has long been so deeply entrenched in popular culture that few people who read the tale now can share in what for its original audience was the shock effect of the denouement revealing the repulsive Mr. Hyde and the eminent Dr. Jekyll to be one and the same man. However, a plot surprise in another direction may lie in wait for today's readers. Those who turn to the text assuming they know the outline of the story on the basis of film renderings are likely to be startled to discover that the tale as Stevenson wrote it contains absolutely no women in any major roles.

How significant is the divergence of film from text in this regard? Do performance adaptations that insert women into the story as love or sex objects for the male protagonist merely fill in the gaps left in the text by Victorian reticence? Or is there some other purpose behind Stevenson's exclusion of women from the bachelor world of Jekyll and his friends, and behind the tale's lack of specificity concerning the secret, habitual night-time pleasures that Jekyll seeks to pursue with impunity in his guise as Hyde?

To explore these questions, I want first to profile differences between the 1886 tale and its major film versions in their treatment of sexual issues. I'll then briefly review what various literary critics have proposed about

why there are no central female characters in the text. In the final section
of the paper, I advance a hypothesis of my own, based on considering the
text in the framework of what Stevenson's biographer Jenni Calder
identifies as his devil tales.

I.

Popular notions of the plot of *Strange Case of Dr. Jekyll and Mr.
Hyde*—beyond the generally well-known association of those two names
with a split personality—may derive from any number of twentieth-cen-
tury entertainment spin-offs. TV channel-surfers are especially likely to
have encountered the 1941 film version with Spencer Tracy in the dual role
of Jekyll and Hyde, and an against-the-grain casting of Ingrid Bergman
as Hyde's prostitute and Lana Turner as Jekyll's high-society girlfriend.
John Malkovich fans may have made a point of seeing the 1996 movie
Mary Reilly featuring Malkovich as Jekyll and Hyde and Julia Roberts as
the sympathetic housemaid who learns Jekyll's secret. Lovers of musicals
might have seen or bought the original cast recording for the recent Broad-
way hit, *Jekyll and Hyde: The Musical*, with Linda Eder as Hyde's ill-fated
girlfriend, Lucy. Art-film buffs may have sought out either of the two early
film classics, the 1920 silent version with John Barrymore or the 1931 sound
version with Fredric March, directed by Rouben Mamoulian. Both Barrymore and March turn out virtuoso performances in the double role of the
respectable doctor courting the respectable girlfriend, and the animalistic Hyde who ends up not only abusing his prostitute girlfriend, but mur-
dering the father of Jekyll's fiancee. The list goes on, with the titular dual
role in movie versions being played by, among other people, Paul Massie,
Jack Palance, Ralph Bates, and Michael Caine; and with Jekyll being portrayed as, among other things, a married man on the verge of losing his
wife, a widower in love with his deceased wife's sister, and a Freudian analyst whose own sexual repressions have a field day when Hyde comes on
the scene. One of the most inventive variations presents Hyde as Jack the
Ripper in drag: this is the film *Dr. Jekyll and Sister Hyde*, in which Jekyll
is a research-mad bachelor whose transformation into Hyde involves a sex
change that lets him move effortlessly in on London East End prostitutes
in order to cut their throats and rip out their ovaries for use in his exper-
iments.

Amidst these many plot variations, a near-constant of the major film
renderings is the graphic representation of something which in the text is
merely a possibility open to interpretation, namely, that the pivot for

Jekyll's transformations into Hyde is sexual repression. Historically, this goes back to the first serious stage version of the novel, authorized by Stevenson, which opened in Boston in May 1887, riding the wave of the book's immense popularity in England and America. The play stayed in performance for almost two decades, becoming an influence on the makers of the earliest silent film versions of the tale. The play's co-creators, playwright Thomas Russell Sullivan and actor-manager Richard Mansfield, knew that American audiences were hungry for domestic melodrama. So they made Jekyll a noble, hard-working young doctor undergoing agonies of conscience over the way his well-intentioned research miscarried in the creation of Hyde; they created for Jekyll a generous-hearted fiancee who is the light of her lonely old father's life; and they made Hyde the scene-stealing monster who bursts into the house of the fiancee, grows peeved when the father sends her out of the room to protect her, and proceeds to strangle the old man.[1]

When we turn to Stevenson's 1886 text, we find many things putting us at a farther remove from the sexual repression premise than is the case in the vast majority of performance versions. Stevenson's Henry Jekyll is no handsome youngish man frustrated by impeded availability to a wife, girlfriend, or fiancee; he is a professionally distinguished, paunchy, fifty-year-old confirmed bachelor, who socializes with a few same-aged male cronies, high-placed professionals like himself. The two given distinctive roles in the tale are Jekyll's "old mates" from schooldays, Hastie Lanyon, the hot-tempered doctor who has long scoffed at Jekyll's neurochemical research, and John Gabriel Utterson, the loyal lawyer friend through whose eyes we follow the action of the tale.

None of these male characters gives the slightest evidence of involvement with a female friend or relative, let alone any indication of interest in sexuality. The only female characters who appear even momentarily in the story are unnamed background figures of low social status: a little girl from a poor family whom Hyde knocks down and tramples when their paths cross at an intersection, a few of her indignant female relatives, the maid who observes Jekyll's murder of Sir Danvers Carew, Hyde's Soho landlady, the cook and maids in Jekyll's household, and a woman selling matches on the street. To be sure, we learn late in the tale that Jekyll has from an early stage of his life indulged in night-time pleasures that he finds uncomfortably inconsistent with his cherished public image of himself—so uncomfortably inconsistent that he had dreamed for years of creating a physical alter ego to free himself from his own pangs of remorse as well as from the possibility of detection. Yet we never learn exactly what those secret nocturnal pleasures are. The document entitled "Henry

Jekyll's Full Statement of the Case," which is put into Utterson's hands at the end of the tale, seemingly as a solution to its mysteries, remains carefully elusive on this point. Jekyll merely writes that a "certain impatient gaiety of disposition" had from early in his life begotten an appetite for "pleasures" inconsistent with the desire to "carry my head high and wear a more than commonly grave countenance before the public." He speaks of those pleasures as being "to say the least, undignified," but he suggests that for years they remained a matter of being "merrily disposed." Only after he ventured on the body-morphing experiment that produced Hyde as a chemical precipitate of the evil element within his own mixed nature, he reports, did those undignified pleasures begin to "turn towards the monstrous."[2] As for what he means by "the monstrous"—again we get no clues about sexuality. Jekyll simply defines his monstrosity broadly in terms of narcissism and sadism:

> This familiar that I called out of my own soul, and sent forth alone to do his good pleasure, was a being inherently malign and villainous; his every act and thought centered on self; drinking pleasure with bestial avidity from any degree of torture to another; relentless like a man of stone [86].

This fits with the two acts of violence we hear eyewitness accounts of Hyde committing. Those acts are not sex crimes, but brutal responses to accidental street encounters. The little girl Hyde tramples is running across the intersection in quest of a doctor to deal with a family medical emergency; the man against whom Hyde erupts into homicidal violence is a benevolent-looking elderly stranger who stops him on the sidewalk to ask a question.

II.

Of course, the force of Victorian publishing taboos can support the possibility that sexual debauchery is the obvious reference point for the night-time merriments in Jekyll that turn to cruelties in Hyde, and Stevenson simply could not say so directly. Many Victorian readers certainly took that view. The poet Gerard Manley Hopkins wrote to Robert Bridges: "[T]he trampling scene is perhaps a convention: he [Stevenson] was thinking of something unsuitable for fiction." Literary man F.W. H. Myers commented to Stevenson about the murder scene: "If you think it needful to avoid a female victim ... it might be some relation of a tacitly-understood victim."[3]

However, many other possibilities have been urged to explain why there are no women at the core of the story, and how that relates to the mysteries surrounding Jekyll's night-time activities. The spectrum of views available from critics offers rich testimony to this text's enduring power to respond rewardingly to an immense variety of interpretations.

Indeed, some critics focus precisely on the idea that Stevenson maintains a sense of uncertainty about Jekyll's pleasures in order to challenge readers' imaginations to explore a wide range of possibilities, with the effect of increasing both allegorical breadth of meaning and Gothic intensity of dread. Andrew Jefford, for example, in a 1983 essay, proposes that Jekyll's mysterious pleasures "have the variety and attraction that they do for readers, precisely because we can play with various notions—gluttony, excessive drinking, regular brothel trips, orgy and debauchery, homosexuality, sado-masochism, pederasty, rape, pornography, gambling, street fighting, cock fighting—and virtually nothing is ruled out."[4] Judith Halberstam works along similar lines when she argues in her 1995 book *Skin Shows* that "within Gothic novels … multiple interpretations are embedded in the text and part of the experience of horror comes from the realization that meaning itself runs riot."[5]

Other critics argue for particular hypotheses on Jefford's list that are nonsexual but more easily pursued by a man living alone than with a wife or family, and in that way consistent with the absence of women from the center of the story. One such conjecture is that Jekyll engages in excessive drinking or drug use, with Hyde standing as a figure of the ugly personality transformations growing out of addiction. This interpretation matches well with what becomes Jekyll's uncontrollable bodily craving for the "heady recklessness" and sensuous vitality he gets from his transformations, in spite of his initial assurances to himself and to Utterson that he can banish Hyde from his life any time he chooses. Another conjecture is that Jekyll enjoys the Victorian gentleman's sport of slumming, hobnobbing with the poor in their gin palaces, music halls, and brothels, with the result that his Hyde epitomizes rabble-rousing rowdiness and belligerence. This supposition has been used to support politically oriented readings of the tale in two opposite directions: as a radical protest against bourgeois repression, or, alternatively, as a conservative evocation of a threat of degenerative, apelike savagery among the British working class, the rebellious Irish, the immigrants of Soho, or the foreign subjects of empire.

Critics who see sexual activity as the basis of Jekyll's secret pleasures obviously have a particularly strong argument for the exclusion of women when they read that activity as homosexuality. Vladimir Nabokov, lecturing on *Strange Case of Dr. Jekyll and Mr. Hyde* at Cornell University in the 1950s, was one of the first to suggest that readers might easily suppose Jekyll's clandestine adventures to consist of the "homosexual practices so common in London behind the Victorian veil," whether or not Stevenson intended that interpretation.[6] Elaine Showalter, in a chapter entitled "Dr. Jekyll's Closet" in her 1990 book, *Sexual Anarchy*, claims that there are many reasons to suppose that homosexuality, or at least nervous male homoeroticism, is exactly what Stevenson intended. In the background for the book's composition, she suggests, we find heightened public concern about homosexuality brought about by recent medical theories concerning male hysteria and the 1885 Parliamentary debate on new anti-homosexuality legislation. The text itself, Showalter proposes, trades on socially familiar overtones of secret liaisons between cultured middle-aged men and young roughs, as well as on repeated imagery of forced penetration into private places, and on narrative use of phrases playing on the words "queer" and "gay" (which she argues had code connotations in British homosexual subculture earlier than the early 20th-century date many dictionaries assign).[7]

Critics who have seen heterosexual appetite as the motive for Jekyll's night-time escapades and Hyde's acts of brutality have relied not just on publishing taboos to explain the absence of women as main characters. Stephen Heath in an article entitled "Psychopathia sexualis" proposes that while Stevenson hovers on the threshold of understanding Hyde as what the new sexologists were soon to define as a "lust murderer," he ultimately remains too steeped in traditional Victorian gender ideology to see sexual neurosis as anything but female and therefore does not complete the conceptual leap to imagining Hyde's aggression as sexually directed.[8] William Veeder, in his 1988 essay, "Children of the Night: Stevenson and Patriarchy," attributes the absence of any main female characters to Stevenson's desire to dramatize the weakness of an entire generation of professional men suffering from arrested emotional development. Jekyll, Lanyon, and Utterson all lack the ability to enter into mature forms of either heterosexual or homosexual partnership, Veeder suggests; they instead seek the security of self-mirroring male bonds, and meanwhile Hyde serves as the expression of their underlying oedipal angers and sibling-style rivalries. For Veeder the idea that sexual repression and compensatory illicit sexual activity are at the heart of the story is reinforced by the manuscript history he traces at the start of his co-edited book, *Dr. Jekyll and Mr. Hyde after One Hundred Years*. The key features of that history revolve around a first draft reportedly burned in response to criticisms from Stevenson's wife Fanny and then a mid-compositional draft fragment in which Jekyll speaks more glaringly than in the final version of becoming "from a very early age ... the slave of disgraceful pleasures"; "vices ... at once criminal in the sight of the law and abhorrent in themselves."[9]

Insofar as it matters to our reading of the story to know what Stevenson himself might have had in mind for Jekyll's "undignified pleasures," the original Victorian hypothesis of womanizing or prostitution receives roundabout support from a November 1887 Stevenson letter that critics have variously interpreted or ignored. Writing to American journalist John Paul Bocock, Stevenson mentions the issue of heterosexual desire in Jekyll, if only to de-emphasize it: "The harm was in Jekyll, because he was a hypocrite—not because he was fond of women, he says so himself."[10] Puzzlingly enough, Jekyll *cannot*, so far as I can see, be found in the published text mentioning fondness for women, whether as a lesser sin than hypocrisy or in any other light. Perhaps Stevenson was forgetting having edited out a line he had given Jekyll in the process of composition. At any rate, if we can trust that Stevenson had at one point had the idea for such a line during his writing of the book—and meant it to refer to an actual rather than a hypothetical fondness for women in Jekyll—then the letter to Bocock at least affords a glimpse of Stevenson's personal conception of Jekyll as a womanizer.

The real interest of the Bocock letter for our topic, however, lies all in another direction. It is a direction that points us towards an understanding of why attention to what Stevenson calls the true "diabolic" in man is much more important than decoding Jekyll's habitual night-time activities if we are to probe what I would argue is the deepest level of the question of why women are largely excluded from the main action in Stevenson's text.

The letter is prompted by Bocock's report to Stevenson on how the Sullivan-Mansfield play had been received in New York. Ten months earlier, Stevenson had assured the playwright Sullivan that he didn't mind Sullivan's putting a fiancee for Jekyll into the play. Now, with the performance piece entitled *Dr. Jekyll and Mr. Hyde* apparently receiving a reputation for exhibiting the dangers of lust unsanctified by marriage, Stevenson wrote in a tone of heated indignation:

> Hyde ... was not ... Great Gods! a mere voluptuary. There is no harm in a voluptuary; and none, with my hand on my heart and in the sight of God, none—no harm whatever—in what prurient fools call "immorality." The harm was in Jekyll, because he was a hypocrite—not because he was fond of women, he says so himself; but people are so filled full of folly and inverted lust, that

they can think of nothing but sexuality. The Hypocrite let out the beast Hyde—malice, and selfishness and cowardice: and these are the diabolic in man—not this poor wish to have a woman, that they make such a cry about. I know, and I dare to say, you know as well as I, that bad and good, even to our human eyes, has no more connection with what is called dissipation than it has with flying kites. But the sexual field and the business field are perhaps the two best fitted for the display of cruelty and cowardice and selfishness. That is what people see; and these they confound [*Letters* 6: 56–57].

When we look at the story in light of this statement and compare it with other tales by Stevenson that deal with "the diabolic in man," the theological underpinnings of *Strange Case of Dr. Jekyll and Mr. Hyde* begin to take shape more clearly.

By this I mean that we begin to see how in this story inspired by "a fine bogey tale"[11] he dreamed one night, Stevenson is working with the idea that Jekyll's true sins, not of sex but of pride and selfishness, years ago gave an inroad to the devil, that supernatural embodiment of human evil deeply lodged in Scots Calvinist anxieties about sin. And Old Bogey himself being ever ready to take an inch and steal a mile, the result is that by the time we meet Jekyll in the story, he is half inhabited by the devil. Theological overtones are deliberate in this tale's allusions to *Genesis, Paradise Lost,* and *Faust,* as Stevenson presents another version of the story of a mortal tempted by the thrill of power, pride, and forbidden knowledge to break all sanctified bonds and bounds. Stevenson's working out of that myth shows Jekyll, selfish to begin with but at least capable of friendship, making a fatal choice that leads him deeper and deeper into a pit of tormented isolation, struggling to preserve the shrinking remains of his soul.

As I turn the prism of this many-faceted story to explore it from this angle, I'll aim to demonstrate that the aura of mystery, of unanswered questions surrounding the appearances and activities of its protagonist serves, in addition to whatever other functions it fulfills, to evoke the haunting eeriness and unfathomability that always accompanies the presence of the devil in Stevenson's devil-stories. I'll further try to show that the absence of women as domestic intimates in Jekyll's bachelor world comments on Jekyll's morally dangerous, self-isolating pride, as underscored through the motif of bonds broken and the imagery of family relations grotesquely inverted.

III.

However figurative the language of deviltry may be in the expressions used by Enfield and Utterson to register their shocked first impressions of Hyde, both men certainly fall back centrally on imagery of Satan and damnation in their attempts to account for the mystifyingly powerful sense of evil the stranger conveys. Enfield describes Hyde to Utterson as being "like some damned Juggernaut" trampling the child in a scene "hellish to see" and then facing down his accusers "with a kind of black sneering coolness ... carrying it off, sir, really like Satan" (31–32). Asked to describe this villain's physical appearance, Enfield says, as does everyone else who sees Hyde, that the man inspires instant revulsion and hatred for reasons somehow impossible to pin down and that he gives a strong feeling of deformity for reasons somehow impossible to trace to any particular physical characteristic. When Utterson, his imagination now haunted by ceaseless visions of this loathsome creature's persecutions of Henry Jekyll, finally gets a look at Hyde, he ends up more disturbed than he began. The "pale and dwarfish" appearance, the "impression of deformity," the "displeasing smile"—"not all of these together could explain the hitherto unknown disgust, loathing and fear with which Mr. Utterson regarded him.... 'God bless me, the man seems hardly human! Something troglodytic? ... or is it the mere radiance of a foul soul that thus transpires through, and transfigures its clay continent? The last, I think: for, O my poor old Harry Jekyll, if ever I read Satan's signature upon a face, it is on that of your new friend!'" (40).

This sense of contact with the uncanny and the ungodly is exactly what marks confrontations with the frightening, often apparently supernatural strangers who turn up to egg a main character on to evil or self-destruction in Stevenson's other four devil stories—"Thrawn Janet," "The Merry Men," "The Body-Snatcher," and "Markheim."[12] As Markheim peers at the wavering outlines of the figure who emerges out of thin air to address him on the scene of the murder he has just committed, one clear impression cuts through all his confusion: "Always, like a lump of living terror, there lay in his bosom the conviction that this thing was not of the earth and not of God."[13] The Reverend Murdoch Soulis in "Thrawn Janet" reacts with an instinctive, deathly cold shudder on a stiflingly hot day when he encounters in the church graveyard a strange black man—the form the devil was said to take in Scots folklore, as Stevenson explains in a footnote. The stranger has come to visit the minister's witchlike, wry-necked old housekeeper Janet M'Clour. When in the aftermath of that visit, the minister catches sight of Janet's now "fearsome" face, he is seized with another involuntary cold shudder. That moment of chill instinct, as the narrator tells it, marks for Mr. Soulis the point at which "it was borne in upon him what folk said, that Janet was deid lang syne, an' this was a bogle [a bogy; a terrifying supernatural being] in the clay-cauld flesh."[14]

As these examples suggest, in the plots of all of these tales there repeatedly turns out to be a closeness of identification between the mystery visitor suggestive of the devil and the human being whom this demon turns up to beguile or invade. In *Jekyll and Hyde*, where Hyde emerges as a chemical precipitate from within Jekyll, Stevenson leaves no room to doubt the entire unity of identification between his protagonist and the bogey who mirrors that protagonist's worst capacity for evil.

On that basis, consider again Utterson's sorrowful exclamation, "O my poor old Harry Jekyll, if ever I read Satan's signature upon a face, it is on that of your new friend" (40). Might not Stevenson be subtly inviting the reader to hear the echo of a folk-term for the devil—"Old Harry"— passing through Utterson's accidental conjunction of "old" with the nickname "Harry" for "Henry"? And when in the next chapter we find Jekyll described as "a smooth-faced man of fifty, with something of a slyish cast perhaps, but every mark of capacity and kindness" (43), might we wonder whether Satan's name can be read not only on Hyde's face, but also on Jekyll's?

More importantly, consider what we find when we reconstruct Jekyll's moral history. I would suggest that whatever Jekyll says about gaiety of disposition being the worst of his faults, we are in fact meant to see that Jekyll's worst fault—his original sin, if you will—is the spiritual pride that begets duplicity. Even as a youth, he tells us, he was governed by an "imperious desire to carry my head high, and wear a more than commonly grave countenance before the public" (81). It is this Luciferian pride that made him so rigid about concealing forms of pleasure that he saw as compromising his dignity: "Many a man would have even emblazoned such irregularities as I was guilty of; but from the high views that I had set before me, I regarded and hid them with an almost morbid sense of shame" (81). He has thus stood "committed to a profound duplicity of life" for several decades by the time he comes, some years before the narrative present of the tale, to what he calls "the fatal crossroads" (81, 85) where he swallows the potion that calls out the ruling principle of evil in his character. Jekyll responds to that opportunity for undetectable self-indulgence with a rebellious gusto so flamboyant that we can hardly fail to find it—well, devilishly appealing: "I knew myself, at the first breath of this new life, to be more wicked, tenfold more wicked, sold a slave to my original evil; and the thought, in that moment, braced and delighted me like wine" (84).

Time runs on through the remaining years leading up to the story's opening action, with little visible change in Jekyll's life except a quarrel with Lanyon that drives the friends apart. Yet as we learn from Jekyll's "Full Statement," it was "soon" after the first transformation that the hidden selfishness and arrogance in Jekyll began snowballing towards Hyde's bloodthirsty pleasure in sadism, culminating in the acts of impulsive, gratuitous cruelty towards a little girl and an old man that we see in the novella's early chapters. What we also learn in this final chapter of the novella is that despite all his horrified attempts to rid himself of the increasingly willful inner being through whom "the balance of my nature might be permanently overthrown" (89), Jekyll remains fatally vulnerable to the morally corrupting effects of self-indulgent, self-congratulatory pride. After he has destroyed the key to the laboratory and undertaken months of benevolent activity in expiation of the Carew murder, there comes a moment in which Jekyll undergoes the involuntary transformation which seals his enslavement to Hyde, simply through a "brief condescension" to that self-exonerating pride. Sitting on a park bench on a fine January day, he reports, "the animal within me licking the chops of memory; the spiritual side a little drowsed.... I smiled, comparing myself with other men, comparing my active goodwill with the lazy cruelty of their neglect." It is "at the very moment of that vainglorious thought" that he is seized with the nausea and shuddering that signal the return of a now relentless sequence of involuntary transformations (92). The moment when Jekyll is most blindly self-regarding provides the cue for the Satanic Hyde to step forward and claim the soul to which he had been given ready entry years ago.

In Stevenson's novella, then, as in Sophocles' *Oedipus Rex*—a play Stevenson had been studying just a year before he wrote *Strange Case of Dr. Jekyll and Mr. Hyde*—by the time we as an audience meet our hero of vaunted intellect and pride, his weaknesses of character have been decisively tested at a fatal crossroads and his long-delayed nemesis is at hand. In Stevenson's tale, however, lacking a Greek chorus to supply us with information about what the main characters are failing to see, we move through the drama anchored in Utterson's absolute bewilderment and profound unease. The narrative's closeness to Utterson's perspective, combined with the aura of unfathomable mystery characteristic of Stevenson's evocations of the devil, insures that the story as a whole is suffused with the strangeness Stevenson's title aims to suggest, all the way down to its omission of the definite article "the" (often mistakenly inserted by editors or critics) before "Strange Case." This air of eerie, unsettling indeterminacy pervades the tale's language, characterization, and scene painting as well as its larger meanings. It is hardly surprising that it extends to the matter of Jekyll's night-time pleasures, somewhat along the lines of that Andrew Jefford and Judith Halberstam suggest in talking about multiplication of meanings.

To be sure, Stevenson's crafty narration always leaves the door open in these tales to skeptical readings that would see the devil as merely an emanation of the human capacity for superstitious dread of darkness, danger, or the abysses of evil or madness possible within human nature. Stevenson clearly enjoys playing things more than one way at once. However, he does still want the reading experience itself to carry the full-blooded devil association, partly for the spook story thrill of raising the hairs on our necks, and partly for the purposes of charging moral responsibility on those who commit what are indeed for him the true sins of "the diabolic" in man.

To make a connection, finally, between the role of the diabolic in Jekyll and the absence of women at the center of the tale, we need to go back for a moment to the moral vision implied in Stevenson's letter to Bocock. Consider in particular the statement, "There is no harm in a voluptuary ... malice and selfishness and cowardice ... are the diabolic in man—not this poor wish to have a woman, that they make such a cry about." For Stevenson, the "war in the members"—a biblical phrase that Jekyll uses in the story—is not defined puritanically as a battle between virtuously celibate spirituality and wickedly fleshly sexuality. Instead, it involves a struggle to channel healthy, blameless physical appetites towards spiritually generous ends, so as to remain true to what one recognizes as one's best self. The danger lies in life's many temptations to compromise that best self by narrowly serving only a mean sort of self-gratification. Stumbles along the way are inevitable, so a degree of humility is indispensable to honest acknowledgement of mistakes made and of new efforts needed.[15]

Intimate friends, family members, and most of all well-loved spouses can in Stevenson's view have the enormous value of serving as reflectors of one's faults while simultaneously serving as sharers in and encouragers of one's attempt to improve on those faults. In the following quote, taken from his unfinished 1880 essay, "Reflection and Remarks on Human Life," Stevenson celebrates the role a marriage partner can play as this particular type of Significant Other:

> To take home to your hearth that living witness whose blame
> will most affect you, to eat, to sleep, to live with your most
> admiring and thence most exacting judge, is not this to domes-

ticate the living God? Each becomes a conscience to the other, legible like a clock upon the chimney-piece. Each offers to his mate a figure of the consequence of human acts ... and though I continue to sin, it must be now with open eyes.[16]

Not so for Henry Jekyll, of course. The only mirror to Jekyll's faults is the neutrally silent cheval glass in which, in an act of typically self-isolating narcissism, he admires his transformed image as Hyde. It is unthinkable that a wife, or for that matter a sister, mother, brother or father would be present. Jekyll never allows anyone from the respectable side of his life close enough to witness his fallible acts or remind him about what painful consequences they might entail. The absence of domestic intimates thus helps insure that such bonds as do initially help keep him in check—bonds of old acquaintance, bonds within his compound nature, and bonds of social responsibility—are violated with ever greater recklessness as he proceeds on his juggernaut career as Hyde.

The imagery of the story consistently highlights the danger of Jekyll's betrayal of the ties that bind body to soul, self to society, and family member to family member. The moral is intimated even before the story begins, in the opening line of Stevenson's dedication to his cousin Katharine de Mattos: "It's ill to loose the bands that God decreed to bind." The motif of sanctifying bonds is then quietly echoed in the first chapter's description of Mr. Utterson's faithfulness to "the bond that united him to Mr. Richard Enfield, his distant kinsman" (29).

Jekyll, on the other hand, broke a "bond of common interest" with his old schoolfriend Lanyon when they quarreled over what Lanyon calls Jekyll's "fanciful" scientific ideas. Moreover, Jekyll is driven to pursue his experiment because he considers it "the curse of mankind" that the "polar twins" of two inner aspects of our being—righteous conscience and selfish desire, are incongruously "bound together" (82). Stevenson in his 1879 essay "Lay Morals" had acknowledged that humans can live all too easily "with our opposing tendencies in continual seesaw of passion and disgust," but he had argued that the remedy lies in fusing parts of the self; allowing "the soul and all the faculties and senses [to] pursue a common route and share in one desire." His explanation of how we can honor the bonds between spirit and flesh finds its touchstone example, as did the passage I just quoted from "Reflections and Remarks on Human Life," in that best form of sexual love between a man and woman in which devotion serves to educate and elevate selfish animal instincts:

> Man is tormented by a very imperious physical desire; ... the doctors will tell you, not I, how it is a physical need, like the want of

food or slumber. In the satisfaction of this desire, as it first appears, the soul ... often unsparingly regrets and disapproves the satisfaction. But let the man learn to love a woman as far as he is capable of love; and for this random affection of the body there is substituted ... a consent of all his power and faculties which supersedes, adopts, and commands the other. Life is no longer a tale of betrayals and regrets; for the man now lives as a whole."[17]

Jekyll, however, remains too much the selfish child at the emotional level even to glimpse this possibility of the way that such bonds between two people who love each other physically and spiritually can promote bonds within the self. His blindness to the self-integrating value of profoundly interpersonal unions exceeds that of his bachelor friends, particularly Utterson with his unshakable loyalty to old acquaintances. Jekyll's complete flight from bonds in every sense of the word is reflected in the story's repetition of a striking phrase to describe the sensation Jekyll experiences as Hyde: "a solution [i.e., a dissolving] of the bonds of obligation" (82, 93). As that unnatural freedom from accountability to self and other gives license to murderous impulses, he rains blows upon the body of an old man in a scene that the maid who witnesses it describes by saying that "Mr. Hyde broke out of all bounds" (47). With Hyde now a hunted murderer and Jekyll ever more subject to involuntary transformations, Jekyll withdraws from all social contacts. The man who broke all bonds and bounds is described, in our last glimpse of him through Utterson's eyes, immured in a "house of voluntary bondage" (59) and destined for suicide.

One of the moments of apparent moral reliability in Jekyll's sometimes shifty "Full Statement" comes when he says that he has learned—too late—"that the doom and burthen of our life is bound for ever on man's shoulders; and when the attempt is made to cast it off, it but returns upon us with more unfamiliar and more awful pressure" (83). Stevenson plays on the words "familiar" and "unfamiliar" in the story, as he does with variations of "bond," to underscore that moral. Jekyll's diabolically self-serving attempt to substitute Hyde as a "familiar" (even in the sense of attendant spirit) or a "friend" for the more morally demanding and educational bonds of actual family relations and self-revealing friendships ends up backfiring in ways that imagery at the end of the story makes painfully clear.

Let me end by briefly reviewing that imagery. Jekyll had thought to avoid the war among the members which he imaged in terms of polar twins wanting to go their different ways. By the end of the tale the dissociated halves of himself are locked in a hate-filled, fratricidal warfare to the death reminiscent of Cain and Abel, the biblical siblings invoked by Utterson in the opening paragraph of the story.

Jekyll had temporarily flattered himself that he had towards Hyde "more than a father's interest," even if Hyde had towards him, "more than a son's indifference" (89). In time, Jekyll is describing Hyde as "that child of Hell," and by the end of Jekyll's "Full Statement," this suggestion of paternity has regressed to an *Aliens* image of Jekyll's body invaded by "the slime of the pit" as it "lay caged in his flesh where he heard it mutter and felt it struggle to be born" (94, 95).

Jekyll had congratulated himself on escaping the eye of moral observation—observation such as Stevenson in his prose writings on morals suggests that spouses can painfully but valuably provide to one another. A crowning punishment for Jekyll is that the blob of malevolent, soulless materiality brought forth by his pride, intellect, and selfishness has become, in the final stage of convulsive, involuntary transformations, an "insurgent horror ... knit to him closer than a wife, closer than an eye" (95).

Henry Jekyll does indeed have a significant other. You can call him Hyde, or you can call him the original Old Harry, Prince of Darkness.

NOTES

1. Undated variant typescript copies of the play have recently been located in the New York Public Library, Lincoln Center Branch (microfilm available at the Ohio State University Theatre Research Institute) and the Smithsonian Institution, National Museum of American History (Mansfield Costume Collection).

2. "Strange Case of Dr. Jekyll and Mr. Hyde" in *The Strange Case of Dr Jekyll and Mr. Hyde and Other Stories*, ed. Jenni Calder (New York: Penguin Books, 1979, reprinted 1981), pp. 81, 85, 86; further citations from this edition of the story will be in parentheses in the text.

3. *The Letters of Gerard Manley Hopkins*, ed. Catherine Phillips (Oxford: Clarendon Press, 1990), 243; W.H. Myers to R. L. Stevenson, 27 February 1886, in *Robert Louis Stevenson: The Critical Heritage* (Boston: Routledge & Kegan Paul, 1981), 215.

4. Jefford, "Dr. Jekyll and Professor Nabokov: Reading a Reading," in *Robert Louis Stevenson*, ed. Andrew Noble (Totowa, NJ: Barnes & Noble), 1983, 61.

5. Halberstam, *Skin Shows: Gothic Horror and the Technology of Monsters* (Durham: Duke University Press, 1995), 2.

6. Nabokov, *Lectures on Literature*, ed. Fredson Bowers (New York: Harcourt Brace Jovanovich, 1980), 194.

7. Showalter, *Sexual Anarchy: Gender and Culture at the Fin de Siecle* (New York: Viking Penguin, 1990), pp. 105–114. Janice Doane and Devon Hodges, writing a year before Showalter, also call for viewing Stevenson's text in relation to an upheaval in conventional notions of gender taking place late Victorian England. However, where Showalter sees Stevenson focusing on homosexuality, Doane and

Hodges argue that Hyde embodies his mixed feelings about feminism's "wild" if vital "New Woman."   (See Doane and Hodges, "Demonic Disturbances of Sexual Identity," in *Novel*, Fall 1989, 63–74.)

8. Heath, "Psychopathia Sexualis: Stevenson's *Strange Case*," in *Critical Quarterly* 8:1–2 (1986), 93–108.

9. See Veeder's "The Texts in Question", "Collated Fractions of the Manuscript Drafts" and "Children of the Night," in *Dr. Jekyll and Mr. Hyde after One Hundred Years*, ed. William Veeder and Gordon Hirsch (Chicago: University of Chicago Press, 1988).

10. *The Letters of Robert Louis Stevenson*, ed. Bradford Booth and Ernest Mehew (New Haven: Yale University Press, 1994–95), 8 vols; 6:56.

11. Stevenson's wife Fanny quotes him as using these words about the dream that inspired the tale when she woke him (see *The Life of Robert Louis Stevenson* by Graham Balfour; London: Methuen and Co., 1901; 2:13); Stevenson's own account of the dream origin of the tale occurs at the end of his January 1888 *Scribner's Magazine* article, "A Chapter on Dreams."

12. These four stories, published respectively in 1881, 1882, 1884, and 1885, are the ones that Jenni Calder in her biography of Stevenson links with *Strange Case of Dr. Jekyll and Mr. Hyde* as featuring "Satan's entry on the scene of Stevenson's writing" (see Calder's *Robert Louis Stevenson: A Life Study* [Hamish Hamilton, 1980; reprinted Glasgow: Richard Drew Publishing, 1990], 165 and 221–22.) Stevenson himself, when listing stories in 1894 for a proposed collected edition of his work, created nearly the same grouping, bracketing *Strange Case of Dr. Jekyll and Mr. Hyde* with "Olalla," "Thrawn Janet," "Markheim" and "The Merry Men" (*Letters*, 8:225).

13. "Markheim," reproduced from the autograph manuscript, in *Tales from the Prince of Storytellers*, ed. Barry Menikoff (Evanston: Northwestern University Press, 1993), 310.

14. "Thrawn Janet," as reprinted from the first English edition, in *Tales from the Prince of Storytellers*, ed. Menikoff, 323.

15. My case for viewing this philosophy about love relationships as the burden of Stevenson's fictional and prose treatments of male-female relations can be found in my article, "Revaluing Women and Marriage in Robert Louis Stevenson's Short Fiction," in *English Literature in Transition*, 40:1 (1997), 34–59.

16. Stevenson, "Reflections and Remarks on Human Life," Addenda: V in *The Works of Robert Louis Stevenson* (New York: Scribner's, 1924) 22:633.

17. Stevenson, "Lay Morals," *Works*, 22:560.

The Hand of Hyde[1]

Richard Dury

Dr. Jekyll, after one of his nocturnal "adventures" in the safe disguise of Mr. Hyde, slowly emerges from sleep in his comfortable middle-class bedroom, yet feels that he is somewhere else, feels strangely that he is waking in the Soho apartment he rents for Hyde. Dozing off and reawakening he tries "in my psychological way" to understand this illusion. It is then that

> my eyes fell upon my hand. Now the hand of Henry Jekyll (as you have often remarked) was professional in shape and size: it was large, firm, white, and comely. But the hand which I now saw, clearly enough, in the yellow light of a mid–London morning, lying half shut on the bed-clothes, was lean, corded, knuckly, of a dusky pallor and thickly shaded with a swart growth of hair. It was the hand of Edward Hyde [JH 87–8].

Like Crusoe seeing the footprint in the sand, he stares first in incomprehension and then in sudden alarmed awareness that his whole situation has changed from previously assumed safety to sudden danger.

This memorable scene is one of those when (as Stevenson says in "A Gossip on Romance" [1882: 123]) "the threads of the story come ... together and make a picture in the web; the characters fall into some attitude to each other or to nature, which stamps the story home like an illustration." These "pictures" make a direct appeal to the collective imagination (in Stevenson's words: they are "the realization ... of the daydreams of common men") and are perhaps easily stored in the mind because they associate a strong emotion with a simple spatial configuration. In the case of Jekyll staring in horror at the hand of Hyde, the scene also calls into play a whole series of age-old feelings concerning this privileged yet often alien-seeming part of the body.[2]

References to the hand permeate the whole of Stevenson's text,[3] and the motif has been taken up by some perceptive illustrators and film directors. The twelve illustrations by Barry Moser, for example (JH 1990), open with Jekyll's father and end with the portrait of Jekyll's father mutilated by Hyde. At the centre of the sequence, in sixth and seventh position, we find the hand of Jekyll and the hand of Hyde. The two hands are symmetrical: Jekyll's hand is a left hand hanging down, passive, yet suggestive of male genitalia, especially the rather large thumb; Hyde's hand is a right hand raised upward, actively clutching a small liquid-filled glass, deformed and hairy.

The hand is also given prominence in Mamoulian's film of *Dr. Jekyll and Mr. Hyde* (1931), where the opening titles are followed by a sequence of Jekyll playing the organ, in a montage of three elements: (1) the musical score of a Bach Prelude and Fugue (suggesting both doubleness and attempts to escape it in the fugal structure, or the divine control of destiny in its pre-written nature, or the arts of man opposed to death), (2) the butler, Poole (whose wrinkled face may remind us of mortality), and (3) the hands playing. The sequence ends with the hands of Jekyll (or the hands of the viewer, since this is part of Mamoulian's famous long subjective opening) playing the final chord, thereby associating the hands with movement, life, and creation but also with closure, doubleness, destiny, and death. In the transformation scenes it is the hands that are the most prominent changing feature, and it is to these that Jekyll looks to confirm that he is changing.[4]

The use of the hand to check identity is also found in Jean Renoir's *Le Testament du Docteur Cordelier* (1959): after falling to the floor in the first transformation scene, Dr. Cordelier immediately looks at his "Hyde hands." In the symmetrical first re-transformation scene, the doctor lying on the floor of his laboratory raises his right hand, looks at it, turns it round and smiles, while his voice-over says, "I was Cordelier once more."[5]

In Stevenson's text, it is only in the two spontaneous and unwilled transformations into Hyde (while musing in bed and while thinking animal thoughts in Regent's Park) that Jekyll knows that he has changed into Hyde by looking at his hands. Mamoulian and Renoir have added visible functions to the hands to compensate for all the other (especially metaphorical) uses of the motif in the text that are difficult to translate into pictures.

Of course, the hand is often perceived as far from alien, as familiar and (with the face) as the most "spiritual" part of the body. Superior to words in the direct expression of feelings and emotions, the hands are "so expressive that they cannot lie" (Bronne 1970: 23). They are as closely associated as the face with the persistent identity of the individual: palmists see individual destiny in the hand, criminologists accept fingerprints as a unique mark of identification, graphologists identify an individual from his written "hand" and see therein indications of personality, and most people see in the form and habitual style of movement of the physical hand similar indications. For Pierre Reverdy (1956: 22), the hand is "possibly the best summary of the individual and his whole personality.... The hand represents psychological individuality perhaps better even than the face, which learns to play a role, to wear a mask and to lie."[6]

And yet even those who praise the hand seem to find it slightly disturbing, as does Focillon in his "*Eloge de la main*" (1939: 137) when he says of hands that "they are almost animate beings...faces without eyes and without voices."[7] The hand is an expression of the individual, yet somehow seems separated from him, with a life and a will of its own in competition with the Ego. As Roquetin (in Sartre's *La Nausée*) observes, his hand seems to be himself but also different from himself: "It's alive.... It's part of me, those two animals that move at the end of my arms.... I feel its weight on the table as something apart from myself"[8] (Sartre, 1938: 30).

The strange and alien nature of this most familiar part of the body seems to act against the individual's desire for unity. In R.S. Thomas's poem "The Hand" (1975), even God is disturbed by the hand he has made, which calls out, "Tell me your name" and boasts "the world / is without meaning, awaiting / my coming." God does not reply, knowing that "this was the long war with himself always foreseen." Here we see Intelligence challenged by the contemplation of the material hand, which reminds him of a division within himself that he is unable to resolve—the same situation in which Jekyll finds himself as he looks at his hand on awaking.

This feeling of division is also reflected in the story (in Genesis ch. 27) of Jacob obtaining his blind father's blessing by putting goatskins over his hands. Although Isaac thinks that "the voice is Jacob's voice," he accepts the proof of identity given by the hands, which are "hairy, as his brother Esau's hands." In this way Jacob obtains the blessing that confirms his previous appropriation of the inheritance from his elder but "less evolved" twin brother. Psychologically, we could see this tale as the effective rejection by the individual of the hands, body, instinctive nature, and sexuality (the disinheritance of Esau and his "hairy hands") and the granting of preeminence to the mind and soul (Jacob, the "voice"), thanks to the collaboration of the super–Ego, Isaac.

An even clearer example of the hands warring against the mind is found in Aldous Huxley's short story "Farcical History of Richard Greenow," in which the protagonist finds that at night a part of his personality writes the sentimental romances he detests, assuming a feminine name and "flamboyant feminine writing." In the end he goes mad, shouting and gesticulating with his left hand, while his right hand, now taking possession even in daytime (rather like Hyde at the end of *Dr. Jekyll and Mr. Hyde*) crosses out what he has written in favour of pacifism and writes patriotic speeches against the Germans (rather as Hyde writes blasphemies in the margins of a pious work much valued by Jekyll). In both cases, we have a hand that takes possession of the whole body.

The hands of others are also disturbing, perhaps because they resemble one's own. The monster's hand is large, ugly, dirty, and hairy, yet it can easily be seen as a feared part of oneself, a part beyond the control of one's conscious will. In Tennyson's "Lucretius," the philosopher's unconscious happiness is destroyed as "some unseen monster lays / His vast and filthy hands upon my will / Wrenching it backward into his: and spoils / My bliss in being." Here, the monster's "vast and filthy hands" may well be taken for the speaker's self-awareness, or the awareness of his own body—an awareness indeed that may be stimulated principally by the contemplation of his own hands.[9]

Any non-human hand is potentially disturbing, an eloquent reminder, especially for the Victorians, both of the evolutionary theories of Darwin and of the ideas of a constant animal element in human nature. The hairy hands of Hyde are a reminder of these fears, especially when combined with the many suggestions of his primitive or animal nature.[10]

The association of animal hands with degenerative moral nature is seen in George MacDonald's *The Princess and Curdie* (1882). Curdie is given the power to know the moral nature of others by the feel of hands: a hideous (but virtuous and faithful) animal has a paw that feels like the hand of a little child, while the hands of the King's evil counsellors feel like the claw of a bird of prey or the underside of a snake. Stevenson's tale has a similar message: appearance and inner nature are often different, and both writers take the hand as a special indicator of degenerate animal nature.

Even the hands of those of different classes can be disturbing; the hand of the worker being clearly different from the soft white hand of those who do no manual work. Jean Macé in his child's guide to the workings of the body (1861:14) reveals the fear felt by the privileged few for "that workingman with his rolled-up sleeves, whose black and dirty hands you would fear to touch."[11] While Jekyll's is that of a "professional" gentleman, Hyde's hand is reminiscent of the excluded proletarian: powerful, hairy, dark. Indeed, one can easily see Hyde both as the socially excluded (Jekyll's butler quickly reassures Utterson: "Oh dear no, sir. He never *dines* here," JH 41), and as the threat to established authority (in his destruction of the letters and portrait of Jekyll's father).

One important source of our equivocal relationship with hands is that they can be a reminder of mortality. Death, often shown to inhabit the mirror in sensational narratives, also inhabits the hand (as is suggested by the frequent use of dead hands and skeleton hands in horror films and by the frequent poetic metaphor "the hand of death"). In Stevenson's *Treasure Island* (ch. 3) it is Blind Pew, the "eyeless creature," characterized by his hand which "gripped in a moment like a vice," who brings the pirates' Black Spot, the warning of death, to place in the hand of the transgressor. When Billy Bones (the name itself another reminder of mortality) sees the small black disk placed in own left hand he knows that he is going to die.

We may see four major sources for this association: (1) the hand is the most visible part of the individual's own body and contemplation of it (like contemplating one's mirror-image) reminds the individual of his corporality and hence mortality, (2) the lifeless hand, a plaster-cast hand, or the depiction of a hand cut off at the wrist all contrast starkly with the mercurial movements of the living hand, the most mobile part of the body, (3) the hand is associated with striking and punishing and the causing of death, and (4) manual acts like signing and sealing, or the handshake to confirm a deal, associate the hand in acts whose irrevocable finality makes them similar to death or the sexual act: they are irreversible, they create a new situation.

The most direct expression of the connection between the hand and Death is the "hand from the grave" that snatches the individual from life. The sensational mystery novel by Sheridan Le Fanu, *Wylder's Hand* (1864), ends with a murderer being killed as his horse rears in fright at the sight of a hand with a ring on the little finger (the hand of the man he has murdered) emerging from the ground:

> In this livid hand, rising from the earth, there was a character both of menace and appeal; and on the finger, as I afterwards saw at the inquest, glimmered the talismanic legend "Resurgam—I will rise again!"[12]

The idea of the dead hand pursuing and wreaking revenge is also present in Maupassant's short story *"La main d'écorché"* (1875),[13] where the dead hand brings death to the student who has stolen it from the grave and who has placed it as a joking *memento mori* in his bedroom. This repulsive hand ("frightful, black, dried, very long and slightly clenched"[14]) apparently strangles the student while he is sleeping and then returns to its corpse.

The hand coming from the grave to bring death reminds us of the statue of the man whom Don Juan has murdered, holding out his hand to him with the order "*Dammi la mano intera!*" (Da Ponte/Mozart). Here the hand of death combines with the idea of the *kolossos*, the stone double of the buried corpse, which holds down the dead person, but also represents him and allows a disturbing dialogue between the dead and the living (Castoldi, 1989: 11–12). This double appropriately calls for Don Giovanni's reminder of doubleness and mortality, his own hand. Hyde (like all Doubles, a reminder and bringer of death) is himself explicitly compared to a *kolossos*, when Jekyll says that he commits his unnamed sadistic acts "relentless like a man of stone" (JH 86).

Death may also be represented by a person close to death, whose outstretched hand may well provoke the instinctive rejection felt by the wedding guest in Coleridge's *Rime of the Ancient Mariner* (1798), who cries, "I fear thee, ancient Mariner! / I fear thy skinny hand!" In Stevenson's short adventure story "The Pavilion on the Links" (1880), the aged but repulsive and hypocritical Northmour (who shares some affinities with Jekyll) is found in bed looking pale and feverish. The narrator, after telling the reader that Northmour was to die shortly afterwards, continues, "He held out to me a hand, long, thin, and disagreeably hairy." The hairy hand reminds us of Hyde, and we find a similar sick hand held out when Utterson goes to visit Jekyll after the Carew murder: "There, close up to the warmth, sat Dr. Jekyll, looking deadly sick. He did not rise to meet his visitor, but held out a cold hand" (JH 51).

The hand held out by the representative of death is disturbing because it invites the interlocutor to place himself in a symmetrical configuration with the Other, a mirroring situation, with the two very similar hands in direct contact.

Other disturbing presences may hold out their hand to the viewer, like that of Parmigianino's "Self-Portrait in a Convex Mirror" (1524).[15] The half-closed eyes and the dreamy expression combined with the apparent unfocused awareness of his own hand, grotesquely enlarged by the convex mirror, seem to give us a situation similar to that of Jekyll as he wakes and contemplates his hand on the bedclothes. In another sense, this painting has affinities both with Stevenson's tale as a whole and with the equally cognitively unsettling work of Escher: there is the same feeling of unease produced by a combination of the perturbing with the paradoxical, the contradictory, the unresolvable. The painting represents Parmigianino and his hand painted on an actual convex surface like that of the mirror—making it is impossible to decide if this is a painting of the real Parmigianino and his left hand viewed via a mirror, or a painting of Parmigianino's mirror-image and its right hand.

The viewer, assuming that the artist has a reason for giving the hand such prominence, is stimulated to search for meaning—and so will revisit all its possible meanings, many of them rather disturbing. Another troubling element is the gesture made with the hand: not only displayed, enlarged, and deformed by the convex surface but held out towards the viewer, as if he would break out of the globe, break through the circle of art to touch the Other.

The viewer is drawn into the problematic visual situation since, standing in front of the painting as in front of a mirror, he is the virtual origin of the mirror-image. As John Ashbery says in his long poem dedicated to the picture *Self-Portrait in a Convex Mirror* (1975): "You feel then like one of those / Hoffmann characters who have been deprived / Of a reflection, except that the whole of me / Is seen to be supplanted by the strict / Otherness of the painter in his / Other room."

One feels equally deprived of a reflection in Mamoulian's film when the subjective camera turns towards a mirror and we see Dr. Jekyll's face, and also in Hulme Beaman's illustration (Stevenson 1886/1930) of Hyde holding up a small rectangular mirror and seeing his own face for the first time. We see the mirror and Hyde's image, but of Hyde himself only the left hand grasping the mirror's frame. Hyde/Jekyll looks at himself contentedly, admiring even the reflection of the virile right hand holding up the candlestick. In contrast, Escher's similar and complementary "Hand with Reflecting Sphere" (1935) shows a vertical left hand securely supporting the sphere in whose reflection we see the wan and questioning image of the artist, with its right hand coming towards the viewer, getting larger as it does so. The hand of the image seems to be the frightening hand of the Other, reducing the image's left (and artist's right) hand, small and laid on the artist's knee, to passive resignation. It is almost the picture of Dr. Jekyll after he has seen his own hand on the bedclothes as the hand of Hyde.

Contemplation of the hand by those particularly aware of the brief span of life left to them is especially poignant. The hand is a reminder of death (which seems certain), but since it is alive and moving, it is also a reminder of present life (which seems equally certain). Perhaps the most chilling example of this uncomprehending contemplation is the short poem written by Keats in 1819, shortly before his early death:

This living hand, now warm and capable
Of earnest grasping, would, if it were cold
And in the icy silence of the tomb,
So haunt thy days and chill thy dreaming nights
That thou would'st wish thine own heart dry of blood
So in my veins red life might stream again,
And thou the conscience-calmed—see here it is—
I hold it towards you.

The poem ends with the hand being held in front of the reader and the dying writer, the short unmetrical last line breaking out of the poem's own rhythmical frame.

If the hand is a reminder of corporality and mortality, it is also a clear reminder of sexuality. While attention to ugly, hairy hands suggests rejected corporality or sexuality, any artistic "framing" of hands with positive characteristics (as in the description of Jekyll's hands) will suggest sexual desire and erotic contemplation. In *Treasure Island*, for example, the sexual attraction of the dominant male is shown in the way Silver offered his hand to Jim and then "took my hand in his large firm grasp" (ch. 8), and in Stevenson's *Catriona* a character with some affinities with Silver, the untrustworthy James More, offered another young protagonist "his large, fine hand" (ch. 25).

The hand has natural associations with sexuality, since it falls naturally to about the same level as the sexual organs, may be placed to cover them and is employed in intimate caresses. It is also an unclothed part of the body that may represent the rest (as when Rita Hayworth sensuously "undresses" her gloved hand in *Gilda*). With the hand representing the naked body, we may understand the Victorian insistence on the wearing of gloves on most social occasions: at church and the theatre and at balls and evening parties.

The hand may assume formal similarities with the male sexual organs in its shape and position (as we have seen in Barry Moser's illustration and in the heavy right hand of Michelangelo's "David"—strangely large with respect to the rest of the body), in its contrasted active and passive forms, in the darker coloring than the rest of the body and the body hairs associated with it, as well as in the similarity of instrumental roles—the penis being referred to as "tool" and the hand as "the instrument of instruments." Showalter (1990: 115) refers to "the implied phallic image" of Stevenson's description of the Jekyll/Hyde hand in the bedroom scene.

However, the hand may be seen as feminine when it contains, caresses and calms; hence, as a synthesis of abstract masculine and feminine qualities: passive and feminine when it contains, active and male when it grasps. Stevenson's description of Jekyll's hand as "large, firm, white and comely" seems to exploit these contrasting gender associations: the words "evoke stereotypically masculine (large, firm) and feminine (white, comely) characteristics" (Doane and Hodges, 1989: 70).

The hand may also be the object of self-contemplation by the subject, and Jekyll's pleased sleepy contemplation of his own hand seems like dreamy autoerotic narcissistic contemplation. On the other hand, his alarmed view of his new hand "of a dusky pallor and thickly shaded with a swart growth of hair" may correspond to repressed memories of metamorphosis in puberty and the shock of the subject in contemplation of the new growth of body hair.

This last possibility is clarified by the use of the basic situation of Jekyll's wakening in Ian McEwan's *The Daydreamer* (1994), a book ostensibly for children but perhaps principally for adults. In the final chapter, the boy Peter undergoes the last of his fantasy metamorphoses, this time into a "grown-up." Like Jekyll, he wakes to feel that something indefinable is different with the room and with himself. The most shocking and convincing sign of his transformation is the sight of his own changed hand:

> before he could stir, he was startled by the sight of his hand. It was covered in thick black curly hairs! He stared at the great fat thing with its sausage-sized fingers and began to laugh. Even the knuckles sprouted hairs [McEwan 1994: 136].

Continuing to borrow from the first transformation scene in Stevenson's tale, McEwan then narrates how Peter gets up (naked) and goes to the mirror. Shocked, he has to cling to the basin as he examines his transformed face: "With its mask of black stubble, it looked like an ape was staring back at him." Here, then, the hand is the first unsettling sign of a change to bodily and sexual maturity.

The disturbing hand that rebels against the will of its owner is a recurring motif in horror films. The story of the pianist who, after an accident, receives the transplanted hands of an executed murderer and who then cannot resist murderous impulses (based on Maurice Renard's novel *Les mains d'Orlac* [1920]) has been filmed several times: *Orlacs Hände* (Germany, 1924); the classic expressionist film with Peter Lorre *Mad Love* (USA, 1935); *Orlac's Hands/Les mains d'Orlac* (GB/France, 1960); and *Hands of a Stranger* (USA, 1962). The rebellious hand even without transplant is a feature of *Idle Hands* (USA, 1999) in which a lazy teenager finds his right hand has a murderous will of its own.

Particularly disturbing is the animated detached hand, now a cliché of the parody horror film. *The Addams Family* (1964, 1973), for example, includes a disembodied hand named "Thing." The couple lost in the wax-works in *Waxwork 2: Lost in Time* (1992) are pursued by a dismembered hand, which kills the girl's father (Sir Wilfred). There are clearly similarities here with the pursuing Double, Hyde, who kills the father (triply represented by Sir Danvers Carew, by Jekyll's father [whose portrait he destroys] and by Jekyll himself). In *The Evil Dead 2: Dead by Dawn* (1987), a hand tries to kill its owner, who is obliged to cut it off, and even then it continues to attack him. In the above mentioned *Idle Hands* the owner finally chops off his hand, which continues its murderous rampage and even threatens to take to Hell the soul of the girl he is sexually attracted to. Here we may see the hand as the rejected body and everything connected with it, which returns strengthened by repression.

The detached horrific hand (thankfully in a more subtle form) is found in Rilke's *Die Aufzeichnungen des Malte Laurids Brigge* (1910/1966: 792–7), when the narrator tells of a traumatic incident from childhood when he went under the table to look for a dropped pencil. In the darkness he gradually distinguishes objects, especially his own stretched-out hand moving over the floor, all alone, rather like a water animal on the sea-bed. He looks at the hand with curiosity and increasingly sees it as a separate entity, thinking of how "it knows things that I had never taught it." Then suddenly "another hand came out of the wall towards it." It is a monstrous, "larger and extraordinarily thin hand" that is however like his own, since it moves in a similar way and the two hands draw blindly towards each other. Terrified, he returns above the table and tries to tell his governess but cannot find the words to do so. This situation is similar to that of Jekyll seeing the hand of Hyde: first the dreamy contemplation of the hand, the curiosity, the sense of detachment from his hand, apparently independent; followed by terror as he sees the other hand.

The various interpretations of the hand as "Double" (as mirror-image, representation, body as opposed to mind, as the reminder of death and sexuality) are additionally complicated (in a way that readers of Doubles stories will find familiar) by a further doubling: the right hand and the left hand. The oppositions on the first level are now repeated on the second: one hand is associated with the body, death, sexuality, instinctive behavior; the other hand with the mind, the non-material, the spirit.

Though it might seem of greater evolutionary advantage to be equally skilled in the use of both hands, all human societies show a massive differentiation in function and value of the right and left hands. The possible origins of this were examined by the French anthropologist Robert Herz in a brilliant essay in 1909. He sees right-left-hand differentiation as deriving from "the fundamental opposition that dominates the spiritual universe of primitive societies: the sacred and the profane," an opposition that is then extended to human society and the whole of the natural world. In such a situation "an ambidextrous man would ruin the economy of the spiritual world" (Herz 1909: 12; 1960: 99), hence the recognition of the same dichotomy in the individual as in the Universe and the clear separation of the good hand from the bad.

What Herz says about the left hand in various cultures could be easily applied to Hyde and helps to explain the extraordinary imaginative charge possessed by this short tale. In the gestural language of the North American Indians, the right hand stands for "me," the left for "not me, others." The right hand when moved above the left hand is associated with "the ideas of *death, destruction* and *burial*" (Herz 1909: 13). Hyde, associated with the Other and with Death, is also associated with the left: his entrance to Jekyll's house is through "a certain sinister block of building" (JH 30) on the left side of the street, the powders for the transformation are in a drawer on the left side of Jekyll's cabinet, and his handwriting slopes to the left ("backwards").

Herz continues with a description of the left hand that could be read as a description of Hyde:

> If, in the world of gods and the living, the left hand is spurned and humiliated, yet it has its own domain where it rules and where the right hand is excluded: but it is a shadowy and ill-famed domain [the left hand] inspires terror and repulsion. Its movements are suspect: people prefer it to be quiet and discreet, hidden, if possible, by the folds of clothing [Herz 1909: 15; author's translation].

Herz concludes that "the systematic paralyzation of the left hand, like other mutilations, expresses man's will to make the sacred predominate over the profane" (1909: 16). One might supplement this with a psychological explanation: since the hand represents the individual, the contemplation of two equal symbols of this individuality stimulates an idea (or reinforces an existing idea) of a corresponding division of the personality. Any subsequent attempt to attain a unitary identity by suppression of one "side" of the personality will then help to reinforce an already-existing idea of a moral distinction between right and left hand.

Primitive mythologies already associate the two sides of the body with two personalities. The Zuñi Indians of North America "personify the left and right side of the body as two gods who are brothers: the former, the elder is reflective, wise, and of sound judgement; while the latter is impetuous, impulsive and made for action" (Herz 1909: 17). Stevenson, then, by associating Hyde with the left hand, with everything that is instinctive, rejected by society, is exploiting a series of correspondences that can be seen as universal.

The multiple levels of doubling that make Stevenson's text such a fascinating structure are especially dense in the frequent use of "hand" with the meaning "writing." When Utterson shows a note written by Hyde to Guest, his head clerk and an amateur graphologist, Guest declares "it is an odd hand." He then places this note in a specular configuration alongside a brief note written by Jekyll. The two documents placed side by side representing the two sides of Jekyll are like the two physical hands side by side. Guest concludes that "the two hands are in many points identical: only differently sloped" (JH 55). Later on, Jekyll tells us that he gave Hyde a signature "by sloping my own hand backwards" (JH 87). The suggestion here is that Jekyll's "hand" slopes in the normal direction (*i.e.*, to the right) while Hyde's slopes "backwards" (*i.e.*, to the left), one like the mirror-image of the other.

It is interesting that, although Hyde is here still associated with the left, his hand(writing) is not monstrous, but like Jekyll's. Stevenson seems to be saying that the left side of the body and of the personality are only monstrous in the eyes of cultural convention.

It is interesting that Stevenson himself had two distinctly different "hands." A few months before the composition of *Dr. Jekyll and Mr. Hyde* he assures a correspondent that he himself has written the whole letter, though it might not seem so because "I have two hand-writings" (Letters 5: 122). A year before (1884) he says that because of illness "I have been obliged to lean my hand the other way, which makes it unrecognisable; the hand is the hand of Esau" (Letters 8: 417). This sounds very much like Jekyll "sloping my own hand backwards" to give Hyde a signature, and the uncouth hand of the instinctive Esau sounds much like the hand of Hyde.

Not only are the "hands" of Jekyll and Hyde mirror-images of each other, but Jekyll and Hyde can write each other's "hand": Jekyll writes a note in the hand of Hyde in order to reassure his friend Utterson, and Hyde writes a letter to Lanyon as if from Jekyll after remembering "I could write my own hand" (JH 93). This self-referring phrase and the general recursive configuration of Jekyll and Hyde writing each other's hand reminds us of Escher's famous "Drawing Hands" (1948), where two hands emerge from a sheet of paper, each hand drawing the other. It is "sloping my own hand backwards" as in Escher's drawing that Jekyll supplies his double with a "hand."[16] The two hands in Escher's drawing are indeed, like the "hands" of Jekyll and Hyde, "in many points identical," apart

from being "differently sloped," one sloping to the right, the other sloping to the left, one a right hand and the other a left.

Stevenson's brief narrative possesses such a notable mythical charge
in part because of the simple fable-like structure, with its few characters
in archetypal antagonisms that involve themes and motifs, such as the
hand, of universal valency. It also constitutes a fascinating structure composed of these same themes and motifs (including the hand) in doublings,
reversals, and self-reference. This riddling form too has its meaning: as in
the case of Escher and Parmigianino, Stevenson's text is disturbing in its
irresolvable complexity, suggesting that the reader, not only Jekyll and
Hyde, is a prisoner in a labyrinth of meaning. There is no final meaning
in this narrative of Escher-like fascination and of equally cunning construction.

In the end, the hand which has been so important in the creation of
the labyrinth finally disappears: Stevenson's last two chapters are two documents, one written by Dr. Lanyon, the other by Dr. Jekyll; the first is
signed, but the second, significantly, is not. So here, at the very end of the
text, instead of Jekyll's "hand" (meaning "signature" in legal formulas),
we find an absence. Jekyll eliminates the feared hand of Hyde at the cost
of his own hand, his own identity, his own existence.

NOTES

1. An earlier version of this paper was published in Naugrette (ed.) (1997).

2. The motif of the hand in Stevenson's novella has been touched on by
Doane & Hodges (1989: 70–1), Showalter (1990: 115), and Dury (1993: 78–80).
Doane & Hodges see the hairy hand as bringing with it associations of feared feminine sexuality; they also note that Stevenson undermines the hand as 'stable sign
of distinction, certainty and identity' by making both Jekyll and Hyde forgers of
the other's hand (handwriting). Showalter points out the association of Hyde
with Jekyll's left hand (which she suggests might have homosexual connotations);
the phallic nature of the hand; and Stevenson's use of 'hand' to mean 'handwriting' and 'signature.' The cultural and literary meanings of the hand are explored
by Bronne (1970) and the hand as a motif in modern French literature by Junker
(1967); the meanings of the right vs. left hand have been studied by Herz (1909).
Rowe (1999), which came to my attention too late for the present study, studies
the 'severed hand' trope in the Renaissance and 19th-century periods in Anglo-
American literature from a cultural and philosophical point-of-view, seeing the
motif as questioning the idea of responsible and non-voluntary acts in periods of
ideological change.

3. *hand(s)* is the most frequent common noun (after *lawyer*, always used to
refer to Utterson), occurring a total of 66 times. The word is made more prominent by some puzzling uses, in particular 'from the days of childhood, when I had

walked with my father's hand' (JH 91), which possibly means 'when I walked hand-in-hand with my father,' or 'when I was in my father's control.' The phrase 'with my father's hand' is a strange mixture of the familiar and the unfamiliar: it sounds like an idiom—yet it is not, and the use of 'with' is far from normal. Another strange phrase (also noted by Wolf 1995: 106 n4) occurs when Jekyll says that if needed he would sacrifice 'my left hand' to help Lanyon (JH 74). Jekyll's expression—the normal idiom is 'I would give my right hand for something'—calls attention to the sinister associations of the left, in this text also associated with Hyde.

4. At the first drinking of the potion, the hands come up to clutch the throat; at the second drinking the camera moves from changing face to changing right hand holding the arm of the chair, back to face, then down to the left hand. Later, after each of the two spontaneous transformations Jekyll looks down anxiously at his hands.

5. In the first involuntary transformation scene, a hairy left, then right hand emerges from the bedclothes; they uncover a drowsy face, still half asleep. Cordelier raises his head slightly and the left hand is turned in inspection; he then looks at his right hand, before moving to the mirror.

6. "La main, peut-être le plus complet résumé de l'homme, de sa personnalité totale.... La main résume l'homme psychique, peut-être plus encore que le visage qui s'éduque, se masque et ment."

7. 'Elles sont presque des etres animeés ... visages sans yeux et sans voix, mais qui voient et qui parlent.'

8. 'Elle vit, cest moi [...] C'est moi, ces deux bêtes qui s'agisent au bout de mes bras [...] je sens son poids sur la table qui n'est pas moi.'

9. For Tennyson and hands see Sanders 1957.

10. For Utterson he is 'hardly human,' with the air of the cave-man about him: 'something tyrogloditic' (JH 40); he attacks Carew with 'ape-like fury' (JH 47), and Poole describes him as a 'masked thing like a monkey' (JH 68); he also utters savage laughs, cries and screeches.

11. "Cet ouvrier aux manches retroussées, dont vous auriez peur de toucher la main noire et sale."

12. It may be of interest to Stevenson scholars that in the same chapter in which this event occurs (ch. 72, "Mark Wylder's Hand") there is a minor character with the unusual name of 'Jekyl' (*sic*).

13. This was an early and influential severed-hand ghost story and may have directly influenced the American horror-film tradition as it was "widely circulated in the 1940s American comic-book version by Classic Comics" ["The Flayed Hand" in *3 Famous Mysteries, Classic Comics* No. 21 (1944)] (Rowe 1999: 128).

14. 'affreuse, noire, sèche, très longue et comme crispée.'

15. Cf. Stoichita, Victor I. (1993). *L'Instauration du tableau: métapeinture à l'aube des temps modernes*. Paris: Méridiens Klincksieck, pp. 235 ff.

16. Escher's Dutch title for his lithograph is "Tekenen," which can mean 'signs,' 'signing' or 'drawing.'

REFERENCES

Ashbery, John (1975). *Self-Portrait in a Convex Mirror*. New York: Viking Press.

Bronne, Carlo (1970). "Variations pour les mains." *Bulletin de l'Académie Royale de Langue et Littérature Françaises* (Bruxelles) 48.i: 22–31.

Castoldi, Alberto. 1989. Per una definizione del doppio (1989). *Quaderni del Dipartimento di Linguistica e Letterature Comparate* (Univ. Bergamo) 5:5–13.

Doane, Janice, and Hodges, Devon. 1989. "Demonic Disturbance of Sexual Identity: The Strange Case of Dr. Jekyll and Mr/s Hyde." *Novel* 23:63–74.

Dury, Richard (1993). *The Annotated Dr. Jekyll and Mr. Hyde. 'Strange Case of Dr. Jekyll and Mr. Hyde' by Robert Louis Stevenson*. Edited with an Introduction and Notes. Milano: Guerini.

Dury, Richard (1997). "Variations sur la main de Hyde." In Naugrette, Jean-Pierre (dir.) (1997): 99–118.

Focillon, Henri (1939). *La vie des formes*. P: PUF/Quadrige (incl. *L'Eloge de la main*). Eng. transl.: *The Life of Forms in Art*. NY: Zone Books, 1989 (incl. "In Praise of Hands", pp. 157–185).

Herz, Robert. 1909. La main droite. *Révue Philosophique* 68.Transl. as "The pre-eminence of the Right Hand: A Study in Religious Polarity," in *Death and The Right Hand*. London/Glencoe, Ill.: Cohen & West/ The Free Press, 1960.

JH—Stevenson, Robert Louis (1886). *Strange Case of Dr. Jekyll and Mr. Hyde*. London: Longman Green and Co. Edited with an Introduction by Jenni Calder. Harmondsworth: Penguin, 1979.

JH 1990—Stevenson, Robert Louis (1886). *Strange Case of Dr. Jekyll and Mr. Hyde*. Foreword by Joyce Carol Oates, Illustrations by Barry Moser. Lincoln, Nebraska: University of Nebraska Press, 1990.

Junker, A. (1967). "Das Thema der Hand in der modernen französischen Literatur." *Die neueren Sprachen* 66 (n.s. 16): 311–323.

Le Fanu, Sheridan. (1864). *Wylder's Hand*. New York: Dover, 1978.

Letters—Booth, B.A. & E. Mehew (eds.) (1994–5). *The Letters of Robert Louis Stevenson*. New Haven/London: Yale University Press. 8 vols.

Macé, Jean [pseud. of Jean Moreau] (1861). *Histoire d'une bouchée de pain, lettres à une petite fille sur la vie de l'homme et des animaux*. Paris: Dentu. Also 68th edition s.d. Paris: Hetzel (Bibl. d'éducation et de récréation).

MacDonald, George (1882). *The Princess and Curdie*. Harmondswoth: Penguin/ Puffin Classics, 1994.

McEwan, Ian (1994). *The Daydreamer*. London: Jonathan Cape.

Maupassant, Guy de (1875). "La main d'écorché." *L'Almanach lorrain de Pont-à-Mousson*. Also in *Contes et Nouvelles 1875–1884* Vol. 2. Paris: Gallimard.

Naugrette, Jean-Pierre (dirigé par) (1997). *Dr. Jekyll & Mr. Hyde*. Paris: Autrement (Collection Figures Mythiques).

Reverdy, Pierre (1956). *En vrac*. Monaco: Editions du Rocher.

Rilke, Rainer Maria (1910). *Die Aufzeichnungen des Malte Laurids Brigge. Sämtliche Werke* 6 Band. Frankfurt-am-Main: Insel Verlag, 1966. Eng. transl. *Notebooks of Malte Laurids Brigge*. New York: Vintage Books, 1990.

Rowe, Katherine (1999). *Dead Hands: Fictions of Agency, Renaissance to Modern.* Stanford: Stanford University Press.

Sanders, Charles Richard (1957). "Tennyson and the Human Hand." *Victorian Newsletter* 11 (spring 1957): 5–14.

Sartre, Jean-Paul (1938). *La Nausée.* Paris: Gallimard/Le Livre de Poche.

Showalter, Elaine (1990). *Sexual Anarchy. Gender and culture at the fin de siècle.* New York/London: Viking/Bloomsbury.

Stevenson, Robert Louis. 1880. "The Pavilion on the Links." Also in *The New Arabian Nights*, 1882. Tus. 1.

Stevenson, Robert Louis. 1882. "A Gossip on Romance." In *Longman's Magazine*, 69–79. Tus. 29: 119–131.

Stevenson, Robert Louis (1886/1930), ill. S.G. Hulme Beaman. *Strange Case of Dr. Jekyll and Mr. Hyde.* London: John Lane Bodley Head.

Stevenson, Robert Louis (ed. Osbourne, Lloyd & Fanny van de Grift Stevenson) (1924). *The Works of Robert Louis Stevenson* (Tusitala Edition). London: Heinemann.

Thomas, R.S. (1975). "The Hand." *Laboratories of the Spirit.* Also in *Collected Poems 1945–90.* London: Dent, 1993.

Wolf, Leonard (ed.). *The Essential Dr. Jekyll and Mr. Hyde, Including the Complete Novel of Robert Louis Stevenson.* New York: Plume/Penguin USA, 1995.

Engineering Influences on *Jekyll and Hyde*

Gillian Cookson

The *Strange Case of Dr. Jekyll and Mr. Hyde*, Robert Louis Stevenson's original and influential story of duality, confirmed the author as a literary celebrity.[1] The story of how *Jekyll and Hyde* was written has often been recounted: Stevenson, ailing, beset by money worries, reeling from the recent loss of a much-loved friend and mentor, completed the book— "conceived, written, rewritten, re-rewritten and printed"—in ten weeks during the autumn of 1885.[2] The inspiration had come to him in a dream when—in his own words—he was looking for "a vehicle" for an idea about "man's double being."

> Then came one of those financial fluctuations... For two days I went about racking my brains for a plot of any sort; and on the second night I dreamed the scene at the window, and a scene afterwards split in two... All the rest was made awake, and consciously.[3]

Stevenson had already enjoyed critical success with *Treasure Island*, published in 1883, and was to taste more with *Kidnapped* and *Jekyll and Hyde* in 1886, although he did not manage to support himself by his writing until after his father's death the following year.[4] Under the circumstances, especially considering that his precarious state of health often left him unfit to work, it seems curious that he spent long periods over the two years, July 1885 to June 1887, engaged upon something which he knew would never bring either critical acclaim or financial reward, a memoir of the friend whose loss had so affected him, the electrical engineer Fleeming Jenkin.[5] It was the only full-length biography that Stevenson ever completed.

By any conventional standard, the Jenkin memoir was not successful. The demands of biography did not fit Stevenson's *modus operandi*, especially when his health had been so bad. Although he claimed to have enjoyed the experience, and to be satisfied with the result, he also confessed that "knowing what I am, and how I work, I do not believe I would accept a similar task again."[6] The memoir was not well-received by critics, especially those who were expecting a more thorough treatment of Jenkin's technical and scientific work. Stevenson was used to writing quickly and imaginatively without much call for factual verification in his work.[7] The demands of *Jenkin* were the exact opposite, requiring much effort in time-consuming research and very little in constructing a story. Stevenson, embellishing and romanticizing where a lesser writer may have resisted the urge, produced an unsatisfactory hybrid. Concluding that biography was not his forte, he abandoned it as he had playwrighting before.

And yet *Jenkin*, for all its faults and limitations, holds a key to understanding *Jekyll and Hyde*. Stevenson was already working on the biography when he wrote *Jekyll and Hyde*, and there is evidence both in its text, and in the circumstances of Stevenson's writing it, that the novel reflects something of his mild fixation with engineering and engineers. The allusions to engineering in *Jekyll and Hyde* are so cryptic that they have gone unremarked, but taken in combination with Stevenson's response to the loss of his much-loved friend Jenkin, they seem to confirm that the author's preoccupation with engineering generated ideas for his novel.

It was noted with mild amusement many years ago that the founders of the Institution of Electrical Engineers included "the curious addition of Jekyll and Hyde."[8] This was assumed to have been coincidental. Yet it now seems that there was more than chance at work. Most of the characters in *Jekyll and Hyde* bear the names of engineers, some of them well-known, others less so. Henry Jekyll, the deviant scientist, shares the name of Lt. H. Jekyll, R.E., a founder in 1871 of the Society of Telegraph Engineers, forerunner of the Institution of Electrical Engineers. Jekyll's alter ego has the same name as Major General H. Hyde of the India Office, also a Royal Engineer and early member of the Society of Telegraph Engineers. Another member of the STE was Frederick C. Danvers of the India Office; Hyde's victim in the book was called Sir Danvers Carew.[9] The murder was investigated by Inspector Newcomen, synonymous with the eighteenth-century steam engine inventor. Dr Hastie Lanyon, friend of Dr. Jekyll, shares an unusual surname with Sir Charles Lanyon, an eminent civil engineer working in Ireland during the 1880s and personal acquaintance of Fleeming Jenkin.[10] There was also a contemporary mechanical engineer called John Hastie (1844–94).[11] The names of other mechanical engineers, Arthur Edward Guest (1841–98) and Braithwaite Poole (1805–88), appear in minor characters, Guest the clerk and Poole the butler. Another lesser character, Richard Enfield, bears the name of a famous government engineering establishment, the Enfield armory. This idea could be dismissed as whimsical, yet as circumstantial evidence it is strong: of the nine characters named in *Jekyll and Hyde*, in only one case, that of J.G. Utterson (perhaps significantly a lawyer—see below), has no connection been found with engineering. Furthermore the names are not common ones, and some are extremely unusual. Stevenson's allusion to engineering was veiled, but it is unlikely that it was accidental.

Stevenson's fascination with engineers and engineering stemmed from his background, especially from his troubled relationship with his father Thomas, the dour lighthouse builder.[12] Their disputes during Stevenson's "ferment of youth"[13] hinged upon spiritual differences and strong disagreement about the course of his career. Louis was intended to join his father, uncle and cousins in the civil engineering business founded by his grandfather. The Stevensons were engineers to the Northern Lighthouse Board, ultimately responsible for the building of 97 lighthouses around the Scottish coast.[14] But Louis's distaste for engineering bordered upon loathing. He finally confessed to his father that he wanted no occupation but writing, and after a brief attempt at practicing law, became an author.

The other engineer in Stevenson's life, Fleeming Jenkin, was in every way a striking contrast with the father, and friendship with Jenkin was the one positive and enduring outcome of Stevenson's career as a student of engineering in Edinburgh. Jenkin (1833–85), professor of engineering in the University of Edinburgh from 1868, a man both practical and intellectual, was an electrical engineer and pioneer of undersea telegraphs. He was an unusual specimen for an engineer, noted for his broad interests and ability to make important contributions to other disciplines—his critique of the theory of evolution forced Darwin to reconsider part of his thesis; his application of graphic forms to economic theory influenced leading economists of the time; he took a thoughtful yet practical interest in technical education; he was concerned with issues of public health. Perhaps most significantly for Stevenson, Jenkin was a lover of theatre and poetry, a keen producer of amateur theatricals in which Stevenson was often cast, a respected literary critic and occasional playwright. In Stevenson's essay "Talk and Talkers" Jenkin appears as Cockshot, a man of "extraordinary readiness and spirit" with a theory on any topic, "bottled effervescency, the sworn foe of sleep."[15] Seventeen years the author's senior, Jenkin had been his mentor and close friend from their first meeting in 1868, when Stevenson was a youth of seventeen. Jenkin was young at heart, an open-minded man who listened to Stevenson's opinions and admired him as a writer. In Jenkin's wife, Anne, the author discovered the first of four significant older women with whom he forged close emotional bonds.[16]

Though Stevenson generally avoided polite society in Edinburgh, he found a new interest in the Jenkins' private theatricals which were staged each spring.[17] Anne Jenkin was a renowned amateur actress, Jenkin the director and producer, and each year in a makeshift theatre in their house two plays were performed, usually Shakespearean comedies, light classics in translation, or melodrama. The audiences were made up of Edinburgh acquaintances and servants. Starting as prompter in 1871, Stevenson graduated through supporting roles to leading parts by 1875, giving his last performance in 1877. His interpretation of Shakespeare included a degree of improvisation and a smattering of practical jokes upon other members of the cast.[18] Though lacking natural flair, Stevenson was sufficiently enthused by acting, and eager to please the Jenkins, to work hard at it. He also advised on casting, and when he could not attend rehearsals was sorely missed by Jenkin, who joked: "You certainly do brighten up a scene wonderfully. Perhaps it is by contrast with the depth of your stupidity that our brilliance stands out...."[19]

The essence of Jenkin and Stevenson's friendship was this shared enthusiasm for literature and drama. Engineering, though, had a role in their relationship, and Jenkin's love of the subject was respected, though not shared, by the younger man.

> The taste for machinery was one that I could never share with him, and he had a certain bitter pity for my weakness. Once when I had proved, for the hundredth time, the depth of this defect, he looked at me askance: "And the best of the joke," said he, "is that he thinks himself quite a poet." For to him the struggle of the engineer against brute forces and with inert allies was nobly poetic.[20]

Jenkin for Stevenson was simultaneously an embodiment of engineering and poetry. Stevenson's fascination with duality, the divided self, the double life, has long been recognized; one appeal of Jenkin, the engineer-poet, was that he held within himself an intriguing combination of contrasting interests.

Jenkin's sudden death in June 1885 profoundly shocked Stevenson, then living in Bournemouth—in a house he had named Skerryvore after one of his family's lighthouses—and in miserable health, even by his own ailing standards. He was also financially straitened, although his fortunes were changing. There were great expectations of *Treasure Island*, completed in 1882, which promised to be 'as rich as Cuba.'[21] But while Stevenson worked on his memoir of Jenkin, he remained sufficiently anxious about his family's inability to repay any debts if he died that he returned a much-needed advance of £100 to his American publisher, Scribner.[22] After Jenkin's death, Stevenson had immediately agreed to write the memoir, and had made a small start before turning his attention to *Jekyll and Hyde*, inspired by the dream while he was also thinking about *Jenkin*.

Not only was there no hope that the memoir, to be published along with Jenkin's edited papers, would earn Stevenson either wealth or fame, but the strain of writing in an unfamiliar genre, when money and intervals of strength and health were in short supply, added substantially to his anxieties. It had been hoped that the work could be done by the spring of 1886, but it took more than another year to complete, in June 1887.[23] Other—paying—projects were delayed. But Stevenson was clear about the purpose of *Jenkin*; it was a labor of love and commemoration. He wrote later to Sidney Colvin: "I owe to you and Fleeming Jenkin, the two older men who took the trouble and knew how to make a friend of me, everything that I have or am...."[24] In a letter to Edmund Gosse lamenting Jenkin's death, Stevenson had mused upon his lack of belief in "the immortality business," adding that "we were put here to do what service we can, for honour and not for hire...."[25] Writing the memoir provided solace for Stevenson in a deeply felt bereavement. Through writing, he was able to assuage some of his grief. By making sense of his friend's character, Stevenson achieved an understanding of his own love for the man: "And give me time, the picture, the face, will rise at last out of these botchings, or I am the more deceived; I do seem to see him clear and whole. I need not tell you, the more I have gained this view, the better I love him."[26] Because he derived personal benefit from the work, it was allowed to occupy many precious hours during two years when he was often too ill to write at all.

Appropriately for one fascinated by dualism, writing about Fleeming Jenkin brought twin benefits to Stevenson. Besides producing an appreciation, paying a tribute which gave solace to the family of the deceased and working through some of his own grief, Stevenson also probed the duality of the engineer-poet, exploring the possibility of two people contained within one. His considered thoughts on this are only marginally considered on the pages of *Jenkin*. But those clues within the text of *Jekyll and Hyde*, and the coincidence in gestation of the two books, suggest that Stevenson's preoccupations during the period of mourning his friend and mentor fed into his imaginative work and helped generate one of his greatest stories.

An earlier version of this paper originally appeared in Notes and Queries, *244 [New Series 46]: 4 (December 1999) and is reprinted with the kind permission of the author and Oxford University Press.*

ACKNOWLEDGEMENTS

The research upon which this paper is based was generously supported by the Leverhulme Trust. Thanks to Jan Hewitt and Neil Cookson for ideas and comments on an earlier version, and to Alan Sandison.

NOTES

1. Emma Letley (ed.), *The Strange Case of Dr Jekyll and Mr Hyde* (Oxford, 1987), xxv.

2. Frank McLynn, *Robert Louis Stevenson: a Biography* (London, 1993), 254.

3. *The Collected Works of Robert Louis Stevenson* (1911), hereafter Swanston, XVI, 188.

4. Letley, vii.

5. "Memoir of Fleeming Jenkin" in *Papers Literary, Scientific, etc., by the late Fleeming Jenkin, F.R.S., LL.D*, eds. S. Colvin and J.A. Ewing (London, 1887), reprinted in Swanston, IX, 165–303. See also Gillian Cookson and Colin A. Hempstead, *A Victorian Scientist and Engineer: Fleeming Jenkin and the Birth of Electrical Engineering* (Ashgate, 2000).

6. *The Letters of Robert Louis Stevenson*, eds. Bradford A. Booth and Ernest Mehew (Yale, 1994–5), V, 422.

7. In *Jekyll and Hyde*, this vagueness about facts causes a problem with the story, for as Rider Haggard and others pointed out, Jekyll's will could not have been brought into force a mere three months after his disappearance. Stevenson, qualified as a lawyer, should have realized this: Letley, 211–2.

8. Rollo Appleyard, *History of the Institution of Electrical Engineers, 1871–1931* (London, 1939), 43.

9. I am grateful to Tim Procter, formerly of the Institution of Electrical Engineers archives, for confirming details of these members.

10. For information about Sir Charles Lanyon, thanks to Carol Arrowsmith of the Institution of Civil Engineers.

11. For information about Hastie, Guest, and Poole, thanks to Keith Moore of the Institution of Mechanical Engineers.

12. For instance, McLynn.

13. The phrase is Sidney Colvin's: *Letters*, I, 211.

14. See Bella Bathurst, *The Lighthouse Stevensons* (London, 1999).

15. In Swanston, IX, 89–90.

16. McLynn, 38.

17. *Letters*, I, 211.

18. McLynn, 88.

19. Yale University Library, Beinecke collection, number 4983, Jenkin to Stevenson, 5 February 1879. See also number 4984, 13 March 1879.

20. Swanston, IX, 205.

21. *Letters*, V, 198, to Anne Jenkin, *c.* 6 February 1886.

22. *Letters*, V, 357.

23. Cambridge University Library, Add.7342, J18, letter from Anne Jenkin to Sir William Thomson, 8 November [1885].

24. *Letters*, VI, 266.

25. *Letters*, V, 172.

26. *Letters*, V, 342.

ESSAYS ON OTHER WORKS

"The Damned Thing in Boards and a Ticket on Its Behind": Stevenson's First Book, *An Inland Voyage*

Jason A. Pierce

On 28 April 1878, Robert Louis Stevenson first became the author of a published book—it was hardly a momentous occasion. There were no crowds outside the booksellers' shops eager for a glimpse of the new title. There were no lines of patrons at Mudie's or any of the other circulating libraries, at least not for this book. There were no copies clandestinely sealed in packets and shipped across the Atlantic for America's ravenous pirates. Indeed, there was no clamor anywhere to indicate that *An Inland Voyage* was a book by an individual who would become one of the late Victorian era's most prolific and most widely read authors. For Stevenson, though, this first book changed everything.

Prior to 28 April 1878, Stevenson had already been recognized both for his flowing style and for his inability to produce anything more than filler for the monthly magazines. His résumé was impressive enough, with essays, reviews, and short fiction in such notable periodicals as the *Cornhill*, *Temple Bar*, the *Fortnightly*, and *Macmillan's*. Still, despite these credentials, he was little more than an upmarket hack. He took what work he could find—writing for the *Encyclopædia Britannica*, contributing an essay and a review (both unsigned) to the first issue of *London*, a new weekly started by a university friend, and sending his prose to two and sometimes three periodicals in hopes of finding a little "lucre."

Not that Stevenson needed the money. As Lloyd Osbourne, his stepson and sometime collaborator, would later recall, though Stevenson was "gloriously under the spell of the *Vie de Bohème*" (Osbourne 3), thanks to his father's generosity he was never in any serious want. Unlike many another denizen of Grub Street, Stevenson rarely found himself lacking any necessity; he was more interested in the appearance of life on the ragged edge than in actually living it. One of his earliest essays, "Beggars," is essentially a middle-class Æsthete's perspective on "life among the lowly"; having never experienced true want, he describes a "beggar-soldier" as "the lover, the artist and artificer of words" and a "needy knife-grinder" as "the maker, the seeër, the lover and forger of experience" (*Works* 15: 272). Here was an individual who, unlike so many other writers of the time, had not wanted for much. Whereas many of his contemporaries were forced to scrabble in the dust for meager recompense, Stevenson, unfettered by any real financial need, could allocate significant effort to book-length endeavors.

For many of his peers, though, a book was beyond consideration. The average late Victorian essayist was effectively chained to the brief essay form; writing brought in just enough money to fend off hunger and the bill collectors. Assuming that such a writer could have secured a publisher for a proposed book (by no means a surety), the writing of it would have required precious time that could have been better spent writing more essays. For a young man whose sole income came from irregular contributions to whatever periodicals would pay for copy, spending time on anything longer than a two-part essay would be tantamount to risking his career. Worse yet, that most Victorian of publishing formats, the three-decker novel, was, in Stevenson's words, "a feat—not possibly of literature—but at least of physical and moral endurance and the courage of Ajax" (*Works* 2: xi).

Victorian travel narratives were typically published by the same general-interest publishers that produced the novels Stevenson found so daunting. It should come as no surprise, then, that they appeared from the outside much like one volume of a three-decker. Typically issued in octavo format, such texts appealed to sedentary readers who sought a minor change from their fiction-reading habits. As to content, however, travel narratives were judged less on the quality of their characterization and, like the guidebooks of the day, more on the information they conveyed. Unlike either novels or guidebooks, though, travel narratives tended to be the products of "amateurs," individuals who wrote not to support themselves but rather merely to record their experiences for posterity and as a secondary function of their primary occupations.[1] This gave the prose of such texts a certain measure of innocence, which was generally acceptable to readers who expected superfluity of detail rather than writing skill.

This was the segment of the market into which Stevenson would make his entrance as a writer of books. In early September of 1876 he and friend Walter Simpson, a fellow Edinburgh University alumnus, set off from Antwerp with an eye toward reaching Paris in their sail-powered canoes, *Cigarette* and *Arethusa*. From the outset Stevenson saw the trip as material for a book, and it is no accident that the narrative begins with a key metaphor: "What would happen when the wind first caught my little canvas? I suppose it was almost as trying a venture into the regions of the unknown as to publish a first book" (*Works* 12: 3). For the author, making the leap from magazine contributor to book writer was like traveling in an unfamiliar land, which he did with no little trepidation. Like Stevenson the traveler, Stevenson the author was a stranger in a strange land who feared the prospects of failure.

But of course success is more easily gained when one follows the lead of others. In recent memory, no fewer than three travel narratives similar to what Stevenson would produce appeared in print. In October and November 1870, a two-part series, "The Log of the 'Nautilus' and 'Isis' Canoes" appeared in the *Cornhill*. The authors, who in the text refer to one another by their canoe names—Stevenson would make use of a similar trope in *An Inland Voyage*—were Thomas Rolls Warrington and George Smyth Baden Powell.[2] Like much of what appeared in the *Cornhill* of the Leslie Stephen era, the "Log" was unabashedly intended for readers of a social standing similar to that of its authors. The tone is almost comical in its dry erudition, exhibiting little narrative style but plenty of Oxbridge refinement. There is little indication that the places Warrington and Baden Powell visit are inhabited; rather, they are a series of interesting sites. The locks of Trollhatten are "a stupendous marvel!" (460), the Femörehufvud lighthouse "a most peculiar building" (535), and Stockholm "a glorious city in the sea" (543). While these sites are off the Grand Tour itinerary of so many Victorian travel narratives, it is nonetheless the sites that are of primary importance for the narrators. The only individuals who rise above the anonymous masses are the pilots of two ferries, Captains Ericson and Owen, and, as their only distinguishing features are their shared occupation, one is left with the impression that they are more important for their rank than for their personalities.

A second model available to Stevenson was James Lynam Molloy's 1876 book *Our Autumn Holiday on French Rivers*. Like Warrington and Baden Powell, Molloy fit the model of the amateur travel writer, having made a successful career for himself as a composer of popular music.[3] While not so tedious a narrative as "The Log of the 'Nautilus' and 'Isis' Canoes," *Our Autumn Holiday* was certainly intended for a similar audience. The travelers are four public school and university graduates, who, along with their dog Gyp, travel from landmark to landmark in France aboard their outrigger canoe, the *Marie*. During their travels, they stay in *auberges* fashionable enough to have *femmes de chambre* and expensive enough to be listed in the guidebooks. Indeed, despite the travelers' somewhat unorthodox mode of transportation, their reliance on the publications of the tourist industry is evident. In Poissy they seek out the Hôtel de Rouen "following Mr. Murray's recommendation" (190); at Castle Blois, Molloy recounts the historical events concerning Charles V and Jeanne d'Arc that one might expect to find in a Baedeker volume (280). What is clear is that *Our Autumn Holiday* is not so much a traveler's tale as it is a tourist's tale. In the preface Molloy indicates that he feels induced "to express the hope that [their journey] may be found worthy of repetition" (vii). This idea of following in another's footsteps is important, not only because the author hoped that subsequent travelers would use his voyages as a model, but also because the author himself was following in the footsteps laid out by the guidebooks. Though their vehicle of transportation was atypical, Molloy and his fellow-travelers were clearly following the beaten track. His narrative exemplifies Buzard's concept of "anti-tourism," that method of travel whereby travelers experience key Cultural sites yet assert their distinction from the ever-growing "mob" of tourists.

The third text available to Stevenson was William Moëns's *Through France and Belgium, by River and Canal, in the Steam Yacht "Ytene."* Moëns, though more experienced with book writing than Warrington, Baden Powell, or Molloy, was nonetheless an amateur as well, having published his only previous work a decade earlier.[4] As in the previous models, it is the sites that receive particular attention. With the travel narrator's typical mixture of personal awe and uninspired rhetoric, Moëns describes the view from Richard Cœur de Lion's Chateau Gaillard as "extensive and beautiful" and the interior of the Cathedral of St. Waudru as "very bold and elegant" (36, 162). Nowhere is Moëns's lack of interest in 1870s French culture more evident than in his exhaustive description of the construction of the screw boats (*mouches*) that ply Paris's waters at the expense of the people who actually use them for travel (62).

Moëns's text was published not long before Stevenson set out on his own journey. In *An Inland Voyage*, the young writer found occasion to raise it in conversation with a French lock-keeper:

Madame reminded her husband of an Englishman who had come up this canal in a steamer.

"Perhaps Mr. Moens in the *Ytene*," I suggested.

"That's it," assented the husband. "He had his wife and family with him, and servants. He came ashore at all the locks and asked the name of the villages, whether from boatmen or lock-keepers; and then he wrote, wrote them all down. Oh he wrote enormously! I suppose it was a wager" [55–56].

Like Molloy and his company, Moëns traveled as part of roving community. The parties aboard both the *Marie* and the *Ytene* were self-contained pockets of English culture traveling about the French countryside. Molloy's and Moëns's experiences of France came to them only through the lenses of their floating enclaves of Englishness, and their experience of another culture was to some degree falsified by their method of travel.[5] While not participating in a package tour organized by one of the excursion companies, Molloy and Moëns were nonetheless insulated from French culture by the presence of their traveling companions. For Stevenson, traveling by canoe necessitated an individual connection between traveler and experience, a point he underscored when, in an 1877 letter to Sidney Colvin, he wrote, "Molloy was not a canoeist; he went in a four oar gig" (*Letters* 2: 231). Though he traveled alongside Simpson in the *Cigarette*, Stevenson was alone with his thoughts aboard the *Arethusa*; as a result, his experience of the journey was not filtered through an intervening layer of home culture. Indeed, often in *An Inland Voyage*, Simpson seems to disappear from the narrative, leaving Stevenson by himself to interact with the locals. Thus, whereas Molloy's and Moëns's experiences of their journeys were communal, Stevenson's experience of his was personal.

This personal experience of travel would seem much more in line with the narrative of Warrington and Baden Powell. They had, after all, paddled their canoes about in canals on the continent much as Stevenson and Simpson would do half a decade later. The quasi–Bakhtinian theory of travel advanced by Barry Curtis and Claire Pajaczkowska in their essay "Getting There: Travel, Time and Narrative," is a useful tool in the distinction between the two voyages:

Like Carnival, this [physical process of] movement implies an inversion of everyday order and, for the traveller [sic], offers a vicarious participation in the pleasures associated with higher status, symbolically marked by exalted points of view, exclusive spaces and privileged services [199].

For Warrington and Baden Powell, the voyage of the *Nautilus* and *Isis* had offered exactly this sort of vicarious pleasure. Though their social standing was of a high status at home, they could afford to live even more extravagantly while they were in Sweden. Whenever possible they took rooms in expensive lodgings—the Gotha Kalary Hotel in Gothenburg, the Grand Hotel in Oxlö, the Rydberg Hotel in the center of Stockholm, and invariably "fine" inns in Mariestad, Norköping, Ytter Järna, and other towns. When unable to secure such comfortable accommodations, the travelers found it difficult to disguise their disdain for the humble cottages and villagers' guest rooms in which they found shelter. In addition to their preference for exclusive spaces, Warrington and Baden Powell also demonstrated their partiality toward privileged services. Though their narrative bears the title "The Log of the 'Nautilus' and 'Isis' Canoes," it might just as easily be called "Travels by Ferry." For canoeists, the narrators appear remarkably uninterested in traveling under their own power; whenever they have the opportunity, the two load their canoes aboard whatever other form of transportation presents itself. For Warrington and Baden Powell, the canoes were more status symbols than vehicles. Their willingness to travel by other means while conspicuously stowing their canoes as cargo indicated to all who saw them—Swedish locals and *Cornhill* readers alike—just how high their social status was during the voyage: these were two individuals who were sufficiently well off to bring canoes on vacation and hardly use them.

In contrast, the journey depicted in Stevenson's *An Inland Voyage* challenges the theory devised by Curtis and Pajaczkowska. While the allusion to Bakhtin's idea of "Carnival" remains appropriate, the disturbance of the norm enacted by travel is more complex than a simple "inversion of everyday order." Curtis and Pajaczkowska's hypothesis depends upon the assumption that travelers seek to experience the unfamiliar in order (at least in part) to provide themselves with a temporary elevation in social class. Besides ignoring the problem of explaining why individuals of the highest ranks would then travel, this theory fails to take into account the allure of "slumming," traveling for the purpose of temporarily experiencing life as a member of a lower social class.

Stevenson saw his canoe trip as a new opportunity to slum about.[6] Adopting Warrington and Baden Powell's vehicles and part of Molloy's route, he could meet people who were not particularly far removed (culturally or physically) from the British working class while being unimpeded by the constraints of a traveling circle of his own culture. As a university graduate, an attorney, and the son of a prominent engineer, his early life experiences were limited by the constraints of the Scottish professional classes. The everyday lives of the rural French peasantry were as foreign (and as exotic) as any that might be depicted in narratives by Mary Kingsley or Isabella Bishop. Stevenson recognized that what the British middle class conceived of as commonplace was in fact well beyond what the average individual would ever directly experience. The world-view underlying middle-class morality could not conceive of the life led by those beneath them, yet it seemed so mundane as to go without notice. The rustics of the continent, though, belonged not only to a different country—or countries, considering that Stevenson's journey took him through both France and Belgium—but also to a different class. In a manner not dissimilar from that in which the writers of exotic travel narratives detailed the people they met at the expense of the places, Stevenson used *An Inland Voyage* to recount the manners and conversations of the characters he encountered while virtually ignoring the sites he saw.

James Wilson has argued that "[f]or Stevenson, travel writing was landscape painting in words, and ... he saw landscape as a background for people" (74).[7] While the latter half of the claim may have some validity, the assertion that Stevenson's travel writing was analogous to the Dutch style of landscape painting that enjoyed a revival in the 1870s is off the mark. Stevenson's interest, both as a traveler and as a writer, was in the exploration of personalities and relationships. Writing about William Blake, Stevenson revealed his own position on the relative values of people and scenery: "His designs are unspeakably interesting. There are little bits of landscape sometimes behind his figures that make one feel more as if that was how landscape should be painted than anything else, mere thin washes of colour" (*Letters* 2: 23).

Stevenson maintained that position during the journey that would become *An Inland Voyage*. Writing to his mother from Compiègne, Stevenson appears to have been completely uninterested in the village itself yet keen to describe "the French folk who hold up their hands in astonishment over our pleasure journey" and a "pretty girl at the window of a floating house" that proved to be a "washing establishment" (*Letters* 2: 189–90). The places or landscape were of little interest to Stevenson; it was the people or figures who were of primary importance.

What interest, then, did Stevenson find in the people he encountered, and why was his travel narrative so different from other examples of the genre? He hinted at an answer in his essay "My First Book," where he noted his early tendency "to make a plaything of imaginary series of events" (*Works* 2: ix). Despite his skills as an essayist, Stevenson's original passion as a writer was for fiction, for creating characters, and for examining their reactions to various situations and stimuli. Thus, though he wrote within the travel genre, his ulterior motive, the discovery of character, was at odds with the travel writer's customary attention to Culture. Stevenson argued in his 1879 essay "Truth of Intercourse" that "Veracity to facts"—that is, cultural or anthropological facts—"is easy and to the same degree unimportant in itself" (*Works* 13: 40–41). According to Stevenson, "to tell truth, rightly understood, is not to state the true facts, but to convey a true impression; truth in spirit, not truth in letter, is the true veracity" (48). His *An Inland Voyage* was an attempt at conveying that "true impression" of what he experienced during his canoe trip with Walter Simpson.

Needless to say, Stevenson's first book was not what Victorian readers had come to expect from a travel narrative. On the one hand, it had no exotic peoples or rituals, and, on the other, it didn't give the narrator's impressions of Europe's greatest sites. Instead, it presented people from nearby places in relatively unexciting situations. Further, the narrative voice was all wrong. It presented events from neither the self-avowedly objective perspective of the exotic explorer nor from self-consciously subjective perspective of one taking in the greatest sites the continent had to offer. Instead, here was a travel narrator who was involved in the events taking place, a narrator who seemed to forget that he was part of the nation and class reading his text rather than the nation and class about whom he wrote.

This class issue in particular is important. Members of the Victorian middle class typically interacted with their working-class contemporaries from one of two positions: condescension or removed empathy. Stevenson, though, did neither. Instead, he participated in the life he sought to chronicle. Entering the society of the Belgian and French peasantry allowed him to play at dress-up, to "s[i]nk into commonplace" existence (110), and he clearly reveled in the experience. Being away from home allowed him to take on other personas. He and Simpson appeared to children at one point as "a pair of Bluebeards": "they might speak to us in public places … but it was another thing to venture off alone with two uncouth and legendary figures" (*Works* 12: 31). Later, in Pont-sur-Sambre, Stevenson was pleased to be taken as a peddler—a *marchand*—for it allowed him and Simpson access to a social class that they otherwise would not have known. Travel allowed Stevenson not only to recognize what he called the "infinite … class distinctions" of society (*Works* 12: 35), but also permitted him to experience the lives of members of those distinct classes directly.

The experiences recounted in *An Inland Voyage* thus are exempla of carnivalesque discourse, albeit not of the type Curtis and Pajaczkowska theorized. Rather than using travel to experience a temporary elevation of social status, Stevenson traveled to see how the other half lived. Stevenson concluded that the life of the working class was not necessarily undesirable, even though this conclusion was at odds with Victorian middle-class morality, which asserted the preeminent value of wealth and domestic stability. Stevenson argued that the life of the peasantry could be preferable to the life of those whom he derisively called "bankers": "It is better fun, during the holidays, to be the son of a travelling merchant, than the son and heir to the greatest cotton spinner in creation" (*Works* 12: 38).

Those bankers and heirs of cotton spinners, though, were the text's intended audience, and they did not react particularly favorably to the book.[8] Though Stevenson was pleased finally to see "the damned thing in boards and a ticket on its behind" in 1878 (*Letters* 2: 233), it wasn't selling despite being priced at a relatively affordable 7s 6d.[9] Only 485 copies were purchased in its first year, a significant proportion by the circulating libraries, and, despite the appearance of a half-crown "Second Edition" (actually a second printing) in 1881, Stevenson never saw the shilling-per-copy royalties that were to begin after the sale of 1000 copies (Swearingen 30; McKay 1: 8). Even if we believe the stories that Kegan Paul regularly defrauded writers of the royalties due them—stories advanced in no small part by Tennyson, whose acrimonious break with the publisher was legendary—it is still clear that Stevenson's first book was a commercial flop.

While the public response to *An Inland Voyage* was tepid, most critics were at least ambivalent, and some actually recommended it. An unsigned review in *London* applauded Stevenson's work as "a book among ten thousand" and "charming" (qtd. in Maixner 47). While this is likely a piece of puffery—Stevenson was a frequent contributor to *London* in 1877 and 1878, and one of its editors, W. E. Henley, collaborated with Stevenson on several plays—it nonetheless set the tone for much of what was to follow.[10] The term "charming" was used by more than one reviewer, and several made reference to the conviviality (and occasional flippancy) of the narrative's tone.

Those of a less forgiving inclination noted what the *Saturday Review*'s critic called Stevenson's "perverted ingenuities of expression" and "circumlocutory phrases" (qtd. in Maixner 52–53) like the following:

> There is a headlong, forthright tide, that bears away man with his
> fancies like straw, and runs fast in time and space. It is full of
> curves like this, your winding river of the Oise, and lingers and

returns in pleasant pastorals; and yet, rightly through upon, never returns at all. For though it should revisit the same acre of meadow in the same hour, it will have made an ample sweep between-whiles; many little streams will have fallen in; many exhalations risen towards the sun; and even although it were the same acre, it will not be the same river Oise [83].

Despite the pronouncement by one of Oxford's literary societies that *An Inland Voyage* was "the best specimen of the writing of English of this century" (McKay 4: 1625), this is clearly not Stevenson's writing at its best. This first book suffers from what the unsigned reviewer for the *British Quarterly* called "over-consciousness" (124) and what Sidney Colvin, in his unsigned *Athenaeum* review, called "self-consciousness" (qtd. in Maixner 50).

Stevenson's self-consciousness as a writer of books was partially excused by Colvin when he noted that *An Inland Voyage* was the work of "a young writer publishing his first book" (50); it is hardly surprising that one's first foray into so public a medium would make the writer hyper-aware of his role in the narrative. Yet Colvin's explanation is not completely satisfying. Stevenson's self-consciousness is also a product of his interest in personalities and human nature. Just as the traveling merchant Hector Gilliard of Maubeuge and the strolling artist M. de Vauversin are characters with more depth than was typical of the mundane travel narrative, so too is the narrator more fully fleshed out. Stevenson-as-narrator is no pasteboard sham of a figure, expressing awe at impressive vistas and pathos before touching scenes; rather, he is a real person, one whose ideas were not completely in line with those of his nation and class, yet one who was not willing to subjugate those ideas for the purposes of financial gain. Though he claimed that "[t]he first duty in this world is for a man to pay his way" and that a writer cannot "plunge into what eccentricity he likes" until he has made a success of himself (*Works* 15: 285), Stevenson was an individual who did not really need for his book to be successful. Just as his parents' financial support had helped him escape the essay's constricting bonds, so too did it allow him to experiment with the travel narrative genre.

For his intended audience, though, this was hardly acceptable. While some of the critics and *literati* found in Stevenson's prose a new approach to narrative, average readers—those who paid for their copies rather than receiving them *gratis* from the publisher—were alienated by the elevated, affected voice in this travelogue. Moreover, his treatment of the journey made it difficult for readers to place Stevenson's text generically. Neither a factual tale about a distant culture (small "c") nor a detailed account of an individual's responses to Culture (capital "C"), Stevenson's first book didn't accord with readers' expectations and so was left to sit on the bookshelves. Thus, *An Inland Voyage* was a commercial failure yet a qualified critical success; though it didn't garner the popular regard necessary to make an occasional essay writer into a self-sufficient professional author, it drew the attention of several influential figures who would prove instrumental in Stevenson's subsequent career.

WORKS CITED

Altick, Richard D. *The English Common Reader: A Social History of the Mass Reading Public 1800–1900.* Chicago: University of Chicago Press, 1957.

Curtis, Barry, and Claire Pajaczkowska. "'Getting There': Travel, Time and Narrative." *Travellers' Tales: Narratives of Home and Displacement.* Ed. George Robertson et al. London; New York: Routledge, 1994. 199–215.

Gattrell, Simon. Introduction. *The Ends of the Earth: 1976–1918.* Ed. Gattrell. Vol. 4 of English Literature and the Wider World. Gen. ed. Michael Cotsell. London; Atlantic Highlands, NJ: Ashfield, 1990. 1–66.

McKay, G. L., ed. *A Stevenson Library: Catalogue of a Collection of Writings by and about Robert Louis Stevenson Formed by Edwin J. Beinecke.* 6 vols. New Haven: Yale University Press, 1951.

Maixner, Paul. *Robert Louis Stevenson: The Critical Heritage.* London: Routledge & Kegan Paul, 1981.

Moëns, W. J. C. *Through France and Belgium, by River and Canal, in the Steam Yacht "Ytene."* London: Hurst and Blackett, 1876.

Molloy, James Lynam. *Our Autumn Holiday on French Rivers.* London: Bradbury & Agnew, 1874.

Osbourne, Lloyd. *An Intimate Portrait of R. L. S.* New York: Scribner's, 1924.

Review of *An Inland Voyage*, by Robert Louis Stevenson. *The Examiner* 25 May 1878: 659–60.

_____. *British Quarterly Review* 68 (July 1878): 124.

Stevenson, Robert Louis. *The Letters of Robert Louis Stevenson.* 8 vols. Ed. Bradford A. Booth & Ernest Mehew. New Haven: Yale UP, 1994–95.

_____. *The Novels and Tales of Robert Louis Stevenson* ("Thistle Edition"). 25 vols. New York: Scribner's, 1898–1925. (Referred to in the text as *Works* followed by a volume number.)

Swearingen, Roger. *The Prose Writings of Robert Louis Stevenson: A Guide.* Hamden, CT: Archon, 1980.

[Warrington, Thomas Rolls, & George Smyth Baden Powell.] "The Log of the 'Nautilus' and 'Isis' Canoes." *Cornhill* 22 (1870): 457–69, 534–45.

Wilson, James. "Landscape with Figures." *Robert Louis Stevenson.* Ed. Andrew Noble. Critical Studies Series. London: Vision; Totowa, NJ: Barnes & Noble, 1983. 73–95.

NOTES

1. The best-sellers listed by Richard Altick in his book *The English Common Reader* give some indication of just who wrote travel narratives. Under the heading "Travel, History, and Biography," four nineteenth-century travel narratives appear: David Livingstone's *Travels*, Francis Leopold McClintock's *Voyage of the "Fox,"* Paul Belloni Du Chaillu's *Explorations in Equatorial Africa*, and Queen Victoria's *Leaves from a Journal* (388). (I have chosen to exclude John Wilson Croker's expanded edition of Boswell's *Journal of a Tour of the Hebrides*, which, though it sold very well, was a combination of the *Journal* and the *Life of Johnson*.) Each of the authors was first a professional in a field outside of writing: Livingstone was a missionary for the London Missionary Society, McClintock a naval officer, Du Chaillu a purveyor of stuffed African animals and birds for American museums, and Victoria a monarch. (Boswell was a lawyer.)

2. Warrington, later Baron Warrington of Clyffe, was a Cambridge graduate who would later serve as a member of the Privy Council for more than a decade. Baden Powell, an Oxford alumnus, would become a Conservative MP for the Kirkdale Division of Liverpool.

3. Though several collections of his music appeared in print, this was the only narrative work he ever published.

4. Moëns's first book, *English Travellers and Italian Brigands* (1866), was an account of his experiences as a captive of bandits in southern Italy. The son of a Dutch merchant, Moëns worked briefly at the Stock Exchange before retiring to devote himself to yachting, photography, and antiquarian research.

5. In his 1887 essay "The Regrets of a Veteran Traveller," Frederic Harrison suggested that, because of hostilities on the continent during the mid-nineteenth century, travelers tended to associate with fellow-travelers from their own country. He noted that "our modern mania is to carry with us our own life, instead of accepting that which we find on the spot" (qtd. in Gattrell 10).

6. He had already had some experience with the practice. During his years as a student at Edinburgh University, Stevenson spent considerable time among "seamen, chimney sweeps and thieves" in "an old public house frequented by the lowest order of prostitutes—threepenny whores" (qtd. in *Letters* 1: 210).

7. It is interesting that *The Examiner*'s review of *An Inland Voyage* disagreed with Wilson: "He is not a landscape painter in words; if he had suppressed geographical names and occasional scraps of the French language, we might have read his book without knowing in which hemisphere or continent his route lay" (659). Interestingly, Wilson begins his article with a quotation from the painter John Everett Millais praising Stevenson's style. Millais' primary interest, like Stevenson's, was in people and not in landscape.

8. In later years, Stevenson would come to recognize just how much power the audience held over the artist. In his 1888 "Letter to a Young Gentleman Who Proposes to Embrace the Career of Art," Stevenson, with an eye toward his early book writing days, noted, "It is doubtless tempting to exclaim against the ignorant bourgeois; yet it should not be forgotten, it is he who pays us, and that (surely on the face of it) for services that he shall desire to have performed" (*Works* 15: 284–85).

9. Typically, each volume of a three-decker novel was priced at 10*s* 6*d* (half a guinea) to the retail purchaser, making the entirety of a new novel cost 31*s* 6*d*.

10. Henley so liked *An Inland Voyage* that, in a letter to Stevenson, he wished the book "were in ten volumes" (McKay 4: 1389).

A World Made for Liars: Stevenson's *Dynamiter* and the Death of the Real

Alan Sandison

> Art is the only serious thing in the world. And the artist is the only person who is never serious.
> —*Oscar Wilde*

On the 18th of April 1884, an editorial in the *New York Tribune* struck a prophetic note when it observed that the power of making war was no longer the prerogative of governments:

> Dynamite, in fact, has put a tremendous power in the hands of individuals, and has reinforced all revolutionary and seditious tendencies enormously, making mere folly and fanaticism seriously dangerous, and increasing the natural bent of all lawless movements to gather strength as they go on....Indicators are that the new problem forced upon the world by the fertility of modern invention will give it serious trouble in the future.[1]

The *Tribune* was, of course, extrapolating from current events, and many amongst Europe's Heads of State and Heads of Government would have mournfully concurred. Britain's forces of law and order had been forced to the same conclusion a good deal earlier.

The last quarter of the nineteenth century was distinguished by many kinds of excess, but conspicuous amongst them was the number of bombs thrown. A popular target was European royalty, which appears to have dashed from one ceremony to another under a veritable hail of explosive missiles, mostly the violent expression of distaste by one group of anarchists or another. The object of attack does, however, seem to have had a better than fifty-fifty chance of escape since neither the bombs nor the bombers were notable for their efficiency.

Italian anarchists were a particularly highly motivated and resourceful lot, though their efforts fell a long way short of their aspirations. When Victor Emmanuel II died in 1878, the bomb thrown into a parade being held in his memory wounded several people but killed no one. Later that year, a twenty-nine-year-old cook launched an attack with a knife (inscribed with the words "Long live the international republic") upon the new king, Umberto I. He inflicted no more than a slight scratch on the royal person but did considerable collateral damage to the Prime Minister on the recoil, as it were. Rashly, monarchists held another parade in Florence to celebrate the king's escape, whereupon the anarchists threw another bomb which killed four people.

Still slow to draw some rather obvious conclusions, the monarchists held another parade two days later to mark the Queen's birthday when, of course, another bomb was thrown into the crowd, further depleting the monarchists' ranks. Wiser than her devoted followers, the Queen herself had sensibly stayed at home.

About the same time as the attempt to kill Umberto, there were two unsuccessful attempts on the life of the German Emperor and one on the King of Spain. Tsar Alexander II was less fortunate, being despatched by another blast of dynamite some two years later. In the midst of this regicidal pandemic, Umberto alone appears to have displayed something of the imperturbability of Stevenson's Prince Florizel, commenting that such episodes were "professional risks." So relaxed was he, in fact, that he commuted the death sentence passed on his assailant and gave the lad's mother a pension. His *sang-froid* clearly stood him in good stead since he wasn't finally despatched until 1900.

One of the more interesting anarchists was Francois-Claudius Ravachol, who may have been at heart no more than a common murderer but aspired to the degree of anarchist having, as he claimed, lost his faith in God as a result of reading the detective stories of Eugene Sue. He took enthusiastically to bomb-making, helped along by the numerous articles on "Chemistry in the Home," which were a popular staple in anarchist journals. In the early nineties he decided to initiate himself by blowing up certain judges who had handed down excessive sentences to demonstrators. Alas, though he duly set off bombs in the vicinity of two of the judges' residences, he got the wrong door each time, inflicting a certain amount of damage on the masonry but none at all on the unjust judges.

Emile Henry was unquestionably an anarchist by conviction. According to one commentator, his behavior at his trial showed him to be "an intellectual to the end." Challenged with killing and maiming innocent people when he threw a bomb into a cafe crowded with ordinary, low-income Parisians, he delivered himself of the memorable words, "*Il n'y a pas d'innocents*" and proceeded to read from the dock one of the most lucid defenses of anarchism given on such a stage.[2] Though not without friends—an intimate of his, a young poet, later became a friend of Oscar Wilde—he was a good example of the coldly logical anarchist with a fanatical hatred of society, slightly less common in reality than might be suggested in the pages of Conrad or Zola.

Many anarchists fled to England, where they found solace and sympathy among socialites and the intellegentsia, but a *quid pro quo* seems to have been that they did no bombing there. (Conrad's *The Secret Agent* takes as its *point de depart* the irritation of the Russian authorities at Britain's failure to expel these anarchists.) Had they attempted to do so, they would have found that able competition was supplied by the Fenians, who had embarked on their "dynamite campaign" in 1881 and brought it to a peak in the next six years. In 1885, the year of the publication of Stevenson's audaciously titled *The Dynamiter*, bombs had gone off in the Tower of London, Westminster Hall, and the House of Commons. Three years before that, Great Britain had been shocked by the murder of the Chief Secretary of Ireland, Lord Frederick Cavendish, and his Permanent Secretary, who were stabbed in Dublin's Phoenix Park. But there had, in fact, been no fewer than twenty-five "agrarian murders" (*i.e.*, the assassination of landlords and agents) in 1880 and 1881; and 1882 itself turned out to be a bumper year, there being, in addition to the Phoenix Park tally, a further twenty-seven agrarian murders.

So how on earth, in view of all these bloody events brought about by anarchists and Fenians, could Robert Louis Stevenson come to write such an anarchic tale as *The Dynamiter*? One factor might be the relaxed detachment with which quite a lot of influential opinion regarded continental anarchists. The aristocratic Kropotkin was widely received in London society, lectured to the Royal Geographical Society, and gave tea to William Morris and G-F Watts. (There was even a wild rumor that he was going to be given a Chair at Cambridge[3].) More daringly, Stepniak, a fellow-revolutionary, gave tea to young ladies from Lady Margaret Hall. Such hospitality apart, Stepniak was much the more dangerous character, specializing in homemade explosives which he applied with notable success to the chief of the Russian Secret Police. He, too, was received in society, and Edward Garnett's wife, Constance, a distinguished translator of Russian literature, went on a secret mission to Russia on his behalf. Garnett's aunt was the wife of the Secretary of the Board of Inland Revenue, but she allowed her daughters to edit an anarchist journal called *The Torch* in her own home.

Oscar Wilde is therefore not all that wide of the mark when, in "Lord Arthur Savile's Crime," he has *his* dynamiter, Herr Winckelkopf (who, like Zero, lives for his art), recognize Lord Arthur, having seen him "one evening at Lady Windermere's." The explosive clock which he gives Lord Arthur for the purpose of assassinating his uncle, the Dean of Chichester, like so many real bombs, fails to explode, much to the chagrin of the bomb-maker who offers Lord Arthur, in compensation, a case of nitroglycerine bombs at cost price and later an explosive umbrella.

Fanny Stevenson's Prefatory Note to *The Dynamiter* in the Tusitala edition might also suggest a reason for the bombers being taken less than seriously, telling us that there had been "several dynamite outrages in London about this time, the most of them turning out fiascos." As I have already intimated, the efforts of these acts of terrorism on the Continent and in Britain were indeed frequently farcical, even risible; nonetheless, they also frequently killed. The first attack of the Fenians' dynamite war was carried out on the 14th of January 1881, when a bomb was placed inside a ventilation grid on a wall at Salford Barracks. It destroyed a butcher's shed, a satisfyingly metonymic effect one might think, but, unfortunately, it didn't end there: a boy of seven was killed, and serious injuries were inflicted on a number of others.

The Stevensons had lived outside Britain for a number of years, which might have diluted the impact of the Fenian campaign on both, but Stevenson himself was certainly not indifferent to what was happening in Ireland. Some eighteen months after the appearance of *The Dynamiter*, he took up the cause of the Irish Curtin family, whose head—a farmer— had been murdered and the survivors condemned to the dreaded "boycott." Outraged at this, Stevenson proposed moving in with the family even though he might have ended up a martyr to their cause. Only the death of his father put an end to the quixotic scheme.

My interim conclusion would therefore be that a story about dynamiters is not simply a peg on which to hang a jester's cap. A virtuoso piece it certainly is, but this is the Stevenson who a year later will produce his enduring masterpiece, *Strange Case of Dr. Jekyll and Mr. Hyde*, not some callow youth so desperate for money that he will indulge himself in a bravura performance of dubious taste—which is rather the impression we are left with from Fanny's preface when she describes the tale as "an amusement for my husband during the tedious hours of his illness" and then "as a means of replenishing our depleted bank-account."

Every critic of our own day genuflects before the illuminating analysis provided in G.K. Chesterton's prescient book *Robert Louis Stevenson*, published in 1927, and rightly so. What he has to say about the *Arabian Nights* stories is as perceptive as everything else in the book—particularly since he was probably the first major critic to rate them so very highly. Of the first book he concluded, "I will not say that the *New Arabian Nights* is the greatest of Stevenson's works; though a considerable case might be made for the challenge. But I will say it is probably the most unique; there was nothing like it before, and, I think, nothing equal to it since."[4] Of the second collection, *More New Arabian Nights: The Dynamiter*, he makes one tentative criticism:

> [P]erhaps we might take exception to the slight element of political irritation that makes itself felt, of all places in the world, in the amiable nightmare of *The Dynamiter*. It is really impossible to use a story in which everything is ridiculous to prove that certain particular Fenians or anarchist agitators are ridiculous. Nor indeed is it tenable that men who risk their lives to commit such crimes are quite so ridiculous as that.[5]

But is this what Stevenson is doing? Do we not get nearer the truth if we invert Chesterton's statement? In an absurdist world why should the bombers be exempt? As he says approvingly of *New Arabian Nights*, what Stevenson has created is "a medium in which many incongruous things find a comic congruity."[6] It seems to me that the Fenians are disrespectfully—and daringly—included in just such a "comic congruity" which the tales establish. I would suggest that Stevenson, well ahead of the field, is already postulating an absurdist, modernist world (not dissimilar to that of *The Secret Agent*), in which the would-be heroics of the bombers are shown to be an extravagant part of a grotesquely comic, futile whole. There might even be more of a symbiosis between those two harbingers— or symptoms—of modernity, dynamite and a sense of impotence and futility, than first meets the eye. Certainly, "futile" is a word we are introduced to early in the first chapter, and it is linked to an allusion which, in the context, suggests explosives:

> "This is a very pathetic sight, Mr. Godall," said Somerset: "three futiles."

"A character of this crowded age," returned the salesman.

"Sir," said Somerset, "I deny that the age is crowded; I will admit one fact, and that one fact only: that I am futile, that he is futile, and that we are all three as futile as the devil.... [H]ere I stand, all London roaring by at the street's end, as impotent as any baby. I have a prodigious contempt for my maternal uncle; but without him, it is idle to deny it, I should simply resolve into my elements like an unstable mixture.[7]

Unstable mixtures make frequent appearances in Stevenson's work, and they tend to end in an explosion or disintegration and death. Thoughts of such instability are not whimsical but would seem to derive from an insecure moral identity. Stevenson was afraid of, and fought hard against, his own skepticism, but he was never able to vanquish it; and he saw his own condition reflected in society.

Furious with Gladstone for not sending aid to General Gordon in time to prevent his death and taking it as a sign of a morally vacillating age, Stevenson's tirade against the Prime Minister drew a puzzled query from J.A. Symonds (whom Stevenson had corresponded with since getting to know him in Davos). In reply, Stevenson indicts himself:

But why should I blame Gladstone when I too am a bourgeois? When I have held my peace? Because I am skeptic: i.e. a Bourgeois. We believe in nothing, Symonds; you don't and I don't; and there are two reasons why England stands before the world dripping with blood and daubed with dishonor. ... Police-Officer Cole is the only man I see to admire. I dedicate my New Arabs [*The Dynamiter*] to him and Cox in default of other great public characters.

What Stevenson is principally deploring here is something he has identified earlier in the same letter – his own "want of piety": "yet I pray for it, tacitly, every day; believing it, after courage, the only gift worth having."[8] By piety he means, of course, something other and wider than devotion to religious principles. What he is regretting is his own lack of commitment or devotion to some bedrock belief—a "deficiency" that Chesterton also noted, seeing it as an obstacle to his development as a writer. In one of the essays he contributed to *The Illustrated London News*, he observed that what was wrong with Stevenson's "method," as he called it, was that it was "too subjective": "What it lacked was something Stevenson sought but never found: a religion in the sense of a rule; a real trust in some external standard as a reality." Chesterton castigates those critics who, though they "seem to have something very like a spite against Stevenson," fail to realize what, to Chesterton, constitutes his real defect: the fact "that he had not the clear and ultimate idea of truth."[9]

It seems to me that Stevenson would have found little to disagree with in this mordant observation; but neither would he have seen any way of making amends. That truth, which was an accessible reality to Chesterton, the Catholic convert, was not available to Stevenson who had, in Chesterton's own words "[come] out of a world of Puritanism into a world of Pessimism." (To qualify an aphorism is to destroy its *embonpoint*, but Chesterton to his credit adds: "rather, the point of his story was that he escaped from the first but did not enter the second") (235). But that "idea of truth" is also not available to Stevenson for another wider, aesthetic reason: as *The Dynamiter* makes quite clear, the art of fiction for him was grounded in irony and skepticism, hence his alignment with the Modernists. And that, too, was something Chesterton could understand: in *Irish Impressions* we find him arguing (albeit with his tongue at least halfway into his cheek) that "there never was Modernism yet but a Calvinist was at the bottom of it!" (188).

Chesterton is altogether right about the uniqueness of his subject's achievement in these Arabian Tales, for Stevenson is once again showing his modernist sympathies by developing what this astute critic, writing of the first collection, calls "a new form of art" (168). But characteristic of this new form is a profoundly questioning attitude to truth, to purpose, to "reality," to meaning—and a peremptory dismissal of the notion that the art of literature might serve as a recovery vehicle. Thus when the dynamiters arrive with their elaborately staged attacks, convinced that their credibility depends on reality being heightened, sensationalized, spectacularized by the bomb, they are delivering themselves into the hands of a deracinated ironist, who is utterly without "piety" and who will burlesque them to death.

It almost passes unnoticed just how relentlessly the pursuit of truth is guyed from the opening pages of *The Dynamiter*. Somerset, Challoner, and Desborough are three men-about-town (or "men of the world" as Somerset repeatedly calls them) who find themselves in a position of near-destitution and totally without an intellectual or professional discipline. ("Do you know nothing, Mr. Somerset?" asks Mr. Godall. "Not even law," Somerset replies, a little oddly, which Godall considers "an answer worthy of a sage"[10]—or an anarchist in the Kingdom of Letters, we might add.) It is Somerset, the most inventive of the three, who suddenly realizes that they might not be without resources after all; their heterogeneous attributes, though modest in the sum, strike him as being precisely of a piece with the new age now dawning: "Here all our merits tell; our manners, habit of the world, powers of conversation, vast stores of unconnected knowledge, all that we have and are builds up the character of the complete detective."[11]

His confreres are not impressed by the proposal, scorning such "a dirty sneaking and ungentlemanly [trade]." Somerset protests volubly against such an adverse view: "To defend society? ... to stake one's life for others? to deracinate occult and powerful evil?" But his newfound moral fervor is as purely (and enjoyably) rhetorical as is the whole hastily concocted plan. The presiding genius of this world is explicitly amoral: "Chance, the blind Madonna of the Pagan, rules this terrestrial bustle; and in Chance I place my sole reliance." This has the agreeable consequence of committing the "three futiles" to a leisurely wait until Chance will happily "drag before our careless eyes a thousand eloquent clues, not to this mystery only, but to the countless mysteries by which we live surrounded."[12] Hardly the attitude of someone burning to right wrongs and mete out justice, we might think.

Somerset's mocking eloquence leaves nothing standing. Values, beliefs, and engagement are parodied remorselessly from the start. When Challoner objects that he has "no plan, no knowledge; you know not where to seek for a beginning," he is reproved as from a great height: "Challoner! ... is it possible that you hold the doctrine of Free Will? And are you devoid of any tincture of philosophy, that you should harp on such exploded fallacies?"[13]

The fact is that the whole of *The Dynamiter* is busy exploding fallacies—primarily literary or aesthetic fallacies, and, in particular, that time-hallowed assumption of a necessary connection between literature and truth. It is the author's hostility to this idea which lies behind his introduction of the figure of the urban detective into *The Dynamiter*. In an *Arabian Nights* world the detective clearly has no proper place. Where tales never end, leading, rather, to the beginning of more tales, reality is undefinable and evidence unverifiable. To a detective, characterized by a penetrating, rational intelligence trained to sniff out truth much as a beagle is trained to sniff out drugs on an airport carousel, that way madness lies. Consequently, in burlesquing the detective as he does here, Stevenson burlesques the whole idea that the "truth" is a commodity a novelist can trade in. It is every bit as unreal as the conventional forms by which it has been traditionally represented in fiction and which *The Dynamiter* continually subverts.

Not only does each of the three main stories (the "adventures" of the three detectives) have its own petard: each is also hoist with it, and the main casualty is truth. The first bomb, which destroys the terrace house and introduces Challoner to "Miss Fonblanque," allows the latter, "with

the greatest appearance of enjoyment, to narrate the story of her life."
Except, of course, that it isn't. Even the somewhat limited Challoner isn't
truly taken in: "It was an excellent story; and it might be true, but he
believed it was not."[14] And so for the rest of the tales until the last explosion erases Zero himself.

However, Stevenson loves nothing more than a clean slate—it is a
metaphor he is fond of—so that even before the triumph and apotheosis
of the "dynamite scientist," the latter's discourse has gone far to explode
something else: Somerset's skepticism. "I thought you were a good agnos-
tic," says an alarmed Zero; to which Somerset replies:

> I boast myself a total disbeliever not only in revealed religion, but
> in the data, method, and conclusion of the whole of ethics. Well!
> what matters it? what signifies a form of words? I regard you as a
> reptile, whom I would rejoice, whom I long, to stamp under my
> heel. You would blow up others? Well then, understand: I want,
> with every circumstance of infamy and agony, to blow up you!

Somerset, overcome with emotion, dashes from the house in the general
direction of a police station, but his pace slows and he begins to have
doubts. He had given his word to Zero that he would not expose him;
could he now break it? Moral destruction seems unavoidable: "His Gods
had fallen. He who had chosen the broad, daylit, unencumbered paths of
universal skepticism, found himself still the bondslave of honor."
Nonetheless, though, he reiterates his conviction that "right and wrong
are but figments and the shadow of a word...there are certain things that
I cannot do, and certain others that I will not stand," and he resolves to
give Zero an ultimatum: to abandon his trade or be denounced to the
police. Finally, after the destruction of the Superfluous Mansion he escorts
Zero to the railway station, freed of any putative debt of honor to the
dynamiter. But the cost to him is high:

> "I begin to doubt; I am losing faith in skepticism. Is it possible,"
> he cried, in a kind of horror of himself,—" is it conceivable that
> I believe in right and wrong ... And must this change proceed?"[15]

After the book's final explosion, however, he is left with "a great content, a sense, as it were, of divine presence, and the kindliness of fate,"
now that Zero has been "expunged" (201). But that is not the last word
in his emasculation. Well might he have adopted the quotation Zero uses
so mournfully when he is confronted by what he sees as the definitive
failure of his dynamiter's art: "Othello's occupation's gone." Stumbling

into Mr. Godall's "Cigar Divan," he is exhorted by the tobacconist, alias Prince Florizel, alias Shahryar, alias God, to "suffer me to choose you a cigar of my own special brand, and reward me with a narrative in your best style." But Somerset, shattered by the possibility that he might actually believe in something, cannot continue to play the role of Scheherazade now that his erstwhile identity as skeptic and poser has been exploded. Narrative can no longer be all, however much it may appear to be endorsed by Mr. Godall; but, of course, the treatment meted out to him ensures that not even his apostasy will escape Stevenson's destructive irony. Somerset's refusal of the cigar raises Mr. Godall's concern: "[N]ow I come to look at you more closely, I perceive that you are changed. My poor boy, I hope there is nothing wrong?"[16] Somerset replies by bursting into tears, and we understand why. In the words of John Barth, "To cease to narrate, as the capital example of Scheherazade reminds us, is to die—literally for her, figuratively for the rest of us."[17]

Apart from "The Destroying Angel" and "The Story of the Fair Cuban," which are clearly Fanny's work in that they operate in a patently different "key," Stevenson sustains a narrative discourse of brilliant artificiality that advertises the presence of the author in every graceful line of the ensnaring arabesque. It is a discourse which relies enormously on the deployment of an all-consuming irony that constantly shades into burlesque and the absurd. I have written at length on this aspect of Stevenson's art—and his literary iconoclasm—in Chapter Three of *R.L. Stevenson and the Appearance of Modernism,* so I shall content myself here by merely reiterating that a principal target of the writer's subversive irony throughout is realism and the realist school. Of course we get carried along on the wings of illusion—Stevenson's storytelling is as persuasive as ever— but he is his own dynamiter and as he spins his outrageous stories he plants a charge underneath them which, when it explodes, reveals the hand of the illusionist. "He juggles with his readers and with his characters," noted a perceptive New York reviewer, H.C. Bunner, in 1883. "He dresses up a puppet and tells you it is a man, and you believe it, and hold your breath when the sword is at the puppet's breast. Then he holds up the stripped manikin and smiles maliciously."[18] Though this was written of *New Arabian Nights,* it is equally applicable to its successor.

I have said that a principal target of Stevenson's writing in this book is realism and realists, but, as has already been indicated, along with that goes an assault upon the notion of the writer as the purveyor of truth. Earlier, I described *The Dynamiter* as an anarchic text, and I should like to underline this description, for what Stevenson does in this book is not just knowingly to disappoint traditional expectations of nineteenth-century storytelling, he also deconstructs the reader's traditional moral universe. The writer of fiction as Stevenson redefines him is not there to offer a special avenue to "truth," far less to confirm the complacent in their characteristic habit of mind. He well knows that, as Anthony Kerrigan puts it in his introduction to Borges's *Ficciones*, "men long for their deceits"; but he denies them such comforts through that ironic process so well described by Linda Hutcheon in *Narcissistic Narrative*, which entails unsettling the reader so that he is

> forced to scrutinize his concepts of art as well as his life values. Often he must revise his understanding of what he reads so frequently that he comes to question the very possibility of understanding. In doing so he might be freed from enslavement not only to the empirical, but also to his own set patterns of thought and imagination.[19]

Even in recent times and by otherwise sensible critics, it is still possible to find Stevenson being fundamentally misunderstood in this crucial area of his theory of fiction (which by and large is a theory of art) for which *The Dynamiter* provides such a litmus test. Robert Kiely, for example, deplores what he sees as his addiction to "faking": "Stevenson insists upon presenting an illusion, often a very compelling one and then turning to the reader and saying, 'This is a fraud. Not one word of it is true.'" There couldn't be a better example of the persistent undervaluation of Stevenson based on this complaint that he failed to stick to the rules laid down by the novelists who preceded him. Writing of *The Dynamiter*, Kiely claims that "we get the uncomfortable sense that Stevenson is almost compulsive about forcing his various narrators in these tales to plead guilty to telling lies." But such discomfort is self-inflicted, for Stevenson knows exactly what he is doing, and Kiely himself provides the evidence:

> Not only did most of the adventures not happen, but those who told them are posers and triflers. By repeating this pattern of deception followed by remorse, he implicitly casts aspersions on certain kinds of narrative art ... and on the integrity of artists like himself.[20]

But his integrity would only suffer if he were seriously espousing the "certain kinds of narrative art" Kiely has in mind; whereas, in actual fact, Stevenson is gleefully engaged in exploding them.

Gabriel Josipovici, in *The Lessons of Modernism*, describes the revised conception of the authorial self in an analogy which applies particularly well to Stevenson and his attitude to the writer's relationship to truth:

> the artist is no longer either thinker or prophet, looking inwards or upwards for the truth and then conveying it to a grateful multitude; rather he is a gymnast, developing his potential with each new exercise successfully mastered.[21]

The description of artist as gymnast fits Stevenson very well, though, occasionally, he might seem to some to be just a little bit more like Ariel since the difficulty in identifying him—or where, precisely, he stands—threatens, at times, to become the most notable thing about him. But, it must be emphasized that he, like Ariel, is *au fond* a liberator; and he is so by consequence of his theory of art which, dispensing with Victorian strait-jackets, binds no one to a discovered truth insecurely anchored in a highly subjective "reality."

For a writer of the period to involve dynamiters in his "comic congruity" might seem to risk alienating his readers, yet Stevenson was not, of course, the only writer to run such a risk – if, indeed, it were one. Even Gilbert and Sullivan, in *Utopia Ltd.* (1893), have a Public Exploder whose job it is to blow up the King with dynamite "on his very first lapse from political or social propriety." This innovation, it would appear, has resulted in an almost-ideal Republic "which may be described as a Despotism tempered by Dynamite."

But it is Oscar Wilde who comes nearest to Stevenson both in the comic ingenuity of his incorporation of the dynamiter and in the range of possibilities which underlie the dynamiter's exploits. Leaving aside Lady Bracknell's sanguine response to the news that Bunbury had been "exploded" ("Exploded! Was he the victim of a revolutionary outrage? I was not aware that Mr. Bunbury was interested in social legislation. If so, he is well punished for his morbidity."), his short story "Lord Arthur Savile's Crime," written two years after the appearance of *The Dynamiter*, rivals Zero's tale in its burlesquing of the dynamiter. As in the case of Stevenson, however, the target is again traditional assumptions about the literary representation of reality and truth.

When Lord Arthur Savile stumbles out of Lady Windermere's "last reception before Easter" at Bentinck House burdened with the knowledge of the fate which hangs over him (a palmist has revealed that his destiny is to commit a murder), he wanders off into the back alleys of the sleeping city. There he is confronted by the impoverished and degraded fringe-dwellers of the metropolis and is seized by "a strange pity," asking himself,

"Were these children of sin and misery predestined to their end, as he to his? Were they, like him, merely the puppets of a monstrous show?"[22]

The human being, deprived of organic life and suspended in a mechanistic universe or else reduced to being the playthings of a capricious Fate or Chance, is a trope which haunts the imagination of nineteenth-century writers at least from *Bleak House* onwards; and the image they often employ to express it is that of the puppet, which becomes a representative figure of humankind caught up in an endless, absurdist performance—in "a monstrous show." In *The Dynamiter*, Chance, "the blind Madonna of the Pagan," has been invited to preside over the destiny of the three "adventurers"—a term which implies the same sort of moral vacuity it is found possessed of in Conrad's work—and Challoner, at least, feels that he now knows what this means: he has become her plaything.

> The conduct of the man with the chin-beard, the terms of the letter, and the explosion of the early morning, fitted together like parts in some obscure and mischievous imbroglio. Evil was certainly afoot; evil, secrecy, terror and falsehood were the conditions and the passions of the people among whom he had begun to move, like a blind puppet; and he who began as a puppet, his experience told him, was often doomed to perish as a victim.[23]

These sentences sum up well not just the nature of the treatment Stevenson metes out to his characters but also the nature of the world he creates for them to move in: a world constantly verging on the grotesque. Those percipient early reviewers of Stevenson's work, the Lathburys, defined *New Arabian Nights* as, "strictly speaking," grotesque romances, which implies a proper recognition of the incongruities and distortions on which these apparently lighthearted stories are constructed. It might be recalled that Thomas Mann, in his preface to a German translation of *The Secret Agent*, claims that it is tragi-comedy which best represents the vision of modern art, and thence it is the grotesque which is its most genuine style.

That style is in evidence again in Wilde's story where the author acknowledges the pressure to view life as absurdist tragi-comedy. As Lord Arthur surveys the human flotsam and jetsam around him his thoughts take an unsettling turn: "[I]t was not the mystery, but the comedy of suffering that struck him; its absolute uselessness, its grotesque want of meaning. How incoherent everything seemed."[24] This incoherence and meaninglessness also lurks amidst the toils of *The Dynamiter*'s arabesques: Challoner isn't the only one there who is caught in "an obscure and mischievous imbroglio." Even London itself, nothing if not concrete one might think, becomes one of those tropes of bewilderment and menace which are everywhere, so that it is hardly ever described except through unsettling metaphors of which Conrad would have been proud. It is "the humming labyrinth"; it is where the "romantic silence" of Bloomsbury is "roared about on every side by the high tides of London"; while, for Challoner, it "sounded in his ears stilly, like a whisper; and the rattle of the cab that nearly charged him down was like a sound from Africa."[25]

For those writers to whom life is a tragi-comedy or an obscure and mischievous imbroglio, the advent and exploits of real-life dynamiters were not just grist to their mill—they became almost indistinguishable from that same (fictional) mill. The means they used—indeed which they were obliged to use—to proclaim their objectives and their achievements in part came to dictate the very character of the acts themselves. In turn, these dynamiters also came to be hoist by their own petard—that is, the narratives of their exploits became exploits-by-narrative which, while it gave them greater access to the public ear, also exposed them to all the hazards of rhetoric and narrative—such as excess, unintended farce, bathos, and histrionics. The net result was less rather than more "reality," an obfuscation of the boundary between fact and fiction, an illustration of E.L. Doctorow's conviction "that there is no fiction or nonfiction as we commonly understand the distinction: there is only narrative."[26] Stevenson and Wilde would have understood perfectly. In the end, like Scheherazade, the bombers became the prisoners of their own narratives for, once started, these could not be allowed to die without taking the movement with them. If their exploits ceased to be written up in the press or elsewhere—if they were, in the threadbare idiom of the 20th century, deprived of the oxygen of publicity—they lost all capacity to create an "outrage."

In view of the risks even journalistic narratives brought with them, one might have a certain sympathy with those Continental anarchists who, apparently abandoning hope in the spoken or the written word, coined the slogan "Propaganda by the Deed!" But if that deed remained "merely" a deed, it would have been meaningless since no one would ever have heard of it. The moment it gets "written up," however—or even spoken about—it takes on a narrative life of its own (or of the writer or the speaker) and moves into that territory where "anarchic" writers like Stevenson, paid-up subscribers to Doctorow's thesis, prowl with their armory of "satiric deviltries," as Bunning called them, fully primed.

The exploits of the anarchists and Fenians so often seem to have been scripted by someone with Stevenson's talents. When Emile Henry tried to blow up the Paris offices of a repressive coal-mining company in 1893, his bomb was discovered by the police. Alas, somewhat foolishly, they carried it in triumph back to the police station, where, of course, it exploded and killed five of them. Is there any way that this episode can be recounted which will fully immunize it against a farcical reading? I doubt it.

Francois-Claudius Ravachol was unquestionably a murderer before he became an avowed anarchist, and a particularly mean one at that: his tally included a decrepit old rag merchant, an elderly hermit, and two old ladies who ran an ironmongery store. However, after some hesitation the anarchists accepted him as a martyr to the cause, even though it was on these early murders—before he had read Eugene Sue and was converted to the honorable calling of anarchist—that he was condemned. After his execution, his exceptionally meagre revolutionary achievements were commemorated and transformed in the alternative reality of song and dance:

> *Dansons la Ravachole!*
> *Vive le son, vive le son,*
> *Dansons la Ravachole,*
> *Vive le son*
> *De l'explosion!*[27]

If all this might seem to diminish the borderline between fact and fiction, one could say that it was on just these margins that both the bombers themselves and Modernist writers played—witness those exemplars, *The Secret Agent, The Dynamiter,* and "Lord Arthur Savile's Crime." Perhaps that borderline has always been more tenuous than we have been willing to admit: "What is a historical fact?" asks E.L. Doctorow:

> Once it has been suffered it maintains itself in the mind of witness or victim, and if it is to reach anyone else it is transmitted in words or on film and it becomes an image, which, with other images, constitutes a judgment.... [H]istory shares with fiction a mode of mediating the world for the purpose of introducing meaning, and it is the cultural authority from which they both derive that illuminates those facts so that they can be perceived.
>
> Facts are the images of history, just as images are the facts of fiction.[28]

But if historians and writers have always played on a borderline more exiguous than it was recognized or admitted to be, Stevenson (and Wilde) did so with a flamboyant self-awareness which was then unparalleled. They would have instantly recognized the force of Robert Scholes's conclusion that "it is because reality cannot be recorded that realism is dead.... There is no mimesis, only poesis. No recording. Only constructing."[29] That, one might suggest, is *their* revelatory truth. But though reality cannot be recorded, Art can perform an Arabesque which skirts and so defines the black hole where it may, forever conjecturally, be; and Art can survive bombs just as the statue of Shakespeare survives Zero's destructive intent. Indeed, the whole of *The Dynamiter* is an act of homage to Art and the theatre of illusion.

A sense of theatre was, one might argue, *de rigueur* for dynamiters who readily conceded that explosions were for effect rather than to inflict significant harm: spectacular outrages—preferably in a very public "theatre" like Westminster or the Tower of London—were the prime objective since they would attract the right sort of "reviews" in the newspapers. The anarchists who planned to blow up Greenwich Observatory must have been consoled for the failure of their enterprise by the headlines secured for the "outrage" (whose only practical outcome was the Zero-style death of the would-be bomber): "Blown to Pieces!" proclaimed *The Morning Leader*. This was followed by the subheading, "Victim an Anarchist? Was he a member of a gang who had fell designs on London's Safety?"[30]

Role-playing was, one might suspect, innate in every aspiring "dynamite scientist," subterfuge and disguise his stock-in-trade. William Lomasney, for example, was credited by the police and their agents with being a master of disguise:

> Though of youthful appearance, his face was a most determined one, and the way it lent itself to disguise was truly marvellous. When covered with bushy hair, of which he had a profusion, it was one face; when clean-shaven, quite another, and impossible of recognition ... this faculty of disguise proved of enormous service, and may very well have had disastrous effects on police vigilance."[31]

In the end, his faculty for disguise availed him little; in December 1894, while trying to attach some explosives to London Bridge, Lomasney, his brother-in-law, and another man were killed when the bomb exploded prematurely. The bridge was more or less undamaged, an effect which Lomasney had expected, telling a friend that he sought only to frighten H.M. Government and England's ruling class.

Sometimes the bombers took to performing quite literally on stage. In 1884, John Daly was sentenced to life imprisonment for being in possession of dynamite with intent to launch a terrorist attack. At his trial he conducted his own defense with what *The Times* described as "great fluency and in a highly declamatory manner." No one should have been surprised at this. For months the police had had Daly under surveillance, in the course of which time he had auditioned for a job at the Birmingham Concert Hall as a storyteller. One of the proprietors of the Hall was persuaded by the police to give Daly a chance in a one-night stand and he duly appeared on the bottom of a fifteen-act bill. It was not an auspicious start and things didn't improve. According to one of a considerable number of police present, he sang two songs very badly and told the story of his life to a deeply unsympathetic audience. He was, however, tenacious: after twenty-five minutes, having failed to respond to the manager's increasingly irritable signals to quit, he suffered the humiliation of having the curtain unceremoniously dropped on his act.[32] It is distractingly difficult to know what order of reality Daly inhabited. When did he (in his own mind) first set foot on the stage and when did he leave it? Released in 1896, Daly was elected mayor of Limerick in 1899, 1900, and 1901.

Pace Chesterton, these bombers seemed perennially to invite burlesque—even their own side saw the possibilities and contributed to the "fictionalising" of their enterprises. For example, on the 30th of January 1885, *The Times* reported that a convention of "dynamite delegates" was to take place in Paris on an island in the Seine. This august newspaper duly followed up its scoop with an account of the convention in which it gave details of "an inspired speech" by James Stephens (the founder of the Irish Revolutionary—later Republican—Brotherhood). In fact, the entire event was a hoax dreamt up by Eugene Davis, Paris correspondent of the *Irish World*.[33]

There were, of course, many devoted Fenians, dedicated to the perfectly reasonable cause of an independent Ireland; but active conspirators are constantly tempted to consider themselves—or their cause—larger than life, and to adopt a matching rhetoric. Now while life itself *may* be, anything larger than certainly *is* fiction. That is why it is simply impossible to take Professor Mezzeroff seriously. Described by the Irish-American press as a great Russian chemist, Mezzeroff placed advertisements in the press offering lectures "within a day's journey of New York" on such subjects as "Dynamite and the Resources of Civilisation."[34] Professor Mezzeroff was, according to K.R.M. Short, almost "a required feature" at meetings of incendiary organizations such as the Fenian Brotherhood. At an important gathering of the Brotherhood in March 1885 he was introduced in terms worthy of *The Dynamiter* as "England's invisible enemy" and at another meeting gave an account of his provenance which could have come straight from the imagination of Clara Luxmore:

I was born in New York. My mother was a Highlander, my father
was a Russian, and I am an American citizen. I have diplomas
from three colleges, and have devoted my life to the study of med-
icine. When I was a boy, I fought in the Crimean War, and I bear
the scars of five wounds.[35]

This sounds perilously like "the fair Cuban": "I am not what I seem. My
father drew his descent, on the one hand, from grandees of Spain, and,
on the other, through the maternal line, from the patriot Bruce."[36]
Mezzeroff's genealogical disclosures were followed by "an exciting
presentation on the joys of dynamite," in which he promised that he "had
recipes for forty-two explosives safely away in a burglar-proof safe."[37]
Mezzeroff did not escape the notice of *The Times*, its Paris correspondent
filing this tongue-in-cheek note on 30 May 1884 (when Stevenson and his
wife were busy on *The Dynamiter*):

The report that "Professor" Mezzerhoff, of New York, the dynamite scientist, is an Irish saloon-keeper, named Rogers, is declared
to be without foundation. The Irish "dynamiters" in Paris assert
that Mezzerhoff is the man's real name, and that he is a Russian
who matriculated with honor and distinction in one of the universities in his own country. His knowledge of chemistry is said
to be very profound, practically as well as theoretically.

The "professor" intends, after his lecturing tour through the
United States, to pay a visit to the French capital, where he is anxiously awaited by some of his former pupils.

Not only Zero, but Conrad's Professor in *The Secret Agent*, might well owe
something to Mezzeroff, who was described by the *New York Sun* on 20
March 1882 as being "very tall, dressed in sombre black ... wearing plain steel-
bowed spectacles."[38] Stevenson's Zero is "of great height" and the "Wanted"
notice in the *Standard* had described him as being "over six feet in height ...
with black moustaches and wearing a sealskin great-coat." He, too, has unbridled enthusiasm for this new invention applied to the Fenian cause:

In this dark period of time, a star—the star of dynamite—has risen
for the oppressed; and among those who practice its use, so thick
beset with dangers and attended by such incredible difficulties and
disappointments, few have been more assiduous, and not many
... have been more successful than myself.[39]

In fact, anarchists and Fenians alike dilated enthusiastically on the
virtues of dynamite. In a letter to the anarchist journal *The Alarm* in
February 1885, Gerhard Lizius, who was, improbably, secretary of the

Indianapolis Group of the International and a compulsive "narrator" via the anarchist press, sounds as rapturous as Zero on the subject, if rather less sophisticated (though, also like Zero, he seems always to be primed with a Shakespearean reference):

> Dynamite! of all good stuff, this is the stuff. Stuff several pounds of this sublime stuff into an inch pipe, gas or water pipe, plug up both ends, insert a cap with fuse attached, place this in the imme-diate neighbourhood of a lot of rich loafers, who live by the sweat of other people's brows, and light the fuse. A most cheerful and gratifying result will follow.... It brings terror only to the guilty, and consequently the Senator who introduced a bill in Congress to stop its manufacture and use, must be guilty of something.... All the good this will do! Like everything else, the more you pro-hibit it, the more will it be done. Dynamite is like Banquo's ghost, it keeps on fooling around somewhere or other in spite of his satanic majesty.[40]

At the conclusion of his trial for his alleged part in what became known as "the Haymarket affair," America's own home-grown anarchist, the remarkable Albert Parsons, proclaimed dynamite's almost mystical powers: "It is the equilibrium. It is the annihilator. It is the disseminator of power. It is the downfall of oppression. It is the abolition of authority; it is the dawn of peace; it is the end of war, because war cannot exist unless there is somebody to make war upon, and dynamite makes that unsafe, undesirable, and absolutely impossible."[41] The argument sounds familiar.

Lucy Parsons, the wife of this articulate anarchist, was busy the while commending propaganda by the deed, exhorting tramps "to learn the use of explosions and petition the capitalists with bombs instead of words." Their enthusiasm for bombs notwithstanding, the anarchists were, in truth, greatly given to words—spoken or sung. In the newspaper *Freiheit*, songs were printed in praise of dynamite:

> At last a toast to science,
> To dynamite, the force....

was how one began. Another started "Dynamite today, dynamite tonight," but failed to sustain this promising beginning.[42]

Parsons made one last appearance "on stage" as it were. Condemned to be hanged in November 1887, he fulfilled the role of the anarchist-hero to the end, spending his last night reciting poems by Whittier and Marc Cook and singing all the verses of "Annie Laurie."[43] The next day, he and three alleged accomplices were put to death in a macabre, ritualized execution so indebted to theatre as to seem quite unreal. Almost certainly all were innocent of the "outrage" for which they were hanged. Commenting on the trial and verdict, William Dean Howells saw the whole business as a grotesque charade, writing that if it were not for the hideous result, the convictions could have been construed as a colossal piece of American humor:

> But perhaps the wildest of our humorists could not have conceived of a joke so monstrous as the conviction of seven men for a murderous conspiracy which they carried out while one was at home playing cards with his family, another was addressing a meeting five miles away, another was present with his wife and children, two others had made pacific speeches, and not one, except on the testimony of a single, notoriously untruthful witness, was proven to have had anything to do with throwing the Haymarket bomb, or to have even remotely instigated the act.[44]

It is very tempting to conclude that Stevenson's unpretentious little book of 1885 is something like a key document in the development of literary Modernism. If that is too much for those recalcitrants who want to keep him forever in a child's play-pen, it is surely impossible for them to deny that *The Dynamiter* defines key elements in the Modernist phenomenon—even that it peers over the horizon to Postmodernist developments to come. Not that that metaphor is altogether acceptable either since it might seem to support the view that these two "isms" are discontinuous, whereas not the least of *The Dynamiter*'s achievements is that it manifests a literary aesthetic and a fictional mode which make it well-nigh impossible to sustain a belief in such separability.

The Dynamiter serves as a powerful antidote to what one critic has described as the "mimetic poison" of traditional fictional modes. Amongst other assumptions, it successfully explodes the notion that reality itself is anything other than a fiction. Humor in many forms—farce, parody, burlesque, irony—is a prominent agent in this effect, but it is in his use of irony in particular that Stevenson best enhances his Modernist claims. The double benefit this confers on the structure of his narrative is captured very well by that far-seeing critic, Friedrich Schlegel, when talking about the "divine breath of irony" in both ancient and modern poetry:

> In such poems there lives a transcendental buffoonery. Their interior is permeated by the mood which surveys everything and rises

infinitely above everything limited, even above the poem's own
art, virtue and genius; and their exterior form by the histrionic
style of an ordinary good Italian buffo.[45]

By taking as its plot a dynamite campaign, which is a scaled-down
version of the real-life campaign going on contemporarily, and by portraying his conspirators (and their opponents) as absurd, Stevenson subverts both orders of reality—the fictional and the nonfictional. At the same
time the merest glance at the actual activities of the anarchist or Fenian
bombers shows how ambiguous their reality is, and how meaningless their
exploits without some kind of narrative embellishment. To recognize this
is to make another observation of Doctorow's sound very apposite: "The
novelist looking around him has inevitably to wonder why he is isolated
by his profession when everywhere the factualists have appropriated his
techniques and even brought a kind of exhaustion to the dramatic modes
by the incessant exploitation of them."[46]

By imposing his own miniature dynamite drama on the real thing,
Stevenson gains a *mise en abyme* effect where image begets image in an
absurdist, meaningless, and endless sequence. He has, in fact, in 1885
developed a narrative method which is well-equipped to deal with what
a writer on postwar American "nonfiction" has called "the elusive fusion
of fact and fiction which has become the matrix of today's experience."[47]

What *The Dynamiter* asserts is that the novelist is no longer to be
regarded as a particularly insightful and veracious analyst of a social or
political reality. Entirely at one with the emerging Modernist age, it reveals
a distrust of the nature of reality and its modes of representation, and
equally strong misgivings about where truth is to be found and who might
be entrusted to find it.

It is altogether plausible to hold that Stevenson involves the dynamiters in his burlesque precisely to dispel any notion of the writer as someone not just uniquely able to represent reality but with a duty to do so.
Of course this is in no way an aspersion on the novelist as a teller of tales;
but it is a reminder that these tales have little to do with whatever is construed as truth and reality—even if illusionists like Tusitala hoodwink us
from time to time. What the tales' authors must not do—and Tusitala
never does—is to hoodwink themselves. Perhaps the last word could be
left to Doctorow:

> As clowns in the circus imitate the aerialists and tightrope walk-
> ers, first for laughs and then so that it can be seen that they do it
> better, we [novelists] have it in us to compose false documents
> more valid, more real, more truthful than the "true" documents

of the politicians or the journalists or the psychologists. Novelists know explicitly that the world in which we live is still to be formed, and that reality is amenable to any construction that is placed upon it. It is a world made for liars and we are born liars. But we are to be trusted because ours is the only profession forced to admit that it lies—and that bestows upon us the mantle of honesty.[48]

NOTES

1. K.R.M. Short, *The Dynamite War: Irish-American Bombers in Victorian Britain* (Dublin, 1979), pp. 241–242. I am indebted to Dr. Short's book throughout this essay.

2. James Joll, *The Anarchists* (London,1979), p. 118. I have been greatly assisted by Professor Joll's work at a number of points in this essay.

3. James Joll, *ibid.*, p. 132.

4. G.K. Chesterton, *Robert Louis Stevenson* (London, 1927), p. 171.

5. *Ibid.*, pp.166–177.

6. *Ibid.*, p. 169.

7. R.L. Stevenson, *More New Arabian Nights: The Dynamiter* (Tusitala Edition, London, 1924), vol. 3, pp. 4–5.

8. R.L. Stevenson, *Letters* (Tusitala Edition, London, 1924), Vol. 33, pp. 37, 36.

9. G.K. Chesterton, "On R.L.S." in *Generally Speaking: A Book of Essays* (London, 1930), p. 239.

10. R.L. Stevenson, *Ibid.*, p. 3.

11. *Ibid.*, pp. 5–6

12. *Ibid.*, pp. 6–7.

13. *Ibid.*, p. 6.

14. *Ibid.*, pp. 17, 50.

15. *Ibid.*, pp. 137, 138, 199.

16. *Ibid.*, p. 201.

17. John Barth, "Tales Within Tales," in *The Friday Book: Essays and Other Non-Fiction* (New York, 1984), p. 236.

18. H.C. Bunner in *Century Magazine*, quoted in Paul Maixner, *Robert Louis Stevenson: The Critical Heritage* (London, 1981), p. 121.

19. Linda Hutcheon, *Narcissistic Narrative: The Metafictional Paradox* (London, 1984), p. 139.

20. Robert Kiely, *Robert Louis Stevenson and the Fiction of Adventure* (Cambridge, Mass., 1964), p. 120.

21. Gabriel Josipovici, *The Lessons of Modernism* (London, 1987), p. x.

22. Oscar Wilde, "Lord Arthur Savile's Crime" in *The Complete Works of Oscar Wilde* (London 1983), p. 176.

23. R.L. Stevenson, *op. cit.*, p. 61.

24. Oscar Wilde, *op. cit.*, p. 176.

25. R.L. Stevenson, *op. cit.*, pp. 48, 140, 126.

26. E.L. Doctorow, "False Documents" in *Poets and Presidents: Selected Essays 1977–1992* (London, 1994), p. 163.

27. Quoted by James Joll, *ibid.*, p.117.

28. E.L. Doctorow, *ibid.*, p. 161.

29. Robert Scholes, *Structural Fabulation: An Essay on the Fiction of the Future* (Notre Dame, 1975), p. 7.

30. *The Morning Leader*, 16th February 1894.

31. Quoted by K.R.M. Short, *The Dynamite War*, p. 50.

32. *Ibid.*, pp. 182, 174.

33. *Ibid.*, pp. 212–213.

34. *Ibid.*, p. 116.

35. *Ibid.*, p. 219.

36. R.L. Stevenson, *op. cit.*, p. 147.

37. K.R.M. Short, *op. cit.*, p. 219.

38. K.R.M. Short, *op. cit.*, pp. 218–219.

39. R.L. Stevenson, *op. cit.*, p. 117.

40. Quoted by Paul Avrich in *The Haymarket Tragedy* (Princeton, 1984), p. 170.

41. *Ibid.*, p. 167.

42. *Ibid.*, pp. 167–168.

43. *Ibid.*, p. 381.

44. *Ibid.*, p. 404.

45. Friedrich Schlegel, *Dialogue on Poetry and Literary Aphorisms* (trans. Behler and Struc, 1968), p.126.

46. E.L. Doctorow, *op. cit.*, p. 162.

47. Mas'ud Zavarzadeh, quoted by Barbara Foley in *Telling the Truth: The Theory and Practice of Documentary Fiction* (Ithaca and London, 1986), pp. 10–11.

48. E.L. Doctorow, *op. cit.*, p. 164.

Scottish Gothic: Robert Louis Stevenson, *The Master of Ballantrae*, and *The Private Memoirs and Confessions of a Justified Sinner*

Eric Massie

Critical discussions of possible intertextual connections in nineteenth century Scottish fiction have thus far failed to establish links between the work of James Hogg and that of Robert Louis Stevenson. This paper will seek to show how Stevenson uses an earlier source to address some recurring themes in nineteenth-century Scottish fiction, and to show that both works rely on the tropes of the Gothic.

There has been much speculation about Hogg's influence on Stevenson, and it was during a visit to Yale in 1998 that the present writer found documentary proof of one such connection. In a letter to the critic and editor George Saintsbury, written on 17 May 1891, Stevenson comments on a passage from Saintsbury's recently published book, *Essays in English Literature 1780–1860*, in which Saintsbury suggests that J. G. Lockhart may have collaborated with Hogg in writing *The Private Memoirs and Confessions of a Justified Sinner*. Stevenson's letter comments:

> I particularly like your Hogg, and your admirable quotations from the unequal fellow. Your theory about the *Justified Sinner* inter-

ests and (I think I may say) convinces me; the book since I read it in black, pouring weather on Tweedside, has always haunted and puzzled me. One felt it could not be Hogg. I had heard Lockhart mentioned, and much as I admire *Adam Blair*, it seemed beyond the reach of Lockhart. But with the two together, it is possible. I would they had collaborated more; we should have been the richer—for the book is without doubt a real work of imagination, ponderated and achieved. I prefer *Adam Blair*, of which I gather I think more highly than you do; but a dozen, and a score of people could come near *Adam Blair*, and ten might have excelled it— but I never read a book that went on the same road with the *Sinner*. It is odd, though I may have heard the story told me when a child, but it is odd that somewhat a similar idea exercised me for some time, and the *Sinner* damped it out; though perhaps unconsciously it came again in a new form. I believe I had not heard the story, for surely the grave would have stuck in a child's mind, and that, when I came to read it some ten years ago—it was fresh to me; and I believe the common ground had been supplied by a common devotion to Covenanting literature—of which I read more as a young man than you could dream.[1]

Saintsbury's theory that Lockhart had assisted Hogg in the writing of the *Justified Sinner* was not supported by any evidence and was comprehensively demolished by Louis Simpson in the 1960s. This paper will not focus on that old debate, but will use Stevenson's letter as the basis for a discussion of the interconnections between *The Master of Ballantrae* and the *Justified Sinner*. In his letter to Saintsbury, then, Stevenson says of the *Justified Sinner*: "The book since I read it in black, pouring weather on Tweedside, has always haunted and puzzled me." Stevenson's letter was written in 1891, and in it he says that he read the *Justified Sinner* "some ten years ago," that is around 1881. Stevenson was back in Scotland, having traveled from Davos, in the summer of 1882, and it was most likely during this interlude that he read the Hogg text: the significance of the timing lies in the fact that he read the *Justified Sinner* some five years before commencing work on *The Master of Ballantrae*.

There are several striking examples of intertextual connections between the two novels that merit mention: both novels emphasize moonlight duels between brothers, Robert Wringhim against George Colwan and Henry Durie against James, Master of Ballantrae; both novels conclude with a preserved body rising from an open grave; both novels reflect families divided along politico-religious lines; and in both novels the Devil is alluded to as an actual presence. In *The Master of Ballantrae*, Stevenson opposes the brothers Durie in descriptive terms that seem to draw on elements in the *Justified Sinner*. James Durie resembles George Colwan in looks and temperament and is cast in the role of Devil Incarnate by the Durie family; the description of Henry, the insipid, pious younger brother, is redolent of the contumacious Robert Wringhim who sets himself against his sibling, citing George as one in the service of Satan.

The Private Memoirs and Confessions of A Justified Sinner is a tale told in three parts: the "Editor's Narrative"; the sinner's confession; and a short account of how the editor and his colleagues came to be in possession of the confession document, garnered from the sinner's grave. The narrative opens in the early years of the eighteenth century and features two rival brothers. The parents are ill-matched, representing opposing natures: the husband is a libertine and his wife is a follower of the fanatical Calvinist minister, the Reverend Robert Wringhim, a narrow-minded bigot. The first-born son is George Colwan, but the father rejects and disowns the younger boy, Robert, believing him to be the progeny of a union between his wife and Wringhim. The young Robert is reared by the Reverend Wringhim, but cut off from his inheritance. He is baptized as Wringhim, he is more intelligent than George, but possesses none of his brother's charm. His mother and the Reverend Wringhim inculcate into Robert a hatred of the Colwans. He is indoctrinated with antinomian beliefs which embrace an extreme Calvinism promoting the view that good works and faith alone are not enough to guarantee salvation: rather, the justified are already known to God and are therefore guaranteed salvation. Hogg suggests that the logic, such as it is, of such a position, may allow the justified to ignore secular notions of morality altogether.

Wringhim is an enthusiastic supporter of the fight against sinners, and pursues his elder brother relentlessly, chastising him and functioning as a grim alternative to the jovial and popular George. The opposition of the brothers extends beyond personality and into the dangerous territory of seventeenth-century politico-religious division. Old Colwan is a Tory Member of Parliament and sympathetic to the cause of the Cavaliers, but Wringhim is a follower of the Covenanters. The conflict between the brothers reaches a crisis as they meet on Arthur's Seat, a hill overlooking the city of Edinburgh. Walking on the crags and admiring the view, George is startled by a grotesque shape in the mist. In the midst of his disorientation he staggers into Robert, lashing out as he does so. Quickly regaining his sour composure Wringhim returns to Edinburgh there to open proceedings against Colwan for attempted fratricide. His case fails when his harassment of George is revealed to the court. George and his associates congregate in one of their favorite public houses to celebrate, and in the course of the carousing, George enters into an argument with a Highlander by the name of Drummond. Later that night, George is found in a lane stabbed to death. Drummond leaves Edinburgh at great speed. The news of his son's death kills old Colwan, and Robert Wringhim falls heir to the estates of Dalcastle. The "Editor's Narrative" ends with the discovery that several eyewitnesses can testify to the fact that Wringhim killed George Colwan, not Drummond, who is cleared of the crime. Robert Wringhim is arraigned, but cannot be found.

The second part of the tale, Robert's "confession," recovered from his grave, restates the material from the "Editor's Narrative," but now they are the subjective impressions of Wringhim himself and show him in an entirely different light. He is righteous and admirable, a fighter for justice and as the narrative develops the reader is drawn into a completely different landscape from that peopled by George Colwan and his friends; their superficial world of carousing and jollity is replaced by an atmosphere of intense religiosity, in which Robert finds a new "guru," a stranger by the name of Gil-Martin. Robert is now haunted by Gil-Martin in a way that resembles Robert's pursuit of George; it is dogged and indefatigable. Gil-Martin instructs the newly justified Robert in matters of doctrine and encourages him in his crusade against sinners, and his brother in particular. The impression dawns upon the reader that Gil-Martin is the Devil. Robert, at this juncture, starts to feel unwell and believes himself to be two people, a compound of Gil-Martin and his brother George, between whom he has disappeared. The lack of balance in his narrative leads the reader to the belief that Robert is presenting the signs of a mind in collapse, but Hogg problematizes this reading of inner deterioration by showing Gil-Martin as a physical presence witnessed by third parties. As the influence of Gil-Martin gains a hold over Robert, the latter's mental stability evaporates. At the last, Robert develops a paranoid fear of Gil-Martin, and, destroyed by alcohol, in a state of total confusion, but still clinging to his belief that he is one of the elect, he publishes his confession as a religious tract, simultaneously swearing to commit suicide.

The text concludes with the Editor's account of how the sinner's grave was found from an essay written in *Blackwood's Magazine* by one James Hogg. The essay deals with the story of the discovery of the grave of an unknown suicide and rumors surrounding the site in the Scottish Borders. Hogg, a shepherd (what else) is invited by the Editor to show him the gravesite, but refuses, stating that he is disinclined to "houk up hunder-year auld banes."[2] The Editor himself is left to exhume the "Confession-document" and to have it republished: he suggests that the document is an allegory and the product of a mind either mad or dreaming and, further, that the author's delusion extended to the belief that he was his own fictional character. Hogg's ability to add a final twist, to set yet another tale within a tale, appears to conform to the Gothic genre and the consequent undermining of certainty would entitle the reader to apply such a description to this most unsettling text.

The *Justified Sinner* is an interesting and challenging study for a variety of reasons, and as an example of a Scottish Gothic novel it deserves attention not simply for its narrative arrangement and for the evocative descriptions of wilderness that are central to the genre, but the novel also highlights radically different human types in the brothers Wringhim and Colwan.

Stevenson's novel, it may be said, refigures some of the arrangements found in the Hogg text, but it is, of course, too simplistic to suggest that the *Justified Sinner* is the only source for the later work.

The idea for the *Master of Ballantrae* may have had its origins in the context of the Jacobite Rising of 1715, although the narrative is located in the period of the '45. Stevenson had planned "A History of Scotland" and would almost certainly have been aware that landed families hedged their bets in their support of the rival Jacobite and Hanoverian factions, often to the extent that brothers fought on opposing sides. In this matter, the arrangements adopted by the Durie family in *The Master of Ballantrae* parallel actual positions adopted within the family of the Duke of Atholl in 1715.

The second Marquis of the first Duke of Atholl, one John Murray, took the side of the Government in the Jacobite Rising of 1715 while his heir, William, Marquess of Tullibardine, suffered sequestration of land for his part in the rebellion. As a consequence, a younger son, James, succeeded to the title. It is possible that this historical source was also incorporated into the ground-plan for *The Master of Ballantrae*. Perhaps a combination of sources are brought together by Stevenson—the seventeenth-century legacy of radicalism that results in the opposition of the Colwan-Wringhim feud and the eighteenth-century division between the Jacobite and Hanoverian factions.

If indeed Stevenson has in *The Master of Ballantrae*, refigured elements of the Hogg text, it is not, even in the context of his own output, a unique occurrence. In a letter to Edward Purcell, dated 27 February 1886, Stevenson confesses to his propensity for adaptation:

> I had no idea what a cruelly bold adapter I was, till I found the whole first part of *Treasure Island* in what I had not read (I believe, but I am not sure) for nearly twenty years: Washington Irving's *Treasure Seekers.*[3]

Later, in *My First Book*, Stevenson went on to restate his awareness of the earlier text:

> It is my debt to Washington Irving that exercises my conscience, and justly so, for I believe plagiarism was rarely carried farther. I chanced to pick up the *Tales of a Traveller* some years ago [...] and the book flew up and struck me. Billy Bones, his chest, the company in the parlour, the whole inner spirit and a good deal of the material of my first chapters—all were there, all were the property of Washington Irving.[4]

Perhaps Stevenson wrote this at least in part ironically, but in any case he demonstrates that the writer of one era may look to the work of a predecessor and find that the tropes of the earlier text reemerge in the later work. That phenomenon need not be plagiarism but rather the reworking of characters and situations which correspond to the constituent ingredients of, for example, the adventure genre—pirates, buried treasure, and, most importantly, dramatic resolution.

It is in the context of creative reworking that the resemblances between *The Private Memoirs and Confessions of A Justified Sinner* and *The Master of Ballantrae* may be traced.

In terms of its narrative configuration, *The Master of Ballantrae* mirrors Hogg's text in its use of multiple layers within which key narrators present personal, indeed biased accounts, of events. For example, Ephraim Mackellar, MA, Steward to the House of Durrisdeer, is inclined to view everything from a standpoint favorable to *his* Master, Henry Durie. Two consequences follow from this bias: firstly, Mackellar is inimical to James Durie, who is by rule of primogeniture the lawful Master of Ballantrae; and secondly, and following on from the previous observation, his reliability as a narrator is therefore seriously compromised. However, with that said, Mackellar is intrinsically important to the action, and his distinctive and dogmatic contribution forms a necessary part of the whole. In terms of balance, if not reliability, James Durie's case is put by the equally partisan Chevalier Burke, soldier and adventurer, and, with James, the antithesis of the rather bloodless partnership of Mackellar and Henry Durie.

In *The Master of Ballantrae*, James Durie is represented, like George Colwan, as the paradigm of evil, but his sins appear similarly understated. He approximates to the Byronic hero: attractive and dangerous in equal measure. Whether he is the "incubus" Stevenson suggests is surely debatable: Mackellar, the sober Calvinist, certainly suspects him of possessing Satanic powers, and the tale derives some order from the assumption that

James is the representative of evil and Henry the put-upon victim of James's mercenary nature.

However, Stevenson undercuts a straightforward opposition of good and evil in devastating fashion by producing in Mackellar, to all intents Henry's man, a reaction which testifies to James's genuine attractiveness. Arriving as Land Steward to the House of Durrisdeer, Mackellar is aware of the actions of the brothers in the Jacobite Rebellion of 1745. The Durrisdeer estate, following the example of the Scottish landed gentry, decide to back both horses as it were, in the conflict between the Jacobite and Hanoverian causes, especially in light of events that looked likely to result in civil war. The Master of Ballantrae, as eldest son and heir, could opt to remain at home and remain aloof, which would result in his younger brother going off to represent the Durrisdeers in Charles Edward Stuart's army. Stevenson subverts any romantic notions of fighting for freedom or independence, or indeed for the Union, by emphasizing the bet-hedging process which precedes the Master's departure for the North and, ultimately, for Culloden Moor and the destruction of the Highland clans. The business, for that is what it is, is decided on the toss of a coin, which means James goes and Henry stays. The process that started as an attempt to cover both options divides the brothers and sparks off a rivalry that operates as a metaphor for internecine strife within Scotland itself. Henry, described by Mackellar as "not very able, but an honest, solid sort of lad," is opposed to deciding the matter in such an arbitrary manner, but his elder brother prevails, stating: "It is the direct heir of Durrisdeer that should ride by his King's bridle...." Henry's riposte is significant: "If we were playing a manly part [...] there might be sense in such talk. But what are we doing? Cheating at cards!"

The Durrisdeer estate, it seems, is morally bankrupt in the matter of which side to back and it is bankrupt financially, relying for survival on a wealthy "kinswoman," Alison Graeme. The old Lord Durrisdeer, prematurely aged and confined to his fireside, is anxious to secure Alison's wealth by marrying her off to James, his heir. When it appears that James has been killed at the Battle of Culloden, the Laird, consummate politician as he is, conjures a marriage between Alison, and Henry, his younger son. It should be remembered that Alison has been entrusted into the care of Durrisdeer and his actions would seem to indicate a less than altruistic regard for her well-being. It is Alison who, enraged by James's decision, picks up the gold coin that has apparently sealed the fate of the Durrisdeer household and hurls it "clean through the family shield in the great painted window." This obviously symbolic act, read simply on one level, indicates the destructive power of random action, as personified by

James, who states: "I have always done exactly as I felt inclined" and "I always go my own way with inevitable motion." His disregard for others is a manifestation of his own hollowness. However, there is a paradox in Alison's throwing of the coin, since it is her fortune that will secure the estate, as old Durrisdeer knows only too well. Like Dalcastle in the *Justified Sinner*, Durrisdeer holds one son in high regard while ignoring the virtues of the other, and with similar consequences as events prove. The head of the House of Durrisdeer is moved to self-interest, and his attitude towards Alison in the wake of the news of the Master's death is worthy of note:

Day in, day out, he would work upon her, sitting by his chimney-side with his finger in his Latin book, and his eyes set upon her face with a kind of pleasant intentness that became the old gentleman very well. If she wept, he would condole with her like an ancient man that has seen worse times and begins to think lightly even of sorrow; if she raged, he would fall to his reading again in his Latin book but always with some civil excuse; if she offered, as she often did, to let them have her money in a gift, he would show her how little it consisted with his honour, and remind her, even if he should consent, that Mr. Henry would certainly refuse.

Henry only enters into Durrisdeer's affections when he becomes a substitute husband for Alison and so secures the future of the estate. Following the marriage, in an arrangement which is certainly not predicated upon love, neither Durrisdeer nor Alison will allow Henry to repair the damage to the family crest, broken by the coin that sent the Master to Culloden and to death. This is significant; the symbol of the broken crest prevents both the burial of the past or the awakening of a new era, and it may be that here Stevenson foregrounds the sense of impasse following the events of 1745 and 1746. Bereft by the death of the Master, Alison and the Laird sit by the fireside in mourning of a sentimental nature that would appear to parallel the mourning for "the King across the water."

In addition to the grief of his father and that of his wife, who has vouchsafed that she brings him no love, Henry must contend with the opprobrium which follows the news that James has been killed at Culloden. The Master's once-tainted reputation is restored, and mention is made of an act of betrayal which led to his demise; Henry becomes the target for the wrath of the local community on the back of a rising sympathy for his deceased brother.

Stevenson describes the scene as follows:

The Master was called up for a saint. It was remembered how he had never any hand in pressing the tenants; as indeed, no more he had, except to spend the money. He was a little wild perhaps, the folk said; but how much better was a natural, wild lad that would soon have settled down, than a skinflint and a sneck-draw, sitting with his nose in an account book to persecute poor tenants! One trollop who had had a child to the Master, and by all accounts been very badly used, yet made herself a kind of champion of her memory. She flung a stone one day at Mr. Henry.

"Whaur's the bonny lad that trustit ye?" she cried.

Mr. Henry reined in his horse and looked upon her, the blood flowing from his lip. "Ay, Jess," says he. "You too? And yet ye should ken me better." For it was him who had helped her with money [*TMB*, 9].

Henry has, clearly, legitimate cause for grievance, as had Robert Wringhim, and the parallel is perhaps valid because the effect in Henry's case is similarly to displace his objectivity and to inculcate a desire for justice as he sees it. It is shortly after he is subjected to open abuse in the community that Henry joins Alison and his father in reclusive withdrawal.

From this point onwards, *The Master of Ballantrae* can be read as a psychological study of the tragic decline of Henry Durie, unloved by his wife, and subjected to the deceit and lies of his brother who did not, as the narrative unfolds, die in battle but escaped in circumstances which are unclear, to adventure abroad. This reading might depend upon accepting the assumption that in this text Stevenson returns to that element in *Jekyll and Hyde* which highlights the importance of reputation, but given that that was an element which exercised Stevenson a great deal, perhaps it does not present such a huge difficulty. It may be that, in returning to this central theme in what is a key text in relation to considerations of duality, as indeed is the *Justified Sinner*, Stevenson, following Hogg, satirizes the mindset predicated upon reputation. Certainly in the context of the Romantic period, examples exist, set in typically Gothic topographies at that, where satire is used to undercut reputation: one has in mind a text such as Peacock's *Nightmare Abbey*, for example.

Henry Durie begins as a strong and charitable figure who is misrepresented not only by the community in which he can expect to enjoy the benefits of status, but also by his father, brother and wife. The point from which his decline is measured is the conclusion of the moonlit duel when he believes he has killed the Master; from this moment forward he is propelled on a complex and convoluted descent into obsessive behavior which leads him to insanity. His *hamartia*, his fatal flaw, is shown in his acceptance of false allegations; he allows himself to be blackmailed by what he knows to be untrue. In short, evil triumphs because good refuses to assert itself: James is elevated from the status of charlatan and sponge on the family's diminishing assets to the status of devil only if Henry believes that to be an accurate estimate of his evil potential.

However, the situation is further complicated by the fact that Henry's sense of justification leads him to the same conclusion as Wringhim; that is to say, he is convinced, in that awareness of justification, that he must destroy his devil brother. The relationship to the Hogg text may be seen in the confusion over what is real and what is false, and that sense of the uncanny central to Gothic fiction resurfaces in *The Master of Ballantrae*— not just in the topography of the wilderness in which the brothers are eventually buried, but in the uncertainties that stem from multiple narration, which functions to destabilize the text. Henry's decline is related by Mackellar, and from his description we can draw parallels between Wringhim and Henry in terms of the corresponding physical and mental deterioration each experiences: it is almost as if in the late nineteenth century there was no better way to portray the deterioration of the mental faculties than there had been in Hogg's day: to portray the internal process, one had to show an external equivalence. Issues relating to perception and reality suggest themselves here, and the role of Mackellar is important in establishing questions of reliability which affect our perception of events. The structure of the novel, in a sense, *requires* Mackellar to be unreliable; he acts as a medium, interpreting actions and translating them into a rather dry account, but he fuses together the various episodes and so gives the text an otherwise lacking unity.

One important observation, by way of conclusion: Stevenson may adopt and he may adapt, but his novel is a major contribution to the same genre as Hogg's; it draws on the culture of Scotland, certainly, but it addresses, at its most profound level, basic human instincts. Like the *Justified Sinner*, *The Master of Ballantrae* extends beyond the conventions of historical romance and uses the tropes of the Gothic to provide an atmosphere that undermines certainty, taking the reader into a bleak landscape consistent with Stevenson's "Winter's Tale."

NOTES

1. *The Letters of Robert Louis Stevenson*, edited by Bradford A. Booth and Ernest Mehew, 8 vols (New Haven and London: Yale University Press, 1994–95), VII, 125–26.

2. James Hogg, *The Private Memoirs and Confession of A Justified Sinner* 1824 (London: The Cresset Press, 1947), p. 223.

3. *The Letters of Robert Louis Stevenson*, V, 212.

4. *My First Book: Treasure Island,* edited by Jerome K. Jerome (London, 1894), pp. 297–309.

5. Robert Louis Stevenson, *The Master of Ballantrae* (Edinburgh: Canongate, 1995), p. 8. All subsequent references are to this edition and are given in brackets in the text.

"Writing Towards Home":
The Landscape of
A Child's Garden of Verses

Ann C. Colley

> … most of us, looking back on young years, may remember
> seasons of a light, aërial translucency and elasticity and per-
> fect freedom; the body had not yet become the prison-house
> of the soul, but was its vehicle and implement, like a crea-
> ture of thought, and altogether pliant to its bidding.
> —*Thomas Carlyle, "Characteristics" (1831)*

At a time when the troubling question of the relationship between
the past and the present lays siege upon a culture's conscience, it is, perhaps, appropriate to consider the role of nostalgia as an organizing force
in the imagination and memory. With this context in mind, I have chosen to examine the nature of Robert Louis Stevenson's nostalgia for his
childhood and the expression of this longing in the poems that compose
A Child's Garden of Verses (1885). Like many of his contemporaries,
Stevenson thought of himself as being alienated and exiled from his home-
land and his childhood by virtue of distance and age. Like them he suffered
from a desire for reunion, for some point of correspondence between the
present and the past, the immediate surroundings and home. Often feeling dispossessed and trapped in the dualities and the tension between the
real and the remembered, he wrote toward home in an attempt to reach
a place where there is a possibility of continuity and where there is a sanc-

tuary from the changes that come with the passing of time. His verses offered him a form of hope, of promise, that he could, for the moment, place himself in the track of his former self and re-enter what was irrevocably absent and seemingly unavailable. He could reclaim what was once himself.

Although Stevenson lived through his nostalgic moments as if alone—recall the solitary voice that at times permeates the lines in *A Child's Garden of Verses*—he was tacitly connected to those who reached for the metaphor of their history to bring what is absent into the present in order more fully to integrate their lives. He took comfort in the past, for he was part of a culture that found in the past a means of resolving (rather than creating) tension or difference. The past gave Stevenson a way of discovering synthesis—an engagement with it did not necessarily expose the antitheses and ironies imbedded in our postmodern sensibility. Even though Stevenson was more than capable of mocking his countrymen, his was not a perspective that tends to distrust what belongs to a former time. Neither did he participate in that part of our contemporary culture that, as Arjun Appadurai suggests, promotes nostalgia without a memory (272)—a world in which people look back to events and places they have never lost and simply take what they need from the past out of a "synchronic warehouse of cultural scenarios" that function as a "temporal central casting" (273) according to the desire of a political moment. On the contrary, Stevenson existed in a context without this disjunctive overlapping. He was part of a sensibility in which there is a distinction and a distance between the past and the present. He belonged to a world that has a memory; consequently, he moved about in places that carry the burden and the authority of what was once in them. For him and his contemporaries, there was, very much, an object to their sadness. They did not subscribe to what Susan Stewart claims is a condition of longing: that nostalgia is a sadness without an object (*On Longing*).

For Stevenson, of course, a primary object of his nostalgia was the landscape of his childhood. Although many critics and biographers have remarked upon the fact of Stevenson's yearning for his childhood and have documented his engagement with the games, the play, the maps, and the interiors of his early years, none has dwelt upon the idiosyncratic nature of their "typography," especially that which he describes in *A Child's Garden of Verses*.[1] In this essay, I concentrate upon the "elasticity" of these childhood spaces and upon their malleable and synthetic landscape. The poems in *A Child's Garden of Verses* are about Stevenson's nostalgia for this flexibility and for its companion, the vicarious violence of play. In these verses the dualities of home and distant skies, land and sea, trees and ships, are not alienating; they do not exile the child, for the child belongs to a larger perspective that collapses the distant and the contiguous. With ease, he journeys back and forth between modes of consciousness and terrain without the experience of difference and duality that can complicate the adult experience and exacerbate the sense of difference. Stevenson's verses offered him a sanctuary that was more durable and satisfying than that afforded by his intermittent nationalism, for they were the means of writing towards home and reclaiming, momentarily, what was no longer fully available to him. These verses helped him walk back into the space of his early years and recover what Carlyle termed the "elasticity" of childhood.

Stevenson's Longing for Childhood

Like one who closely watches passing trains traveling in opposite directions, Stevenson constantly altered his focus and turned his head from one compartment of his life to another. As an adult he kept shifting between childhood and maturity and could not, therefore, regard himself as a "constant" (*Virginibus Puerisque* 59). He was never simply his chronological age. Referring to himself in a letter to his cousin Robert Alan Stevenson, he explained, "You are twenty, and forty, and five, and the next moment you are freezing at an imaginary eighty; you are never the plain forty-four that you should be by dates" (*Letters* 8: 366). Because of this perspective, Stevenson had difficulty in portraying an adult without making some reference to a childish feature or characteristic in the person. Sensitive to the child that lives within the adult, he referred to himself as a grown man who feels "weary and timid in this big, jostling city" and wants to run to his nurse (*Letters* 3: 33), and, at another time, described his aging and infirm grandfather as a person who sits "with perfect simplicity, like a child's, munching a 'barley-sugar kiss'" (*Memories and Portraits* 112). The child adhered to the adult as the shadow sticks to the young boy in the poems "My Shadow" and "Shadow March" (*A Child's Garden of Verses*). Whether it was before or after him, or for the moment invisible, this second self was always in some way attached to the person. Consequently, in Stevenson's fiction protagonists move effortlessly back and forth between childhood and adulthood. At one moment the young narrator of *Treasure Island* speaks of himself as "only a boy" (139) but at another adopts the persona of an adult and imperiously commands, "I've come aboard to take possession of this ship, Mr. Hands; and you'll please regard me as your captain until further notice" (156). Similarly, David Balfour and Alan Breck alternate between "the rude, silly speech of a boy of ten" (*Kidnapped* 172) and the measured phrases of maturity. Their vacillating responses to each other and to themselves reflect the giddiness of their shifting identities.

Stevenson's sensitivity to these fluctuations resulted not only from his recognizing the child within himself and others but also from his yearning for that segment of his life. Reading through Stevenson's prose and poetry, one soon realizes that his nostalgia for Scotland was not nearly as pressing as his longing for his early years there. Even though Stevenson spoke of his childhood as "a very mixed experience, full of fever, nightmare, insomnia, painful days and interminable nights" (*Letters* 5: 97), he also remembered the happier moments that combined with the difficult to make his childhood a more intense time than the present. As an adult he wanted to relive that intensity. Stevenson's attachment to children is an expression of this desire. When he watched them or when he was with them, he could see what he wanted to retrieve from his past and what he hoped still to find within himself. His letters that include passages about children echo this longing. For instance, from Menton in 1874, Stevenson wrote to his mother about a Russian child of two and a half who was staying with her mother at his hotel: "She speaks six languages. She and her sister (*aet.* 8) and May Johnstone (*aet.* 8) are the delight of my life. Last night I saw them all dancing—O it was jolly; kids are what is the matter with me" (*Letters* 1: 429). Like so many other young people, that child was "ever interesting" (*Letters* 1: 441). Periodically, Stevenson also wrote letters to children of his friends. In a letter to Thomas Archer, aged three, for example, Stevenson describes a few moments from his own boyhood and displays an unusually acute memory of what it was like to be Thomas's age. His words reveal his yearning for the games of his youth: "I was the best player of hide-and-seek going; not a good runner, I was up to every shift and dodge, I could jink very well, I could crawl without any noise through leaves, I could hide under a carrot plant, it used to be my favourite boast that I always *walked* into the den" (*Letters* 6: 218).

Significantly, it is in this love of play that one finds the primary expression of Stevenson's attraction to children and childhood. Most of all, he wanted to be back among his boyhood play. Longing to relive these moments, he later devised elaborate war games with toy soldiers, designed maps, printed newspaper reports about the troops' daily movements, and with his willing stepson produced dramas, set up printing presses, and traveled into countries unknown to anyone but themselves. Accompanied by Lloyd Osbourne, Stevenson was able to continue the imaginative play he and his cousin Robert had enjoyed when they had been younger and had eagerly created the lands of Nosington and Encyclopaedia. In his essay "Crabbed Age and Youth," Stevenson, barely disguising his identity, speaks of his wish to reclaim the games of his childhood and admits his reluctance to give up his playthings:

> A child who had been remarkably fond of toys (and in particular of lead soldiers) found himself growing to the level of acknowledged boyhood without any abatement of this childish taste. He was thirteen; already he had been taunted for dallying overlong about the playbox; he had to blush if he was found among his lead soldiers; the shades of the prison-house were closing about him with a vengeance. There is nothing more difficult than to put the thoughts of children into the language of their elders; but this is the effect of his meditations at this juncture: "Plainly," he said, "I must give up my playthings in the meanwhile, since I am not in a position to secure myself against idle jeers. At the same time, I am sure that playthings are the very pick of life; all people give them up out of the same pusillanimous respect for those who are a little older; and if they do not return to them as soon as they can, it is only because they grow stupid and forget. I shall be wiser; I shall conform for a little to the ways of their foolish world; but so soon as I have made enough money, I shall retire and shut myself up among my playthings until the day I die" [*Virginibus Puerisque* 63–64].

Stevenson took his own advice, for, of course, his essays, fiction, and poems are expressions of this impulse to shut himself up with his toys. With their more elaborate versions of hide-and-seek, their dressed dramas, and their arenas of adventurous conflict, *Treasure Island, Kidnapped, The Master of Ballantrae,* and *St. Ives,* for instance, kept the adult Stevenson "halfway between the swing and the gate" (*Letters* 4: 189), and such poems as "Pirate Story" and "A Good Play" from *A Child's Garden of Verses* allowed him to hear "a kind of childish treble note" (*Letters* 5: 85). It is as if he wrote the books and the verses he wished he could have picked up and read—the kind that would have let him re-engage his childhood play. In an 1884 letter to William Ernest Henley, Stevenson exclaimed, "I want to hear swords clash. I want a book to begin in a good way; a book, I guess, like *Treasure Island,* alas! which I have never read, and cannot though I live to ninety. I would God that some one else had written it! By all that I can learn, it is the very book for my complaint" (*Letters* 4: 307).

The Landscape of A Child's Garden of Verses

Stevenson's unwillingness to abandon the pleasures of play issues partly from his sense that a child's spatial orientation differs significantly from an adult's. The boundaries marking the experience of childhood bore no resemblance to those defining adulthood—to become an adult, therefore, was to exchange one kind of map for another and to step outside the child's realm. It was to lose a perspective that might release him from the disturbing dualities that split the attention of his adult life.

This division of worlds is, perhaps, nowhere more visible than in *A Child's Garden of Verses*. Here Stevenson becomes the cartographer-poet who delineates a topography that essentially excludes adults. "Grown ups" stand outside the contours of the child's space, beyond what the poems, with their geographical imagery, survey and map. Adults are outsiders who enter momentarily to put the child to bed. As voices from another "estate," they intrude and call the child home to tea. They are mothers who listen to the patter of feet from another room. None, not even the kindly aunt ("Auntie's Skirts"), is fully part of the child's subjective and self-contained space. Like the nurse who appears to be "very big," they do not even share the same scale ("My Kingdom"). The "we" in the poems, therefore, refers almost exclusively to children, for they are the primary community. Just as the children Stevenson observed on board the *Devonia*[2] found each other "like dogs" and moved about "all in a band, as thick as thieves at a fair" while their elders were "still ceremoniously maneuvering on the outskirts of acquaintance" (*The Amateur Emigrant* 15), the young people in *A Child's Garden of Verses* spontaneously form and dissolve their own society that marginalizes the adult world. Like the child in "Foreign Lands," the young boys and girls search for "a higher tree" so they can see "To where the grown-up river slips/ Into the sea among the ships...." To become an adult is to lose this point of view.

Although Stevenson acknowledged that a phantom of the child stalked the adult and could, at times, seem more real than the adult figure himself, he recognized, of course, that childhood was not fully recoverable. No matter how much he consciously tried to re-enter its domain and how often he tried to take hold of it, his boyhood was always to be somewhat elusive. He remarked that in his adulthood he had "grown up and gone away" from what he once was. Enough remained, though, in memory and impulse, that Stevenson could isolate and long for what was lacking. He did not, of course, regret the passing of the child's terror of chastisement and the suffering that accompanied his frequent illnesses. He did, however, regret the absence of the child's spontaneity and the expansiveness of his imagination—Stevenson envied the child who does not have to travel to activate his mind, who requires merely the stage of his immediate surroundings and the props of the simplest, everyday objects to reach places that he knows only by name. Keenly aware of this loss in his adulthood, he instructed his name-child, at the end of *A Child's Garden of Verses*, to lay down his spelling lesson and "go and play" ("To My Name-Child").

Even more significantly, though, Stevenson deplored the absence of a certain elasticity of perception that is such an integral part of childhood. The child inhabits a malleable space. Like Princes Street (Edinburgh) that can either interminably extend itself and lead the spectator's eye "right into the heart of the red sundown" or "shrink" so that the street "seems to lie underneath" one's feet (*Letters* 1: 330), the child is able to expand and contract his attention, yet never lose touch with himself. He keeps his name and his identity. His shadow moves, grows, and diminishes with him. With ease, the child journeys back and forth between modes of consciousness and terrain without the experience of difference that can complicate the adult experience. In a sense, perhaps, the child is able to realize or make facile the fantasy of empire and eradicate the anxieties attending its displacements.

The poems in *A Child's Garden of Verses* are about Stevenson's nostalgia for this flexibility. They follow the child as he journeys between what is near and far, as he moves from night to day, and as he swings within and beyond the borders of the garden wall, sails in and out of the harbors of home, and grows large or becomes small. In all these situations the child remains intact and secure. The dualities of home and distant skies, land and sea, trees and ships, neither divide him nor cause one part of his consciousness to regard the other as alien—as exiled. In his terrain, beds and books, darkness and light, meadows and seas, pillows and battlefields mingle to form the single subjective topography of his inner landscape. He is part of a larger perspective that collapses the distant and the contiguous and, simultaneously, expands the immediate into the distant— where the rain at the same moment falls "on the umbrellas here" and "on the ships at sea" ("Rain") and where the child senses, although he cannot see them, the presence of other children who, like him, go to bed, play, take their tea, and sing—in Japan, Spain, or India ("Foreign Lands," "Singing," and "The Sun Travels"). There is no layering, no schematic drawing of geological strata. The layers only separate when the adult intrudes with a voice that wrenches what is single apart; then, the child becomes self-conscious and in "The Land of Story-Books" speaks of an otherness:

> So, when my nurse comes in for me,
> Home I return across the sea,
> And go to bed with backward looks
> At my dear land of Story-books.

This looking backwards is a way of perceiving imposed by those who feel the differences of time and place. It is a mode of seeing that belongs to the adult who has difficulty blending the absent and the present and holding what is near and far comfortably within his sight. Unlike the child in the swing, the adult cannot readily see outside and inside the boundaries of his life in one motion. The adult does not have the invisible sweeping eye; he must elicit a mediating object, like the map, to extend his perspective. Recognizing this necessity, Stevenson once recommended to Edmund Gosse (17 March 1884) that in his new office overlooking the Thames he should keep on his table "a great map spread out...." Stevenson suggested that "a chart is still better—it takes one further—the havens with their little anchors, the rocks, banks and soundings, are adorably marine" (*Letters* 4: 260). The child in the poems requires no such mediating object to collect into one space what is near and far, what can be seen and what is invisible. It is only later, as an adult, that Stevenson needs maps and charts to help him reclaim this suppleness of mind so he can compose his fiction.

Because they unite the dualities that leave the adult staring at the space separating the then and the now, the far and the near, the children in Stevenson's verses do not necessarily experience nostalgia—as in "Where Go the Boats?" they look forwards, not backwards. The child's orientation is not, therefore, like that of Dr. Jekyll or the Master of Ballantrae, for his self is not a divided house; it need not turn back to regard itself and stare at its own "imperfect and divided countenance" (*Dr. Jekyll and Mr. Hyde* 83–84). The child blends the nights and days and the open and the secret that come between Dr. Jekyll and Mr. Hyde and cause Hyde, at one point, to look back through the space of his anguish and review his life from his infancy. The child is spared this pain, for he lives in an ever-revolving present—even when he says goodbye, the images he desires sparkle with a presence that keeps them alive. They are, in spite of the valediction, still there ("Farewell to the Farm"). Memory does not continually press against him. In this frame of mind, then, Stevenson's young child considers what it will be like to grow older and does not fear that he will have to recall what he once was ("Looking Forward"). On the contrary, he looks forward to being able to realize and to extend his desires—he will learn to take a ship out to sea ("My Ship and I"), and he will become the lamplighter ("The Lamplighter"). From his perspective, his older self will actualize or confirm his being; it will neither oppose nor diminish it, for his circumference of sight will expand and allow him to see "farther" ("Foreign Lands"). Continuity rather than interruption or retrospection measures the child's globe.

Stevenson's verses emerge from a longing for this circumstance. But as Stevenson realized, he and his nostalgia for the past cannot restructure what had been. One reason they fail is that the adult, unlike the more flexible child, cannot play properly—he has difficulty accepting substitutes and, thus, can never fully entertain the notion of recovery, for he feels cut off from the authentic or legitimate experience. He is, therefore, more than usually sensitive to difference. The child in Stevenson's verses, on the other hand, is constantly using one object for another—a bed for a boat—and that suffices; it becomes the real thing. For him, in the world of play, the shadow does as well as the substance ("Block City"):

> What are you able to build with your blocks?
> Castles and palaces, temples and docks.
> Rain may keep raining, and others go roam,
> But I can be happy and building at home.
> Let the sofa be mountains, the carpet be sea,
> There I'll establish a city for me:
> A kirk and a mill and a palace beside,
> And a harbour as well where my vessels may ride.

When the adult is an exile from this dominion, that possibility disappears. As Stevenson complained, "the mature mind ... desires the thing itself" (*Virginibus Puerisque* 160). The experience of nostalgia, perhaps, also contributes to the failure. Because it gathers bits and pieces from the past and assembles fragments arising from the involuntary memory, nostalgia merely offers vanishing glimpses of what was. This incompleteness denies the possibility of substitution by inscribing the sense of loss or absence and, thereby, awakens a longing for the fuller, more lasting picture. With the exception of its abstracting powers, nostalgia usually confirms the presence of a divided self. In a sense, it signifies the ultimate duality. Stevenson's child, though, for whom the shadow is sufficient, does not have to struggle with memory's imperfections and demands. Moreover, because nostalgia waits in the future, unbeckoned, the child can look out of a moving train's window ("From a Railway Carriage") and without anxiety see the sights fly by. The poem's last line, "Each a glimpse and gone for ever!" can gaily rattle along with the train's repetitive rhythm.

One reason that these passing glimpses are not threatening and do not disquiet the child is that in the elastic space of Stevenson's verses there is, for the child, always the possibility of return, of recovery. No matter how far he roams, he can always go back. Moving through a malleable map that stretches and shrinks, he never really loses sight of where he is. Like Princes Street, home is always, somehow, available; everything is "handy to home" ("Keepsake Mill"). The number of poems in *A Child's Garden of Verses* that convey this sense of security is noteworthy. The poems depict a child who wanders far and wide, yet returns to the safety of his room; who swings high but always comes back down; and who marches round the village and goes "home again." Like the cow, the child "wanders" yet "cannot stray" ("The Cow"). He moves in a landscape of recovery. In this terrain, the continuous revolutions of the "old mill wheel" are the "keepsake" that promises that "we all shall come home" ("Keepsake Mill"). Through this land runs the river, the surface of which once disturbed by the wind, the "Dipping marten," or the "plumping trout," always returns to its former unruffled self:

> Patience, children, just a minute—
> See the spreading circles die;
> The stream and all in it
> Will clear by-and-by ["Looking-Glass River"].

The verses' cycles of sleeping and rising, darkness and light are part of this reassuring rhythm of recovery. They revolve the child in a world of reawakenings. One wonders, perhaps, if Stevenson's desire to travel was not partially a quest for a place where he might re-enter the orbit of the jet-black night and clear day—where he might, as he did on a train between Edinburgh and Chester, travel and feel reborn. Stevenson describes one such experience in a September 1874 letter to Frances Sitwell:

> How a railway journey shakes and discomposes one mind and body! I grow blacker and blacker in humour as the day goes on, and when at last I am let out, and the continual oscillation ceases, and I have the fresh air about me, it is as though I were born again, and the sick fancies flee away from my mind like snows in spring [*Letters* 2: 49].

Obviously, for the ailing Stevenson to go out was not always to be able to come back. The myth of resurrection could not endure. The Master of Ballantrae might return from the dead twice, but not three times.[3]

The Sanctuary of Play and Vicarious Violence

Significantly, Stevenson's nostalgia for childhood includes more than a yearning for the expansive and supple imagination that placed him, as an Edinburgh child, in rooms "full of orange and nutmeg trees" and in "cold town gardens ... alive with parrots and with lions" (*Letters* 7: 355). It is also, it should be recognized, a longing for the vicarious violence of play. Readers often notice that Stevenson's work is replete with violence, but the connection with childhood is not made clear. On the sharp brim of the gentle lines in *A Child's Garden of Verses* sits the disorderly figure of conflict that is somehow sustaining and exhilarating: amid the soft folds of the comforting counterpane hide regiments of soldiers ("The Land of Counterpane") and across the sweet pleasantness of the meadow charge frenzied cattle, galloping destructive winds, pillaging pirates and grenadiers ("Pirate Story," "Marching Song"). When cities burn and squadrons charge ("Armies in the Fire"), there is a vitality, an edge, that seems always to have attracted Stevenson. Indeed, throughout his life the sounds of a ravaging west wind or the "horror of creeping things" (*Letters* 7: 93) stimulated him. For instance, in an 1873 letter, which Stevenson wrote to Frances Sitwell, one hears him responding buoyantly to the wild wind's rousing force:

> It is a magnificent glimmering, moonlight night, with a wild, great west wind abroad, flapping above one like an immense banner and every now and again swooping furiously against my windows. The wind is too strong perhaps, and the trees are certainly too leafless for much of that wide rustle that we both remember; there is only a sharp angry sibilant hiss, like breath drawn with the strength of the elements through shut teeth, that one hears between the gusts only [*Letters* 1: 333].

This is the wild wind that sounds again in "Windy Nights" and "The Wind" from *A Child's Garden of Verses* when the child listens to the trees "crying aloud," feels the strong wind's call pushing against him, and hears its "loud" song.

In a similar manner, murder also animated his imagination. For instance, the soft, yet violent, figure of an "undoubted assassin" doting on his sleeping children intrigued him.[4] In an 1889 letter to Sidney Colvin about the murderer, Stevenson savors the disturbing oppositions between "savagery" and propriety, the presence of the innocents and the memory of the man's violent deed:

The whites are a strange lot, many of them good kind pleasant fellows, others quite the lowest I have ever seen even in the slums of cities. I wish I had time to narrate to you the doings and character of three white murderers (more or less proven) I have met; one, the only undoubted assassin of the lot, quite gained my affection in his big home out of a wreck, with his New Hebrides wife in her savage turban of hair and yet a perfect lady, and his three adorable little girls in Rob Roy Macgregor dresses, dancing to the hand organ, performing circus on the floor with startling effects of nudity, and curling up together on a mat to sleep, three sizes, three attitudes, three Rob Roy dresses, and six little clenched fists: the murderer meanwhile brooding and gloating over his chicks, till your whole heart went out to him, and yet his crime on the face of it was dark: disembowelling in his own house, an old man of seventy and him drunk [*Letters* 6: 327–28].

When one thinks of the coupling of blazing cities, armies, and wicked shadows with the images of dimpling rivers, meadow flowers, and golden sand that quietly play within *A Child's Garden of Verses*, this later taste for violence seems not incongruous with childhood as he depicts it. It is not out of character, then, for Stevenson to write to "the little girls in the cellar"—children at a London (Kilburn) school—and dwell on the "very wild and dangerous" places in the Samoan landscape (*Letters* 7: 225). He is also quick to point out to Charles Baxter a fence "all messed with blood where a horse had come to grief" (*Letters* 7: 229), to dwell upon perilous storms at sea, and to accentuate the dangers and the mysteries of the threatening unknown with which the forest paths are fraught.

Just as he had in childhood, Stevenson undoubtedly found a certain pleasure, if not comfort, in the idea of violence because the fantasy of its aggressiveness compensated for the chronic periods of inactivity when he was ill and for those moments when he was actually strapped motionless to the bed to prevent hemorrhaging.[5] As Jerome Buckley points out, Stevenson's interest in action was an expression of his despising his own weakness.[6] Stevenson feared being passive. To be violent was to engage his surroundings—to do battle with them. Thoughts of such activity offered him a kind of sanctuary from his poor health. He liked the idea of clashing swords; therefore, during times of inactivity he would ask, "Shall we never shed blood?" (*Letters* 4: 259). And he was pleased to think back to the times he had weeded the land around his Samoan estate and partaken in a "silent battle" in which he inflicted a "slow death" upon "the contending forest" surrounding it (*Letters* 7: 27). As he had during his early years, he treasured the notion of being at sea and contending with the elements—these are the moment he relives through "Pirate Story" and "My Bed is a Boat." That possibility was preferable to watching himself slowly grow weaker. It is interesting to note that when Stevenson reflected upon his sickness, he turned to his friends and confided that he wanted to die "violently." In a letter to Sidney Colvin, he wrote: "If only I could secure a violent death, what a fine success! I wish to die in my boots; no more land of counterpane for me. To be drowned, to be shot, to be thrown from a horse—ay, to be hanged, rather than pass again through that slow dissolution" (*Letters* 7: 287).

As an adult, Stevenson obviously never fully realized this fantasy nor grew to be, as he had once dreamed, "the leader of a great horde of irregular cavalry, devastating whole valleys" (*Letters* 4: 259).[7] He had to turn to his fiction to commit such acts. The blood that runs above and below deck in *Treasure Island* and *Kidnapped*, the fighting, dueling, beatings, and murders that accentuate his stories and even his travel pieces reflect this impulse. His words sharpen under the influence of the cutlass and the terror of a "wildly beating heart" (*Treasure Island* 164). Their fury generates the rapidity of Stevenson's style and infuses a vitality that permeates his characters. David Balfour, for instance, is invigorated when he joins with Alan Breck in the protracted killing of the brig's crew. After the fighting, surrounded by broken glass and "a horrid mess of blood" (68), he feels triumphant in spite of his distress and his beginning "to sob and cry like any child" (66), for he has participated in a rite of passage that has taken him from a passive to a more vigorous relationship to his surroundings. Similarly in *The Master of Ballantrae*, the mild-mannered narrator, Mr. Mackellar, is exhilarated and transformed when he discovers that he has the ability and the desire to do harm. Although he does not actually murder the Master, he comes close enough to gain self-respect and to sense his own empowerment.[8]

Fiction was one means by which Stevenson vicariously engaged the exhilaration of the idea of violence; another was, of course, through the games of his boyhood. More than anything else, perhaps, Stevenson was nostalgic for the childhood battles he describes in *A Child's Garden of Verses* and in his letters. In October 1893, for instance, he wrote to his cousin Henrietta Milne (*née* Traquair) and longingly remembered their play: "You were sailing under the title of Princess Royal; I, after a furious contest, under that of Prince Alfred; and Willie, still a little sulky, as the Prince of Wales. We were all in a buck basket about halfway between the swing and the gate; and I can still see the Pirate Squadron heave in sight upon the weather brow." Stevenson concluded, "You were a capital fellow to play" (*Letters* 4: 189–90). It is, of course, this recollection that echoes in poems such as "Pirate Story," "Armies in the Fire," "Young Night-Thought," "The Land of Story-Books," "Marching Song," and "A Good Play" and that, for the moment, carries Stevenson back to a time when he could fully be part of the imagined skirmishes and campaigns. These games were part of his childhood garden's landscape.

Stevenson was especially nostalgic for the child's easy involvement in the fury and passionate bursts of activity—in the vicarious, yet absorbing, violence of play. Unlike the adult, the child enters the game's arena and acts out his part. His whole self is in the scene, and for a few moments he becomes the pirate or the soldier and realizes the figure's gestures. The adult, though, separated by memory, "intellect," and conscience, only partially steps in. He is not committed to its battles. Caught between the silence of a spectator and the voice of a participant, he finds no easy utterance. Stevenson focuses upon this important distinction in his essay "Child's Play":

> [T]he child, mind you, acts his parts. He does not merely repeat them to himself; he leaps, he runs, and sets the blood agog over all his body. And so his play breathes him; and he no sooner assumes a passion than he gives it vent. Alas! when we betake ourselves to our intellectual forms of play, sitting quietly by the fire or lying prone in bed, we rouse many hot feelings for which we can find no outlet [*Virginibus Puerisque* 160].

The adult, essentially, cannot act out the violence, for he performs within the obstructed gap between the character and himself; furthermore, he falls into the space between the then and the now—he cannot locate himself exclusively within the present of the game's circumference. Because he cannot help but "stir up uncomfortable and sorrowful memories, and remind" himself "sharply of old wounds" (160), it is impossible for him to exclude another time. The adult, therefore, carries the burden of reference that throttles the action and translates games into history. Consequently, when he attempts to take his part in play, he finds himself self-consciously repeating the lines rather than actively participating in the scene. He cannot break out of his twofold nature.

This dilemma offers a commentary upon the experience of nostalgia. The adult who cannot fully enter the world of play is similar to the adult who longs for the past. To be yearning for something that is absent is also to be caught in the bondage of self-consciousness and to be trapped in the double vision of Janus. Such a posture makes a history out of the present. It remembers, yet barely touches what it desires; it can never fully revitalize what it hopes to recover—one leaves the ground one longs for as soon as one touches it. Paradoxically, nostalgia is prevented from ever properly resurrecting the past because it relies on a memory that depends upon comparison and a sense of otherness. It cannot fully recover what lies there, for like the adult who attempts to play, it cannot adequately move the limbs and quicken the voices of the absent. Nostalgia, it seems, is always attended by a reference to an "other" that censors by qualifying the player's gestures and discourages by accepting no substitutes.

Even Stevenson, who continued to play war games with his stepson and who gave utterance to the child's voice in his verses, is not spared this circumstance. He understood, though, that if he wanted to recover what he desired, he had to break away from these oscillating rhythms of dualism. One way was to participate in the act or the play of writing. Writing was a vicarious means of warring against a static life. It was what was left to a person who could no longer gather his "allies" and attend to the games of childhood that codify or organize violence without inflicting harm. Writing allowed him to become the child in A Child's Garden of Verses and keep on beginning again. It permitted him to bypass duality by giving him a way of participating in the narrative's continuous present, for its sentences and characters, like the child, acted out the gestures and uttered the passions of play. As Stevenson once observed, "Fiction is to the grown man what play is to the child" (Memories and Portraits 268). His characters, therefore, never have to repeat or remember something they have once said; they belong to an elastic map; therefore, they, even in their exile, are members of a community—the community of an everlasting now that transcends the split consciousness of memory.

Stevenson's experience suggests that nostalgia defeats itself except when it goes around itself to the text and keeps the writer and the reader, for the moment, revolving in a time and a space that is always fully available and, especially in Stevenson's case, needs no otherness, not even a third-person narrator, to explicate or qualify it. The writer becomes Jim Hawkins (Treasure Island); he enters his body and his mind, and that way finds his passage. Writing is the only way home. As Hyde notices, writing keeps what was in the present. Even though he cannot return to the form of Dr. Jekyll, Mr. Hyde can still write in Jekyll's own hand—that part of his "original character" remaining to him (97). It is this original hand that leads Stevenson back into the landscape of his boyhood, into his Child's Garden of Verses.

This article first appeared in a slightly different form in Victorian Poetry, 35.3 (Fall 1997), and is reprinted with the kind permission of the author and the publisher.

NOTES

1. For recent examples of accounts of Stevenson's engagement with the games, the play, the maps and the interiors connected with his childhood, see: Ian Bell's *Dreams of Exile: Robert Louis Stevenson: A Biography* (1992); Jenni Calder's *Robert Louis Stevenson: A Life Study* (1980); and Frank McLynn's *Robert Louis Stevenson: A Biography* (1994). Other accounts may be found in: David Daiches' *Robert Louis Stevenson and His World* (1973); and James Pope Hennessy's *Robert Louis Stevenson* (1974).

2. When Stevenson traveled to America in August, 1879, he sailed on the *Devonia*, a ship carrying emigrants from Scotland, Ireland, England, Scandinavia, Germany, and Russia who "had been unable to prevail against circumstances" at home (*The Amateur Emigrant* 15).

3. In *The Master of Ballantrae*, the Master returns to his estate twice after being thought dead; the third time, however, he does not survive. In New York the Master arranged with his Indian servant, Secundra, to bury him alive and then when all is well to bring him out of his grave, but the plan does not work. With the assistance of Secundra's frantic attempts to resuscitate his body, the master revives but only briefly. The narrator describes the episode:

> Of the flight of time, I have no idea; it may have been three hours, and it may have been five, that the Indian laboured to reanimate his master's body. One thing only I know, that it was still night, and the moon was not yet set, although it had sunk low, and now barred the plateau with long shadows, when Secundra uttered a small cry of satisfaction; and, leaning swiftly forth, I thought I could myself perceive a change upon the icy countenance of the unburied. The next moment I beheld his eyelids flutter; the next they rose entirely, and the week-old corpse looked me for a moment in the face [187].

4. Stevenson met this white "assassin" when he was on tour of the Gilbert Islands on board the *Equator*.

5. One of these fantasies occurred when Stevenson gleefully represented himself as a "murderer" and impersonated "William Figg" (one of the ironic personae Stevenson used in his correspondence with friends) who in "earlier and more thoughtless years" had "been unjustly condemned for forgery, arson, stilicide, public buttery, and rape followed by murder in the person of twelve infant and flaxen-headed children of different sexes ... (Ferguson and Waingrow 113).

6. When Jerome Buckley remarks upon Stevenson's (as well as William Ernest Henley's) coveting a strength beyond his attainments, he attributes it to his being an invalid and refers to Alfred Adler's *The Neurotic Constitution* (1917) in which the psychologist discusses the antithetical nature of the invalid who despises his own weakness (58-59).

7. On 16 March 1884, Stevenson wrote to Cosmo Monkhouse:

> To confess plainly, I had intended to spend my life (or any leisure I might have from Piracy upon the high seas) as the leader of a great

horde of irregular cavalry, devastating whole valleys. I can still, looking back, see myself in many favourite attitudes; signalling for a boat from my pirate ship with a pocket-handkerchief, I at the jetty end, and one or two of my bold blades keeping the crowd at bay; or else turning in the saddle to look back at my whole command (some five thousand strong) following me at the hand-gallop up the road out of the burning valley: this last by moonlight [*Letters* 4: 259].

8. It should be pointed out that Stevenson was too much a realist and too sensitive to contradiction to overlook the fact that violence is not always so enlivening. He understood that it was possible to suffer the consequences of one's actions, to bear "the care of conscience" (Calder, *Robert Louis Stevenson: A Life Study*, 48), and to be left, isolated and diminished like Mr. Hyde and Mr. Henry. Mr. Henry's wounding of his brother in the duel, for instance, reverses rather than advances his fortunes. One moment of actively facing the enemy throws him back upon himself and entrenches him more deeply within the victim's state of compulsive passivity and guilt.

WORKS CITED

Appadurai, Arjun. "Disjunctive and Difference in the Global Cultural Economy" in *The Phantom Public Sphere*. Ed. Bruce Robbins. Minneapolis: University of Minnesota Press. 1993.

Bell, Ian. *Dreams of Exile: Robert Louis Stevenson: A Biography*. New York: Henry Holt and Company. 1992.

Booth, Bradford and Ernest Meyhew. *The Letters of Robert Louis Stevenson 1854–1890. Volumes 1–8*. New Haven: Yale University Press. 1994, 1995.

Buckley, Jerome Hamilton. *William Ernest Henley: A Study in the "Counter-Decadence" of the 'Nineties*. Princeton: Princeton University Press. 1945.

Calder, Jenni. *Robert Louis Stevenson: A Life Study*. New York: Oxford University Press. 1980.

Daiches, David. *Robert Louis Stevenson and his World*. London: Thames and Hudson. 1973.

Ferguson, DeLancey and Marshall Waingrow. Eds. *Stevenson's Letters to Charles Baxter*. New Haven: Yale University Press. 1956.

Hennessy, James Pope. *Robert Louis Stevenson*. Introd. Nigel Nicolson. London: Jonathan Cape. 1974.

McLynn, Frank. *Robert Louis Stevenson: A Biography*. New York: Random House. 1994.

Stevenson, Robert Louis. *The Amateur Emigrant*. Introd. Jonathan Raban. London: The Hogarth Press. 1984.

Stevenson, Robert Louis. *A Child's Garden of Verses*. New York: Airmont Publishing Company, Inc. 1969.

Stevenson, Robert Louis. *Dr. Jekyll and Mr. Hyde*. Toronto: Bantam Books. 1981.

Stevenson, Robert Louis. *Kidnapped*. New York: Bantam Books. 1982.

Stevenson, Robert Louis. *The Master of Ballantrae and Weir of Hermiston*. Introd. M. R. Ridley. London: Dent: Everyman's Library. 1976.

Stevenson, Robert Louis. *Memories and Portraits*. New York: Charles Scribner's Sons. 1897.

Stevenson, Robert Louis. *Treasure Island*. London: William Heinemann, Ltd. 1924.

Stevenson, Robert Louis. *Virginibus Puerisque and Other Papers*. London: Chatto & Windus. 1905.

Stewart, Susan. *On Longing: Narratives of the Miniature, the Gigantic, the Souvenir, the Collection*. Baltimore: The Johns Hopkins University Press. 1984.

Helter-Skeltery: Stevenson and Theatre

John Cairney

> Every generation has to educate another which it has brought upon the stage....
> —*Robert Louis Stevenson, "Lay Morals"*

We all invent ourselves in our own lives, but we do not always get the chance to play as cast. We are often in another play altogether and wander about the stage of our existence in the wrong costume, muttering other people's lines. We keep waiting for our cue and are afraid we might have missed it. It takes skill, perseverance, and a little luck to get ourselves right in the self-drama of personal identity. Robert Louis Stevenson managed to do it with insouciance and panache—and with a spicy ambiguity.

If his writing had its innate theatricality, his own performance was often its best source. His world was a revolving stage and it revolved around *him.* He sold the world a picture of himself as a romantic bohemian, a contrived and posturing hero-figure, and he was unafraid to act it out.[1] He had the voice for it. As his cousin and first biographer, Sir Graham Balfour, noted: "His voice was always of a surprising strength and resonance. ... It was the one gift he really possessed for the stage."[2] From when he could talk, he did so prodigiously; from when he could write, he did so continuously; and from when he could dress himself, he did so outrageously. In short, there was nothing he did that he did not do excessively and with flair. Extrovertism was a convenient personality screen, and almost as effective as the smoke from the cigarette that rarely left his right hand.

192

All this has been touched on in the countless words written about Stevenson since he whirled through his Victorian world to the delight and discomfort of his parents and many friends. However, scant notice has been given to his literal theatrical activity; that is, the writing of plays. Five full-length plays written in collaboration with others plus the fragment of another may seem a skimpy output compared to his fourteen novels, not to mention the nonstop conveyor-belt industry of essays, short stories, articles, poems, and letters which flowed from his pen from the day he could first write those famous initials. But Stevenson's dramatic work has a relevance to his total artistic development.

For the purposes of this essay, mention only will be made of his theatrical juvenilia: *The Charity Bazaar*, a privately printed, four-page folder of dialogue, which sold for half-a-crown to friends and family in 1875; *The Baneful Potato*, the reputed libretto for an opera written at Torquay in 1865; and *Monmouth—A Tragedy*, completed in 1868 with his cousin Bob Stevenson—a piece that had some fine lines in it and a good plot but which was written in the helter-skelter fashion that was to typify most of the author's theatre work.

We will concentrate instead on the three performed plays written with his close friend, William Ernest Henley: *Deacon Brodie*; *Beau Austin*; and *Admiral Guinea*. No consideration will be given to their final work, *Macaire*, as this was an adaptation of an existing melodrama and not an original dramatic collaboration. In the same way, only formal notice is given to *The Hanging Judge*, an original collaboration with his wife, Fanny. It was the last complete play in which Stevenson was involved and takes its place with the first, *Monmouth*, in being notable only for being completed.

But to begin at the beginning. Apart from Margaret Stevenson's reading to her son from the plays of Shakespeare, the first ideas of the stage came to Stevenson in the form of Mr. Skelt's Toy Theatre. A sixth birthday present from his Aunt Jane Balfour, it very soon took precedence over his favorite toy soldiers, and from then until he was sixteen it was his prime preoccupation. The drama sheets "Penny Plain and Tuppence Coloured" bought from Wilson's shop at the corner of Leith Walk and Antigua Street were his passports to his Theatre of the Imagination. In Mr. Skelt's Model Theatre for Juveniles lay the basis of his thraldom to Thalia. "What am I? What are life, art, letters, the world, but what my Skelt has made them? He stamped himself upon my immaturity...."[3] Exposure to Skelt gave him a nursery view of the world and a multi-colored, unreal view of theatre that was never to leave him. Consequently, he remained, in his own words, "no melodramatist but rather a Skelt-drunken boy."[4]

His later attempts at the drama were always at the mercy of these juvenile first impressions. Even though it was only model theatre, it was an unfortunate model. One wonders why this most diligent student of his own writing trade did not look for better dramatic models? He might have taken advantage of the stage work of Sardou rather than Skelt, Augier rather than Reddington, or even the emerging Ibsen as opposed to Pollock. As Balfour mentioned, "The theatre was always a great delight to him,"[5] and he always *thought* theatrically. In an 1894 letter to Henry James, he described his own writing technique succinctly: "I hear people talking, and I feel them acting."[6] Could anything be more precisely dramaturgical?

It was, however, in his Skelt phase, sometime during 1864, that he put down the foundations of what was to be his first performed play, *Deacon Brodie.*

> A great man in his day was the Deacon; well seen in good society, crafty with his hands as a cabinet maker, and who could sing a song with taste. Many a citizen was proud to welcome the Dean to supper, and dismissed him with regret at a timeous hour; who would have been vastly disconcerted had he known how soon, and in what guise, his visitor returned.[7]

Henry Baildon,[8] a school friend of Stevenson's at boarding school in Middlesex, attests that Stevenson read a version of a play he had written about Brodie sometime towards the end of 1864; Edmund Gosse says a complete draft of such a play did not exist until 1869, which accords with Stevenson's own recollection. He told an American interviewer in 1887, when the play was touring in the United States:

> When I was about nineteen years of age, I wrote a sort of hugger-mugger melodrama, which lay in my coffer until it was fished out by my friend, W.E. Henley.[9]

Stevenson had first met Henley in February 1875, when, with the editor Leslie Stephen, who had published both writers in his *Cornhill* magazine, he visited the Englishman in the Edinburgh Royal Infirmary. Afterwards, he brought up some books from Heriot Row for the patient, assuring Stephen that "I shall try to be of use to him."[10] Soon he was visiting Henley regularly, taking up an armchair from Heriot Row for his greater comfort. Henley had come to Edinburgh from Gloucester in 1873 to seek Dr. Joseph Lister's help in saving his one leg from amputation, having lost the other in boyhood to gangrene after tuberculosis. A formidable autodidact, he had taught himself four languages while bedridden and now did literary work from the ward, as well as translations for the *Encyclopaedia Britannica.*

Louis was overwhelmed by the big, burly, red-bearded, loud-talking, loud-laughing *literateur* and his polymathic larger-than-life personality. Talker had met talker, writer had met writer, dreamer had met dreamer, and from their long, lively discussions emerged the idea that they should write a play together for Sir Henry Irving and make their mutual fortunes. Irving had enjoyed a great success at the Lyceum in London in 1871 as Mathias in *The Bells*, a melodrama, which Henley had seen. Stevenson, too, had seen Irving as Hamlet in 1874 but had not been impressed ("interesting ... but not good").[11] He much preferred Salvini's Macbeth of 1876 in Edinburgh ("I revere Salvini...").[12] The two young men were sure they could write as good a play as *The Bells* for England's actor of the day.

It was 1878 before Henley, now married to Anna Boyle from Edinburgh, "fished out" the early Brodie draft at Swanston Cottage, and what had been Stevenson's baby soon became Henley's adopted child. When the Henleys moved down to Shepherd's Bush in the same year, William continued to badger Louis about the project. Draft after draft was churned out at the Savile Club as Henley vigorously pumped the bellows to raise the Stevenson spark. After much debate and disagreement, the two writers returned to Edinburgh and completed *Deacon Brodie, or The Double Life* at Swanston at the end of January 1879. It was immediately submitted to mentors Fleeming Jenkin and Sidney Colvin for opinion. Neither liked it. "This play business is *ignis fatuus*," said Jenkin.[13] "Remember," Colvin commented, "a play is emotion as a statue is marble,"[14] but he agreed to send it on to Irving. On 6 February, he wrote to Henley: "Nothing can be got out of ... Irving."[15] *Deacon Brodie* was aborted.

In order to protect their copyright, the play registered in 1880 by W. E. Henley and R.L. Stevenson had to be produced on stage. Henley undertook to see this accomplished. In the meantime, Stevenson suddenly decamped to California to write *The Amateur Emigrant* and find another kind of partner in Fanny Vandegrift Osbourne. Henley came to St. Pancras to see him off, convinced that he would never see "his Lewis" again. In a sense, he never did. He always believed that *his* Stevenson went off to America and that another one came back.

William Ernest Henley was not only the *alpha* and *omega* of Stevenson's playwriting time; he was, next to Bob Stevenson, and to a certain extent Charles Baxter, the closest male friend Stevenson was ever to have. There was only a year in age between them, but notwithstanding, Henley was to become mentor, critic, agent, manager, and play-partner to Stevenson—and, it must be said, something of a thorn in his flesh as well. But Henley genuinely loved Lewis, as he always called Stevenson, or at least, his own version of him.

Despite his fine mind, wide reading, critical acuity, and gift for verse-portraiture, William Ernest Henley also had the singular disadvantage of being himself. He was his own worst enemy. Even if he had lost Stevenson to matrimony, he was still determined on *Deacon Brodie* and pestered his friend continually about further ideas on the project. Stevenson replied from San Francisco: "I shall make you a full scenario as soon as the *Emigrant* is done. ... When may I hope to see the *Deacon*? ... I pine for the *Deacon*."[16] No doubt due to Henley's contacts in the English provinces, *Deacon Brodie* made its much-delayed debut on stage at Bradford. It was presented by The Haldane Crichton Company at Pullen's Theatre of Varieties on Thursday, 21 December 1882. Billed as "the new Scotch national drama," it had a brief tour around the North of England and travelled in Scotland as far as Her Majesty's Theatre, Aberdeen, but as Graham Balfour remembered, "It played some forty times without any marked success."[17]

The Stevensons by this time were in the South of France. It was while at San Marcel that Louis heard that the piece had been "hissed off the stage at Bradford."[18] This rather blunted his initial enthusiasm. On 2 January 1883, the Edinburgh *Courant* reported:

> The appearance of Mr. Robert Louis Stevenson as a dramatist cannot fail to be interesting to the admirers of that pleasing and very original writer. His play, written in collaboration with Mr. W.E. Henley, and produced, if we mistake not, at Bradford the other day, bears the title *Deacon Brodie, or the Double Life* and is founded on a well-known Edinburgh tradition. ... The play, which has been privately printed, will probably find its way to the London stage.

Which was why the *People* newspaper was interested and announced on 21 January:

> As a joint production of two young writers, who now turn for the first time their attention to the stage, and one of whom has already established himself as one of the first humorists [*sic*] and most picturesque essayists of the day, *Deacon Brodie* has strong claims upon our attention. ... Its chief feature is its psychology. In the hands of an excellent actor, the character of Deacon Brodie ... should be eminently effective.

Unfortunately, the eponymous role was played by Edward Henley, William's youngest brother, who, while a promising cadet actor, was not by any means a great one, although what he lacked in experience he more than made up for in self-confidence. Stevenson was happy to accept Henley's view of his brother's efforts in the part: "I was delighted to hear the good news about Teddy. Bravo, he goes up the hill fast. Let him beware of vanity and he will go higher."[19] However, when Henley asked him to redraft the script yet again, he responded tersely: "The Deacon can't be tackled until my health and head are re-instated."[20] There followed here what might be called a break between scenes, during which the partners discussed other possible dramatic projects.

In *My First Book,* Stevenson refers to the numerous play ideas that came to nothing—reams of paper that were given over to stage projects. Roger Swearingen, in *The Prose Writings of Robert Louis Stevenson* (1980), lists half a page of titles discussed and worked on and rejected by the writers in this time; he also mentions the eleven titles listed by Stevenson himself during Professor Tait's lecture on Natural Philosophy in Stevenson's first year at Old College.[21] These were the plays he intended to write one day—and never did.

It is clear that throughout the Henley years (1875–87), the stage was being cleared for Stevenson if he wanted it enough. To this end, in 1878, Henley had been going through Stevenson's student play-titles, and wrote:

> The second act of *Rogue Denzil's Death* or *Word from Cromwell* or *Hester Noble's Mistake* or whatever it's called, was made yesterday afternoon. It is the funniest act in dramatic literature. "Whaur's Wullie Shakespeare noo?" as they say in Kirkcubright![22]

Louis was now firmly engaged with Buffalo Will, as Fanny called him (he referred to her as the "Bedlamite"), but even she was drawn into Henley's enthusiastic sphere. In 1881, she added a scribbled pencil postscript to a Stevenson letter to his associate:

> My Dear Friend—Do keep your eagle eye upon the stage where I am convinced a gold mine shows out. Something that you and I and Louis may work to our great advantage. A gold mine is so very necessary for us all and you'll find it nowhere else. With brim purses, think what we could do, and the freedom that a little money gives, think what it would do for your wife, to say nothing of Louis's wife who is greedy of gold.[23]

From such unlikely addresses as Braemar and Strathpeffer, while giving main attention to things like *The Sea Cook*, which eventually became *Treasure Island*, Stevenson still made time to write to Henley on play matters. His letters in this phase were playful, to say the least; more Joycean than Stevensonian, and of full of in-jokes, fictitious dialogue, nonsense, and nonsensical ideas such as adapting Dickens's *Great Expectations* for the stage with Magwitch as Pip's father. "I say there's a play as strong as Hell in that," he insisted.[24]

Yet, at the same time, even after receiving, thanks to Henley's efforts, "a hundred, jingling, gold-minted quid" for *Treasure Island*, he could, in the next breath, say, "Shall I ever have enough money to write a play...? O, dire necessity."[25] Dire necessity was something Robert Louis Stevenson was never to know, but it was Henley's live-in companion. Born poor, he had poverty constantly thrust upon him. He knew that to achieve any kind of riches he had to try for a commercial play. It was his only chance to "get stuff on the nail," as he would say, or "rake in the posh." (Henley was an expert on slang.) Stevenson quickly reassured him:

> The required play is in *The Merry Men*. ... I thus render honour to your *flair*: it came upon me in a clap. ... "Help!" cries a buried masterpiece. ... Once I see my way to the year's end clear, I turn to plays. ... I'm morally sure there's a play in *Otto*.[26]

He was obviously still in a theatrical frame of mind.

While Henley moved up and down Grub Street, flitting in an out of various editorial chairs, Stevenson meandered between Switzerland and the South of France trying to keep up with Fanny's mania for moving house and to resist a tendency to cough up blood. In the early summer of 1884, he paid for Henley to come out to see him. "Burly" arrived with Charles Baxter. It was a combustible combination as both were both formidable and well-trained drinkers. Their spree almost killed their host, and when Stevenson hemorrhaged again, Fanny sent the trio packing, especially Henley, and the curtain came down on a much-needed interval.

But only briefly. Edward Henley had meantime come into a small bequest from an uncle, and he proposed to spend it on a special matinee performance of *Deacon Brodie* in London. A date was set for July 2, the place was the Mr. Gooch's Princes Theatre and curtain up was to be at 2:30 P.M. Social London was agog, and anyone who was anybody was there. The only absentee was Stevenson himself. On that day, he was prone in lodgings at Richmond suffering from the effects of the journey from France. It was a pity. He might have learned much.

The reviews weren't exactly ecstatic, even if none was totally damning. By this time it had really become Henley's play, as Stevenson readily admitted. Henley reacted with typical optimism, writing to Austin Dobson: "The play went brilliantly but the critics have scorned it to a man."[27] Henry James, the only friend who had any real theatre experience, said nothing. It was comment enough. Stevenson, however, assured Henley that he would

> spend three or five or seven hot days upon that Deacon's body.... Also this, if the "cause of art" requires this perpetual skating of bugs, damn art. Let the bugs be.... Look here, I'm a bug; Teddy is, as yet, a bug; you're a bug—ay, though the author of the Deacon. If ruddy, truculent people were to make it their business to beetle us in print, and to card us in private circles—I daresay art would profit—but you and I and Teddy would have a bloody good time.[28]

They never did work on it again. Stevenson described the *Deacon* to Colvin as "damned bad."[29]

The gold mine would seem to have been worked out. Stevenson wrote to Henley:

> I have thought as well as I could of what you said; and I have come unhesitatingly to the opinion that the stage is only a lottery, must not be regarded as a trade, and must never be preferred to drudgery. If money comes from any play, let us regard it as a legacy, but never count upon it as our income for the year. In other words, I must go on and drudge at Kidnapped, which I hate, and am unfit to do; and you will have to get some journalism somehow. [30]

The two partners met, and Henley reported:

> We (Lewis and I) have talked the thing over—reconstruction and all; & I can see my way to make a play of it. But frankly, I don't think we shall ever get to work on the thing again; nor for that matter on anything else. The match is no longer equal. Lewis has grown faster than I have.[31]

In something of an embarrassed silence, the curtain came down on *Deacon Brodie*.

Even though *Treasure Island* (1883), *A Child's Garden of Verses* (1885), *Jekyll and Hyde* (1886), and *Kidnapped* (1886) would be among the meaningful things written in the playwriting period along with other stories and articles, *Deacon Brodie* still bobbed about like a cork in the backwash of both men's respective literary activities. It just refused to sink, despite having been torpedoed twice. The reason was it was not a totally bad play. The writers were too good to make it entirely uninteresting, but neither was technically good enough to make it work as theatre.

The other thing was—but tell it not in Gath—the collaborators were all wrong for each other. Had they worked with other collaborators, or even better still, alone, results might have been better. But they never saw things through the same eyes. This was obvious as soon as the Deacon was adopted by Henley. It became a different play immediately; not necessarily a better or a worse play, but a different play—and there was the rub. Evidence of Henley's heavy hand is apparent in the way the revised version looks back to the transpontine dramas of the old Surrey and Coburg playhouses rather than to the new theatre of the day. Its chief demerit is that it was a Scottish play with a Scottish subject adapted by an Englishman for an English audience—or rather for an English actor, Henry Irving.

Whatever the reason, the shift lost the work a vital dynamic. Rich, rough language was ironed out in favor of a city-slickness that owed more to Covent Garden than the Grassmarket. This is the difference between real dialogue and theatrical patter. Stage talk must have its roots at least in a recognizable reality or it becomes trivialized in mere gags or tricks. Stevenson originally had something of the close, narrow Edinburgh world of upstairs and downstairs, high life and low, nighttime and daytime; the character of Brodie straddled both segments with ease. Like Stevenson, he had the voice and style for each environment.

This is shown in Stevenson's *idée fixe,* the duality inherent in Scottish character, or, to be candid, the hypocrisy. This is fundamental to any understanding of Brodie's Edinburgh background. He was a man with two voices because he had two lives—one for day and another for night. His dialogue originally reflected this, but it was gradually buried under the weight of rewrites by Henley. For instance, this was Stevenson: "I was aince a lad mysel', an' I ken fine by the glint o' an e'e when a lad's fain an' a lassie's willing." Much was lost in the translation of the play's essential Scottishness. Stevenson's natural quirkiness would have been invaluable, but all was smoothed out in a bland innocuousness relieved only by slang, in which Henley was strong.

> We don't call it "smuggled" in the trade; it's a wink and a King George's picture between us ... too flash in the feather, that's the rig; what you drop on the square you pick up again on the cross.

There are two voices at work, and they are not always in harmony. Also, the soliloquies didn't hold because we don't know enough about the persons speaking, which is proof again of hurry. More time should have been taken to tell the audience who people were and where they came from. Audiences need the information if they are to ascribe motives to the characters and understand where those characters are going. In this case, it was nowhere.

The use of the aside was outdated and wasted valuable action time. Too many dramatic possibilities in the relationships were only hinted at and not carried through. Even the *denouement* was rushed, and the revised Brodie kills himself (instead of being killed trying to escape) as if he, too, is glad to get it all over with. But the real truth is that Deacon Brodie did not die of his own hand but of rewrites and improvements.

It is all very irritating. There are so many signals throughout the text of what might have been. It is an excellent basic story, which ought to have been told simply in stage terms and not in those of the picaresque novel. A play script is not a work of literature to be read; it is a dramatic blueprint to be acted upon.

The play was Stevenson's, not Henley's, despite his increasing authorial stamp. The setting was Stevenson's own city, Edinburgh, and the character of Brodie was something the Scot had understood instinctively since boyhood. Why did he let the play slip from his fingers into Henley's? He said elsewhere that he had got his fingers caught in the Vandegrift steam press.[32] The other hand, one might say, was caught in the Henley steamroller. Had he been able to pull himself free he might have managed to get the play down as he had first seen it and not through Henley's eyes.

Stevenson adopted a smiling tolerance for Henley's blustering ways, though he still sought in the plays

> the bird-haunted evocation of life's fluctuations ... containing both laughter and tears ... transcending the rigidity of inescapable logic. ... If we are merely the star's tennis balls—we can at least enjoy the game.[33]

He had no wish to be another Zola. He was always in pursuit of the "*eldorado* of romantic comedy."[34] Henley, on the other hand, and not surprisingly perhaps, saw everything in terms of a rigid reality. The problem was in trying to reconcile two very different points of view. The truth was that the two writing friends cancelled each other out. Unfortunately, instead of working to support each other's strengths, they played to their respective weaknesses. From his reading, Henley knew the work of playwrights

Eugene Scribe as well as the work of English stage professionals like Tom Taylor and G.R. Sim, but he knew them only in theory. His approach was intellectual; he had no dramatic instinct. Stevenson, on the other hand, was totally instinctual, but had no practical experience of play *construction*.

And it was to be the same at Bournemouth. It was a lovely autumn in 1884, and Fanny's son, Lloyd Osbourne, remembered that

> Henley came—a great, glowing, massive-shouldered fellow with a big, red beard and a crutch; jovial, astoundingly clever, and with a laugh that rolled out like music ... and he had come to make us all rich![35]

His mother had a rather different reaction. Fanny had always a more considered view retrospectively, but from time to time she had a point:

> My husband had no particular liking for dramatic production though *Prince Otto* was first outlined as a play; but Mr. Henley possessed an extraordinary facility for infecting others with his enthusiasm.... The plays were invented and written in the fervid, boisterous fashion of Mr. Henley, whose influence predominated. ... It is possible that either, alone, might have been successful, but together they were too much at cross purposes.[36]

In two years between the three addresses Stevenson had in that town during 1884 and 1885, a lot of whisky was drunk, mostly by Henley, a lot of laughs were had, a lot of talking ensued but two full-length plays were written, and an adaptation completed for a professional management. It was a fine frenzy altogether.

Beau Austin and *Admiral Guinea* were virtually created in tandem, although the Admiral was given precedence in publication. Of the two, *Beau Austin* is the better piece and has claim to be the best of their plays. At least, Henry James thought so. It received some excellent notices from discerning critics when Sir Herbert Tree presented it as part of a special matinee season at the Haymarket Theatre, London, on 3 November 1890. Once again it was a social event, and almost a theatre one. William Archer, who was to become a great friend and admirer of both Stevenson and Henley, wrote in *The World* on 12 November 1890: "The production of *Beau Austin* showed triumphantly that the aroma of literature can be brought over the footlights with stimulating and exhilarating effect." Tree staged the piece sumptuously and tailored the script somewhat to suit his own style. As a talker himself, he would have appreciated the quality of some of the dialogue, such as when Menteith, the valet, remarks, "I put a second curl on Mr. George's hair on purpose." Or when Barbara, the maid, says, "When Menteith took me to the play, he talked so much I couldn't hear Mr. Kean."

The play was also presented as "an odd, pretty thing"[37] by Sir Nigel Playfair in London in 1929. The phrase sums up the light, frothy, tongue-in-cheek piece, which deals with the conquest by an aging rake of a virtuous young heroine in light, frothy, tongue-in-cheek language. As actors know, this is the hardest style to play in a theatre, but no less a theatrical authority than actor-playwright-director Harley Granville-Barker considered that *Beau Austin* should be a staple of the National Theatre whenever it came to pass. Lloyd Osbourne noted of RLS that he had "lost not only the last flicker of his youth at "Wensleydale," but also, I believe, any conviction that he might become a popular dramatist."[38] It was true that Stevenson was beginning to tire of the whole play idea, but Henley would not hear of such a thing. *Beau Austin* was dead—long live *Admiral Guinea!* Everyone was summoned into the play circle, even Fanny, who was still quarrying for gold. To her mind, the rumbustious Henley was a small price to pay for theatrical treasure. What must be recognized, however, is that she was then as keen on the plays as Henley was.

In August 1881, Stevenson was three chapters into *Treasure Island* at Braemar Cottage when he stole Blind Pew from Henley's original play line for what was to become *Admiral Guinea*. In August 1884, Pew was to reemerge as the star part in the play completed by both at Bournemouth in the same euphoric burst that produced *Beau Austin*, but hardly with the same results—at least as far as Stevenson was concerned. In March 1885, writing to Henley as it were in the light of the morning after, he said:

> The re-perusal of the *Admiral*, by the way, was a sore blow; eh, God man, it is a low, black, dirty blackguard, ragged piece; vomitable in many parts—simply vomitable.[39]

Admiral Guinea was not performed in Stevenson's lifetime, but it had its admirers, not the least of whom was George Bernard Shaw, who steadfastly held the opinion that Stevenson and Henley were dramatists ahead of their time, not behind it; the term he used for them in the *Saturday Night Review* was "impossibilists."[40] William Archer presented the first performance at the New Century Theatre (now the Playhouse) on 29 November 1900 for a week, but by the time of its opening, Henley had his pen in so many inkwells that he didn't have time to write a prologue for the piece. Archer got his prologue in the end, but it was a half-hearted offering at best. Henley wrote to Charles Whitby, a friend: "I've scribbled a kind of Prologue for the Admiral, which comes off next Monday. Archer's enthusiastic about it. But I've no illusions left."[41] The fact was, with Stevenson gone, he really had no heart for it. "The whole thing's a flam," he said. "That and no more. And I believe not Dryden, nor RLS himself could rise to it."[42] The irony was that Henley was a better poet than RLS, if not a Dryden, but Stevenson was the better dramatist, if not a Zola. It was all crossed wires in the end. The real truth was he had no "Lewis," and it was not the same without him.

Henley did not attend the premiere, as he did not wish to take the author's bow without RLS to share it. As it happened, there were no calls for the author. The best notices were reserved for Miss Elizabeth Robins, an American actress, who spoke the Prologue. Henley did see it again, in the first week of January 1898, and he reported to Whitby:

> The *Admiral* held me—and held the house—with a grip of iron … the house was gripped … I remain of my old persuasion. Give us an actor of genius, and there you are. For myself, a last word. "Here" (Act III) says I to myself, "here's the best English since the big Elizabethans. English better than Congreve's—because it's emotional." And by God, I believe I'm right.[43]

The irony is, he almost was. As always with their work, there were really good things in the play.

A scene in the fourth act presents the Admiral sleepwalking with a candle, when Blind Pew enters upon him. It is a superb conceit—a blind man trying to kill a man who is walking in his sleep. The meeting made compelling theatre and Pew's soliloquy is stunning in its rhythms and cadences. Well-acted, the scene is quite chilling in effect, even to read, but one scene in twenty-four does not make a play. The sleepwalking scene stands out because it is surrounded on either side by Skeltery of the most blatant kind, as if the authors were taking short-cuts across the field of narrative. Pew is the real hero of the piece, but typically, he is killed off too early, and the play dies with him. The play went into production with the Glasgow Repertory Theatre in 1909 (in repertory with Ibsen's *Enemy of the People*), but it has not been produced since. It has, however, received many broadcasts on the BBC over the years, so something lingers.

Stevenson himself has the last word on *Admiral Guinea*. When the published plays arrived at Vailima in 1893, he stated quite categorically that he thought "*A.G.* the very best of the crowd."[44] However, in 1885, Stevenson and Henley were not quite finished. They met for the last time in the spring of that year for their ultimate collaboration—to adapt the old French melodrama *Macaire* for Tree. They did it in their usual rush and delivered it. Nothing happened. Stevenson was as realistic as ever and summed up their final work as "a piece of job work, hurriedly bockled; it might have been worse; it might have been better."[45] It was given a single performance at the Strand Theatre, London, in 1900 and was subsequently performed at His Majesty's in a pairing with *Beau Austin* in 1901. When Irving played Macaire in 1888, he chose to do it in the old version rather than in what Shaw called "a new and vital" Stevenson-Henley adaptation.[46] It was the final insult. It was time to "shut up the box and the puppets." Their play had indeed been "played out."

In the spring of 1885, they both knew then that the great pretense was over and that there was no gold to be got after all. And, although neither man would admit it, a great friendship, even a great love, was lost among the pine trees of Branksome Park. Stevenson had never liked Bournemouth, and he liked it even less now. He returned to his writing and was sufficiently inspired by another cabinet—this time encountered in a dream—to write, not a play, but a book, a "shilling shocker" that would make him rich enough to satisfy even Fanny's dreams of gold. It was now a time for resipiscence.

Stevenson toyed with the idea of working with Thomas Hardy on a theatrical adaptation of that author's *Mayor of Casterbridge*, as he might have toyed with James Barrie or Henry James to make a play of their novels, but none of these schemes came to anything. Both Barrie and James went on to make highly successful plays of their own, so Stevenson's instinct was right. But he had only "toyed" with the idea. Perhaps that was the trouble—theatre was merely a toy thing, and now it had been thrown into the corner along with the toy soldiers. Was poor old Henley thrown into the corner too? He went back to his journalism, his "shot-rubbish" as he called it, but he never really recovered from the failure of the plays. He lost much of his *élan* when he lost *his* Lewis Stevenson.

Their acquaintance went into 1887, a shrivelled figure of its former self, cold now, and distant, mistakes, and misunderstandings having done their mischief. The two now turned away, not only from their joint efforts but also from each other, and left the stage by their respective exits. Stevenson went first: "If I can only get off the stage with clean hands, I shall sing Hosanna."[47] Henley followed, and he was to say of Stevenson: "No better histrion ever lived."[48] In the same article, he ends by finally admitting that, about plays, "I and Lewis knew nothing."

The irony is that within a year of their parting, glasses were to be raised to toast Richard Mansfield's huge success in T.R. Sullivan's adaptation of *Dr. Jekyll and Mr. Hyde* in Boston and New York in 1887. This was the only time Stevenson made any money from theatre. Mansfield was proof of the value of a good leading actor to any production. Irving might have done the same for *Deacon Brodie*, as Henley had always said. Yet before the year was out, this play, too, became part of the American postlude in the rather unsteady hands of the volatile younger brother Edward John Henley. In true Henley fashion, this sometimes engaging but feckless actor alienated audiences, cast, and management all along the way throughout a tour that ought to have been a success but ended in a barroom brawl in Philadelphia. So the saga of the Stevenson-Henley plays ended, not with glasses raised, but with the shatter of broken bottles.

The paradox of theatre is that it is truth revealed in a lie. The tragedy for Stevenson and theatre was that he leaned towards a kind of stage pretense that was never true to itself and was therefore unacceptable to an audience. Theatre is artifice, but plays themselves are not artificial. Neither Stevenson nor Henley ever learned this, and the good lie stayed on their lips. Stevenson always regretted it. As he said:

> To me it is, and must ever be, a dream unrealised, a book unwritten. O, my sighings after romance, or even Skeltery. ... And, O, the weary age that will produce me neither.[49]

NOTES

1. Quoted by Professor Ian A. Gordon. *St. James Guide to Biography* (1991), p. 42.

2. Sir Graham Balfour, *Life of Robert Louis Stevenson* (Methuen, 1901), p. 270.

3. *Memories and Portraits* (Chatto and Windus, 1904) "Penny Plain and Tuppence Coloured," p. 132.

4. Balfour, (12th edition), p. 39.

5. Ibid., p. 98.

6. *Letters*, Tusitala Edition (1924), Vol. V. p. 96.

7. In an interview with the New York *Herald* in 1887 he explained the genesis of *Dr. Jekyll and Mr. Hyde:* "All I dreamed about Dr. Jekyll was that one man was being pressed into a cabinet, when he swallowed and drug and changed into another being. I awoke and said at once that I had found the missing link for which I had been looking so long, and before I again went to sleep almost every detail of the story, as it stands, was clear to me. Of course, writing it was another thing." Of course, a cabinet was also the initial inspiration for *Deacon Brodie* as the cabinet in Stevenson's room at Heriot Row was reputed to have been made by the cat-burglar who was also a noted carpenter. In fact, he designed and made the gallows on which he was hanged in 1788.

8. Henry Belyse Baildon was a school-fellow of Stevenson's at Mr. Wyatt's Burlington Academy, Spring Grove, Middlesex, during 1864 and wrote *Robert*

Louis Stevenson: A Life Study in Criticism (Chatto and Windus, 1901), in which Stevenson recounted to Baildon the outline and early version of the play *Deacon Brodie*.

9. See Note 7 above for same interview.

10. *Letters*, Methuen (1911) Vol. I, p. 180.

11. Balfour, (12th Edition), p. 98.

12. *Letters*, Methuen (1911), Vol. 4, 229.

13. James Pope-Hennessy, *Robert Louis Stevenson* (1974), p. 116.

14. Irving S. Saposnik, *Robert Louis Stevenson* (1974), p. 37.

15. H.V. Lucas, *The Colvins and their Friends* (1928) reported by Swearingen, p. 37. Beineke 4338.

16. *Letters*, Methuen (1911) Vol. I, p. 271.

17. Balfour, (1901) Vol. 2, p. 2.

18. *Letters*, Tusitala (1924) Vol. II, p. 219.

19. *Letters*, Methuen (1911) Vol. I, p. 122. Also National Library of Scotland Letter No. 146. Edward John Henley (1861–98) was the youngest Henley brother of four and began acting in Middlesborough in melodrama before touring with George Fox. At nineteen, he made a great success in *The Critic* at the Gaiety in London and great things were expected from him. However, his unstable temperament worked against his obvious talent and he fell foul of Irving—which was not the best way to further his career. He followed the singer Mary Hampton to New York, where he married her and both returned to London when Teddy was engaged by his brother for *Deacon Brodie*. He was too young and too inexperienced to lead a company and his behavior increasingly hampered both his career and personal life. He married again but his health failed and he died young, having thrown away what might have been a useful theatrical career.

20. National Library of Scotland Letter No. 29.

21. The plays (listed in Swearingen , page 5) were as follows: "Edward Ferren" (3-act tragedy) (Sometimes listed as "Darren"); "Edward Bolton" or "The Last Will" (5-act comedy); "Ananais Proudfoot, Baker and Elder" (3-act comedy); "The Witch" (5-act tragedy); "A Poor Heart" or "The King's Pardon" (5-act tragedy); "The Brothers" (3-act comedy); "Charlie is my Darling" (3-act tragedy); "Francis Nesham" (5-act tragedy); "The Point of Honour" / A Partie Quaree on the Bass (3-act comedy); "The Duke's Jester" (5-act tragedy); and "The Sweet Singer" (5-act tragedy).

There was enough dramatic material in this catalogue to stimulate any playwright but somehow, due to circumstances or lack of decision, or natural dilletantism, or to some delay, little was ever finished. There was always something to deter or distract, and Stevenson was easily distracted. Henley also made an extensive list for the partners to work on, some of which overlapped with Stevenson's titles. For a full list of Henley titles, see Roger G. Swearingen, *The Prose Writings of Robert Louis Stevenson: A Guide* (1980), p. 91.

22. Ibid.

23. N.L.S. Letter No. 37.

24. N.L.S. Letter No. 128.

25. *Letters*, Methuen (1911) Vol. 2, p. 17.

26. *Letters*, Methuen (1911) Vol. 1, pp. 120–121.

27. John Connell, *W.E. Henley* (1972) p. 102.

28. N.L.S. Letter No 37.

29. *Letters*, Methuen (1911) Vol. 2, p. 188.

30. *Letters*, Tusitala (1924) Vol. 3, p. 44.

31. Saposnik, Notes, No. 10, p. 142.

32. Around December 1892, Stevenson had confided to Henley: "I got my little finger into a steam press called the 'Vandergrifter' and my whole body and soul had to go in after it. I came out as limp as a lady's novel."

33. Saposnik, p. 39.

34. Lloyd Osbourne, *Stevenson at Thirty-Five*, Tusitala, Vol. V.

35. Saposnik, p. 36.

36. *Stevenson at Thirty-Five (Intimate Portrait of RLS)* Introduction, pp. 56–57.

37. Kennedy Williamson, *W.E. Henley* (1930), p. 87.

38. *Stevenson at Thirty-Five.*

39. *Letters*, Methuen (1911), p. 235.

40. *Saturday Review* (November 1890).

41. Connell, p. 325.

42. Ibid.

43. Ibid.

44. N.L.S. Letter No. 291.

45. *Letters*, Methuen, Vol. 2, p. 236.

46. *Saturday Review* (November 1890).

47. *Letters*, Methuen, Vol. 3, p. 227.

48. *Pall Mall Gazette* (December 1901).

49. *Letters*, Methuen, Vol. 2, p. 201.

Prayers at Sunset

Barry Menikoff

Robert Louis Stevenson was the most versatile writer of his generation. Not only did he publish in every genre but he experimented with
them as well. *New Arabian Nights* was the model for the modern short
story. *Travels with a Donkey* and *Virginibus Puerisque* dusted off the travel
book and gave new life to the familiar essay. As for *Treasure Island* and
A Child's Garden of Verses, these defined the imagination of children
while refusing to remain confined to children. And the list continues:
*Underwoods, The Master of Ballantrae, The Amateur Emigrant, Weir of
Hermiston*, this last the tragic novel he had been composing when he was
struck with a brain hemorrhage at his home on the morning of December third.

Stevenson, born in 1850, had just celebrated his forty-fourth birthday a month earlier. He well knew the Greek saying, whom the gods love
dies young, but however old, that is a saying of the living, of those who
mourn and venerate at the same time. Stevenson, although young, need
not have been mourned. Through sheer force of will and an indomitable
discipline, he had compressed a lifetime of thought into a body of work
that was one of the marvels of late nineteenth century literature. Like the
dying novelist in his good friend Henry James's story "The Middle Years,"
Stevenson knew that he had reached his maturity, and had no need for a
second chance. That maturity was visible, even audible, in everything he
wrote during those last years in Samoa, his "final phase," as James later
called it. It was in the engrossing "Vailima" letters he compiled and sent
to Sidney Colvin every month. It was in the complex beauty of the South
Seas he evoked so hauntingly in *The Beach of Falesá*. And it was scored in

209

the elegiac coda to *Kidnapped* that he finished a year before his death, the magnificent *David Balfour*.

Those last years were rich with life as well as literature. The bounty of new sensory experiences that he discovered in the Pacific was matched only by the good health he found there. One of the great travelers of his era, he now had good cause to give over travel: the endless pleasures of a brave new world, and a renewed sense of well being. For all intents and purposes he had found his place on an island in the Pacific, and this years after writing those lines that now read as if they were a foretelling of his destiny: "Under the wide and starry sky, / Dig the grave and let me lie." But what of the *Prayers* that Stevenson delivered at Vailima ("O my beautiful, shining, windy house") and were only published after his death? How can these petitions to God be reconciled with the cosmopolitan writer's documented rebellion against the faith of his father?

Quite simply, Stevenson was always able to sustain contradictory ideas, indeed, his most profound tenet insisted upon the paradox that beneficence and cruelty can coexist in the same person. It was he, after all, who divided the talented Dr. Henry Jekyll into the vengeful Edward Hyde. For Stevenson was as much a son of Charles Darwin as he was of John Knox, the great Scottish theologian, and in late essays like "Aes Triplex" and "Pulvis et Umbra" he explored the matter of faith in an age of evolutionary biology. We live, he said, "in our isle of terror and under the imminent hand of death," an image so strikingly modern that one might easily attribute it to a writer like Albert Camus.

But it is one thing to raise the problem of belief in a formal-colloquial essay (again, Stevenson's ability to balance contradictory elements) and quite another to pose those questions in a series of prayers. For prayers, however occasional, assume a God, or god, who can hear and even possibly grant the petitioner's requests. So what is Stevenson doing? Is he invoking the God of his father's faith and asking for the intercession of Jesus Christ for the salvation of his family and his friends? Or is he employing a traditional language and drawing upon a common culture to offer his own view of how to live in the world? Since Stevenson did not believe Christian doctrine it would be easy to say he was simply "using" it, which is what Fanny Stevenson implies in her recollection of the context in which these prayers were composed and delivered. But why would a writer use a language, not to mention a form, that he disbelieved?

At a certain point the language itself, and its representation, becomes the belief. One of the most vivid qualities of these prayers is their invocation of biblical rhythms and biblical language, particularly the *Psalms*, which Stevenson frequently drew upon in his writing. The object was not to imitate the King James Bible but to evoke the sense of awe and importunity associated with its intense spirituality and great literary beauty. The occasions for the prayers were often ordinary, a word offered on the time of day, or the rain (perhaps only a Scot could be so preoccupied with rain), or a friend's departure. Yet the meaning that Stevenson teased out of these occasions could be quite extraordinary.

In "At Morning," a prayer of three sentences, he draws upon Shakespeare and opens up the whole matter of life's incessant routine and daily trivialities. The echo of Macbeth's great soliloquy ("Tomorrow, and tomorrow, and tomorrow") is carried in a single word in the first sentence: "The day returns and brings us the petty round of irritating concerns and duties." Stevenson adopts Shakespeare's image of life as a stage actor and asks for "help" so that we too can "play" the role that has been assigned us, and at the end of the day enjoy the "gift of sleep." That final phrase also recalls *Macbeth* ("Sleep that knits up the ravelled sleeve of care") and reiterates a motif in these prayers for *rest* and *peace* and *quiet*, among the most precious rewards for the day's work, and life's cares. Stevenson had not forgotten his early reading of Swinburne: "I am weary of days and hours ... And everything but sleep."

Although Stevenson's *Prayers* were spurred by occasional concerns (some of his best poetry falls into the category of occasional verse), they are anything but occasional in their representation of his thought. Through them runs the central belief that all men are sinners ("We are evil, O God"). If this sounds harsh, it is so designed. In a very brief compass Stevenson compresses a fundamentally orthodox view of man—that he is an *offender*, *vain* and *egoistic*, that he has *weaknesses*, *deficiencies*, and *frailties*. Yet still he has the capacity to strive for good, or at least to be better, and here Stevenson importunes God—*help us*, *teach us*, *enlighten us*. But what is most striking about his position, and where he departs from the orthodox, is that he makes no assumption that success comes through Christian faith. Rather the struggle is a personal one, and success may reside solely in the intention: "All who have meant good work with their whole hearts, have done good work, although they may die before they have the time to sign it."

It is in the project of the life, what the psychologists would call our behavior, that one finds an alternative to the natural condition of man. And in this project Stevenson upholds behaviors, or values, that were rooted in philosophy and shared by many of his generation. What runs through the prayers with a powerful rhythm and refrain are ideas of *honor* and *courage* and *grace*, of the pleasures of *work* and the glories of the *sun*, of the obligations of *duty* and *loyalty*, of the rewards of *family* and *friendship*. These may seem like simple virtues, or easy pleasures, but they are highlighted and made to shine precisely because they are difficult to achieve, and even harder to sustain. If men were angels, as James Madison once said, we would not have to worry about honor or courage. Yet because men are not angels, as the orthodox would say, we require the intervention of God to see ourselves as we are, and to strengthen our will ("Give us grace and strength to forbear and to persevere").

But Stevenson goes only so far in asking for help. Although he petitions God he is addressing men and women. If life is a battlefield, as he wrote in *The Suicide Club*, then whatever victory is won must come on the ground of the contest. And it is in this arena, the battlefield of life, that Stevenson's prayers prove most powerful. "Sunday," delivered the day before his death, is both a distillate of Stevenson's thought and one of the most poetic passages in his writing: "Be patient still; suffer us yet a while longer." The request for patience is directed to God, on this His day, who must surely have lost patience with his weak and offending children. But after asking for more time, and sufferance, Stevenson in four sentences offers a poignant sketch of human endeavor, of striving, of backsliding, of resolving yet again while knowing that all our resolutions may be futile. And still we go on, thankful for our good fortune, hopeful that we can hold ourselves up in the face of misfortune, eager to take pleasure in the day, and determined to brace ourselves for the night.

There is in this passage, as in all the prayers, a resonant call for courage and endurance that looks back to the classical stoicism of Marcus Aurelius and forward to the lyric existentialism of Ernest Hemingway. If death is our fate, and who knew that better than Stevenson, who lived close to death all his life, then how are we going to live? How will we keep hope alive? Or bring back the joy of splendor in the sky? Perhaps in a house set against the base of Mount Vaea on one side, facing the sea on the other, with work in the morning, friends and family at home and abroad, grateful for the beauties of nature and the inexhaustible gift of imagination.

BIOGRAPHY,
POPULAR CULTURE,
AND PERSONAL RESPONSE

The Squire and the Gamekeeper: RLS and Miss Adelaide Boodle

Olena M. Turnbull

In "A Humble Remonstrance" (1884), Robert Louis Stevenson opposes "the art of narrative" to "the art of fiction" as discussed by Walter Besant and Henry James, and contends that "No art ... can successfully 'compete with life' " ("A Humble Remonstrance" 158). Stevenson's precept that "Life is monstrous, infinite, illogical, abrupt and poignant; a work of art, in comparison, is neat, finite, self-contained, rational, flowing and emasculate" ("A Humble Remonstrance" 160) is well-known. For Stevenson, life is complex, but art is "a simplification of some side or point of life" that stands or falls by its "significant simplicity" ("A Humble Remonstrance" 166). I have previously argued in relation to *Catriona* (1893) that Stevenson is much more sympathetic to women, both in his novels and in real life, than his reputation as the father of "the modern masculine novel" and a writer of "books for boys" would lead one to believe; it now seems appropriate to examine one of his real-life associations with a woman for this *festschrift*. The most obvious relationship that Stevenson had with a woman is that between himself and his wife, Fanny. This essay, however, considers Stevenson's friendship and correspondence with a young woman named Adelaide Boodle and her narrative of life in the Stevenson household at Skerryvore.[1]

J.C. Furnas describes Adelaide as "a young Bournemouth gentlewoman who played the violin and had literary impulses" (Furnas 241).

James Pope Hennessy portrays her and her mother, Julia Boodle, as "two Bournemouth residents who might have been classified as obscure, if not precisely humble" (Hennessy 170), and Ian Bell parenthetically depicts Adelaide as "a local who was more observant than she was wise, and left an account of life at Skerryvore" (Bell 166). Driven from the Continent by the threat of cholera, Stevenson and his wife had moved to rented accommodations in Bournemouth in 1884. They chose to settle there, first, because the climate seemed to suit Stevenson's health and, secondly, because his father, Thomas Stevenson, offered to buy Fanny a house and gave her five hundred pounds sterling towards the cost of furnishing it.

Jenni Calder gives the following account of Adelaide Boodle's first meeting with Stevenson and his wife:

> Adelaide Boodle came to call with her mother, and found Louis perched on a packing case.... She fell in love instantly with both Louis and Fanny. Louis delighted her, Fanny she revered as his dedicated and tender protectress. She came frequently to the house, at first spending most of her time with Fanny, whose "quiet heroism" impressed her greatly [Calder 204].

While hero-worship certainly played a part in Adelaide's relationship with Stevenson and his wife, it did not "blind her to ... realities" (Calder 204). Her memoir entitled *RLS and His Sine Qua Non: Flashlights from Skerryvore* (1926), written many years after the deaths of Louis and Fanny Stevenson, gave an apparently truthful account of what she saw and heard at Skerryvore. On the frontispiece of Adelaide's book, Stevenson's cousin and biographer, Graham Balfour, is cited as stating: "She is one of the very few people who did know Louis and Fanny intimately in their home life, and saw them as they were towards one another, with the warmest affection, but without illusions of any kind." Calder writes that "Fanny and Louis were patient and kind with Adelaide, and Fanny enjoyed having a helper and, in effect, an acolyte" (Calder 205). She explains that "When they left Skerryvore [in 1887], Adelaide was asked to keep a watchful eye on the house and a number of pets who had to be left behind. This task earned her the name of 'gamekeeper,' by which Louis referred to her in subsequent years" (Calder 205). Stevenson frequently signed himself "the Squire" in his correspondence with Adelaide Boodle. She reciprocated by signing herself "the Gamekeeper"—an appellation to which she adhered when she wrote *RLS and His Sine Qua Non*. Her own name appears in brackets underneath.

Hennessy might have classified Adelaide and her mother (a nervous woman who had burst into tears on the doorstep when the Stevensons' maid had not immediately opened the door on the occasion of their first memorable visit to Skerryvore) as "obscure, if not precisely humble," but even now Adelaide is very far from being obscure. If she had never written her memoir about the Stevensons and their life in Bournemouth, she would still be as immortal as any of Stevenson's fictional characters if for no other reason than that she figures in his correspondence.[2] His letters to her record a very human relationship that had its share of ups and downs. Adelaide's letters do not seem to have survived, but her memoir reflects this aspect of her relationship with Louis and Fanny, and more particularly with Stevenson himself.

It was Adelaide's "literary impulses" that had led her to persuade her mother to call on the Stevensons at Skerryvore and, as Furnas tells us, "Her prime purpose was to sit at Louis's feet" (Furnas 242). Adelaide's hope was that Stevenson would agree to teach her how to write. Having asked Fanny whether she should show her "scribblings" to Stevenson, Fanny had offered to help Adelaide because she felt sure that Stevenson would "slash [her work] to ribbons and break [her] heart" (Furnas 242). She knew her husband's "extravagant moods" (Calder 204) much better than Adelaide did. In fact, she was aware that it was not so much any extravagance of temper that Stevenson was apt to display. Instead, it was likely that he would voice a completely honest and brutally direct opinion, especially where a work of literature was concerned. Adelaide therefore became Fanny's pupil, but when Stevenson was approached about teaching a weekly course for young writers at the British Museum, she volunteered to become what Furnas describes as "a sympathetic guinea-pig" (Furnas 243) on whom Stevenson could try out his prospective lectures. Adelaide recounts his reaction to one piece that she had written as follows: "Suddenly there was a low (but crescendo) rumble of thunder: 'Oh, but this work is disgracefully bad! It could hardly be worse. What induced you to bring me stuff like this?'" (*RLS and His Sine Qua Non* 57). According to Adelaide, Fanny sprang to the rescue, and the following excerpt from the book that Adelaide wrote in later life not only depicts that scene, but gives one an idea of what the young Adelaide's writing skills must have been like if this brief extract represents an example of her more mature style:

> All in a moment she reared her glorious head, and from the divan at the far end of the room rang out this scorching denunciation: "Louis! You are a brute! I told you it would kill the child— and it *will*."
> "No, it won't," gasped the (somewhat elderly) child. "I want

him to say just whatever he thinks. I don't mind a bit. I *will* learn to write. *I'm going* to do it or die."

"Of course you are!" he cried triumphantly.

In a moment, all his anger gone, he was on his knees beside me on the hearth-rug, my trembling hand firmly clasped in his own.

"Of *course* you are!"

Then in a tone which, even in memory, still sends a glow to my heart, he went on eagerly:

"And *I'm going* to teach you" [*RLS and His Sine Qua Non* 58–59].

Stevenson did teach Adelaide, although he knew that neither her heart nor her talent lay in the profession of letters, and what he taught her becomes apparent as one studies the written record of her life which was for a time bound up with the lives of the inhabitants of Skerryvore. The Stevensons were kind and tolerant towards Adelaide, who seems to have been a very intense and emotional young woman, somewhat given to histrionics if her prose affords any indication of her character. In a letter to Ida and Una Taylor dated 7 September 1890, Fanny described her as follows: "She always seemed to me to be damping down 'internal fires' (holy fires) and ready at any moment to burst into flames" (Booth and Mehew 5: 385 Note). However, there was a childlike quality in the young woman that appealed to Stevenson and his wife. Adelaide describes how her literary lessons with Fanny were sometimes abruptly cut short when Stevenson "would glide into the room like a stage conspirator, with finger on lips, and beckon me away." Fanny had reportedly smiled and said, "Oh yes! Of course you must go. Louis is tired of being alone. He wants another child to play with him. Run along, both of you!" (*RLS and His Sine Qua Non* 35). It seems likely that Louis and Fanny Stevenson had entered into a pact to humor and amuse their young guest.

Adelaide's "internal fires [which seemed] ready at any moment to burst into flames" were in evidence early on as far as her enthusiasm for writing (and music) was concerned. Later in life, she helped to run a convalescent home for working girls and then became a missionary, so it is clear that the "holy fires" that Fanny Stevenson had noted remained a mainstay of her character. Stevenson seems to have understood and sympathized with the young woman and her need to find a mission or vocation in life, perhaps because he had been subject to more than a few enthusiasms himself before finding his own calling, as he explains in an essay entitled "Crabbed Age and Youth" (1878). He writes:

All my old opinions were only stages on the way to the one I now hold, as itself is only a stage on the way to something else. I am no more abashed at having been a red-hot Socialist with a panacea of my own than at having been a sucking infant. Doubtless the world is quite right in a million ways; but you have to be kicked about a little to convince you of the fact. And in the meanwhile you must do something, be something, believe something.... Even in quite intermediate stages, a dash of enthusiasm is not a thing to be ashamed of ... ["Crabbed Age and Youth" 127–128].

Stevenson recognized that Adelaide's enthusiasms were prompted by her need to "do something, be something, believe something," even if her opinions were only stages "on the way to something else," and his concern for his "gamekeeper" is demonstrated in that he kept up a correspondence with her from the time that he left Bournemouth in 1887 until the end of his life. He sent an annual giftbox to Adelaide, her mother, and her sisters each Christmas via Charles Baxter; he and Fanny invited Adelaide to visit them in Samoa (an offer that she felt obliged to decline); and he was always ready to offer help and advice whenever Adelaide required it. Like his father, Stevenson tended to be chivalrous toward women because he recognized "the falseness of their position in life" ("Talk and Talkers: Second Paper" 107). Adelaide never married perhaps because she also recognized "the falseness of [woman's] position in life" and chose instead to be one of "the noble women who have devoted earnest lives to the intellectual and moral needs of mankind" (Stanton 156–157).

One can glean insights into her character from what she writes, and Stevenson's step-grandson (Adelaide's "adopted grandson"), Austin Strong, provides us with a description of Adelaide in later life that seems in some degree to suggest the Victorian child-woman. However, there are elements of his depiction which jar incongruously with that particular conception of her:

Like most precious things, she is small. She dresses in plain black with white ruching at her neck and wrists. There is nothing much to her bonnet, yet somehow, unconscious to herself, she achieves style; for, as someone has said: "The life of a bonnet is the tilt to it."

Her gait is swift and swallow-like. She never sits, but perches lightly in a chair. Her face is English, strong, aquiline, and beautifully modeled, while her hands are those of a man of action. Put her in small-clothes and a stock, and you'd have Charles Lamb with all his sensitiveness and humour; give her a sword and a cocked hat, and you'd have Lord Nelson to the life [*RLS and His Sine Qua Non* vii–viii].

Strong's odd sketch of Adelaide blends masculine and feminine characteristics in such a way that one is left with the distinct impression
that she was very much a woman to be reckoned with—small, intense,
energetic, strong-willed, motivated, sensitive, and humorous. She was
probably a redoubtable woman, and was perhaps considered eccentric
by her contemporaries. Lady Balfour is said to have described her
thus:

> "If you could tame an angel"—but she is *not* tame. "Her ungovern-
> able charity only matches her rage for righteousness,"—but that
> isn't sincere enough, nor clear, nor simple enough. She is as
> wholesome, as delicate, as disciplined, and yet in all good ways as
> unbridled as a mountain stream. She handles truth like a rapier,
> but she would heal every wound she felt obliged to inflict;—sim-
> ply because she couldn't help it [*RLS And His Sine Qua Non* x].

Certain words and phrases tend to stand out in this description—"*not*
tame," "ungovernable charity," "rage for righteousness," "unbridled,"
"simply because she couldn't help it." The evidence would seem to suggest that Adelaide retained her impulsiveness, her "holy fires," and her
enthusiasms throughout her life.

Having said that Adelaide's relationship with Stevenson had its ups
and downs, a low point in their friendship was reached when Adelaide
declined an invitation to visit the Stevensons in Samoa on the advice of
her local Anglican clergyman. Stevenson immediately wrote to remind
her that "God is no churchman, my dear lady; and no clergyman. The
world is great and rough; he is nearest to that right divinity who can accept
that greatness and that roughness" (Booth and Mehew 7: 73). His letter
continues as follows:

> I am pained that a friend of mine should conceive life so smally
> as to think she leaves the hand of her God, because she leaves a
> certain clique of clergymen and a certain scattered handful of
> stone buildings, some of them with pointed windows, most with
> belfries, and a few with an illumination of the Ten Command-
> ments on the wall [Booth and Mehew 7: 74].

In his letter dated 17 January 1891, Stevenson did not attempt to disguise
his annoyance at Adelaide's decision. However, a few months later he
apologized (after a fashion), owning that he had been very much put out,
that he was sorry he had expressed himself so roughly, and that he had
fallen ill as a result (Booth and Mehew 7: 110). With the same complete

honesty and directness with which he had critiqued her "scribblings," Stevenson ends his letter to her thus:

> I am quite capable as you have seen of exposing my passionate dissent from your opinions—or that which I supposed them; I am incapable from the same sentiment of embarrassing you with any thanks. It is the description of a rather bracing relation, I fear, but a genuine [Booth and Mehew 7: 112].

In declining Louis and Fanny's invitation, Adelaide had retired into what Stevenson refers to as "the fortified camp of the proprieties" ("Talk and Talkers: Second Paper" 107). However, it must be recalled that the standards to which young middle-class women were held in nineteenth-century Britain were suffocating and oppressive as compared with current standards of acceptable civilized behavior between men and women. At that time, women were often treated like children and had few legal rights. They could do little without the permission of their fathers, brothers, husbands, clergymen, or other male relatives or guardians. Victorian double standards permitted the harsh exploitation of working-class women, while those of Adelaide's social class and above were considered to be merely ornamental and completely useless: "fit for nothing but to sit in her drawing-room like a doll–Madonna in her shrine" (Pinney 205). Stevenson himself remarked that:

> The drawing room is, indeed, an artificial place; it is so by our choice and for our sins. The subjection of women; the ideal imposed upon them from the cradle, and worn, like a hair shirt with so much constancy; their motherly superior tenderness to man's vanity and self-importance; their managing arts—the arts of a civilized slave among good-natured barbarians—are all painful ingredients and help to falsify relations. It is not till we get clear of that amusing artificial scene that genuine relations are founded, or ideas honestly compared ["Talk and Talkers: Second Paper" 108].

Adelaide chose to continue her "rather bracing relation" with Stevenson and the following year, on 4 January 1892, he wrote to congratulate her on her new employment as a "schoolteacher." Her pupils were young working girls who, having fallen ill, found themselves in the convalescent home that she was helping to run, and her "school" was located in the cellar of the building. Adelaide's attempt to teach the basics of reading, writing, and arithmetic to these young women was admirable because even if "prospects for the woman who was not going to confine herself to the smooth career of wife and mother were significantly less bleak than at the beginning of the [nineteenth] century" (Cunningham 4), marriage, childbirth, or a life of poorly paid unremitting toil was all that most young working girls had to look forward to.

The letter dated 4 January 1892 constitutes the first of three letters that Stevenson wrote to Adelaide and "the Children in the Cellar," and one wonders whether they were as much intended for the further edification of Stevenson's "pupil" as for the instruction of her students. In that first letter, Stevenson described himself as "a long, lean, elderly man who lives right through on the under side of the world, so that down in your cellar you are nearer to him than the people in the street" (*RLS and His Sine Qua Non* 141). He gave an account of where "the lean man" lived in such a way as to emphasize geographical, physical, and cultural differences. He also described the customs, fears, and superstitions of the people who lived on his island. In the second letter to "the Children in the Cellar," which is dated 14 August 1892, Stevenson reiterated the sentiments which he had expressed fourteen years earlier in his essay "Crabbed Age and Youth" (1878) when he wrote: "Wherever we are it is but a stage on the way to somewhere else, and whatever we do, however well we do it, it is only a preparation to do something else that shall be different" (*RLS and His Sine Qua Non* 151). Perhaps Stevenson already knew that Adelaide would ultimately choose a very different path through life and hoped in some way to help prepare her for it. The final letter, dated 4 September 1892, echoed the first which had described a frightening forest or wood which made the lean man feel "lonely and scared, and he doesn't quite know what he is scared of" (*RLS and His Sine Qua Non* 144):

> The wood has an ill name, and all the people of the island believe it to be full of devils; but even if you do not believe in devils, it is a pretty dreadful place to walk in by the moving light of a lantern, with nothing about you but a curious whirl of shadows and the black night above and beyond [*RLS and His Sine Qua Non* 163].

The forest or wood was obviously a metaphor for the world we live in, much of which might be unknown to us and therefore frightening. However, we are told that Stevenson's protagonists, a black boy named Arick and his own step-grandson, Austin Strong, kept their courage up in spite of their fears.

Barry Menikoff has recently observed that fear and courage are "the most powerful recurrent emotions" in Stevenson's novel *Kidnapped* (1886), which is "marked with incidents of violence as well as danger." Menikoff interprets these elements of Stevenson's tale as highlighting "the central issue of manhood, which is what David must achieve" (Menikoff Introduction xxxi). It is therefore interesting to note that, although the protagonists of Stevenson's letters to "the Children in the Cellar" are male, the letters themselves are initially addressed exclusively to a young female audience. Moreover, Stevenson is completely even-handed in the way he describes the forest "spirits" or "devils" which "are thought the most dangerous," for he writes that they

> come in the shape of beautiful young women and young men, beautifully dressed in the island manner, with fine kilts and fine necklaces and crowns of scarlet seeds and flowers. Woe betide he or she who gets to speak with one of these! They will be charmed out of their wits, and come home again quite silly, and go mad and die [*RLS and His Sine Qua Non* 146–147].

In these letters to Adelaide and "the Children in the Cellar," Stevenson arguably mocks the superstitious fear of the unknown in general and the prurient fear of puberty and sexuality that characterized Victorian society. These letters lend weight to Katherine Linehan's point that Stevenson's "attraction to carefree male fellowship contends throughout his adult life against a principled concern to promote male maturity of vision about the social and psychological realities between the sexes" (Linehan 35). Lloyd Osbourne states that Stevenson "would have written more [letters to "the Children in the Cellar"] but for the fact that his friend left the home, being transferred elsewhere" ("Letters To Young People" 501: Note). However, the letters that Stevenson wrote to Adelaide and her students were collected and published together with seven more that Stevenson wrote for his step-grandson, Austin Strong, so that there are ten of these "Letters to Young People" in all.[3]

Stevenson's fascinated observation of children is apparent in his essay "Child's Play" and in what he writes in "Notes on the Movements of Young Children." He comments: "There is a sincerity, a directness, an impulsive truth about their free gestures that shows throughout all imperfection" ("Notes on the Movements of Young Children" 211). Perceptive and intuitive on the subject of children, he retained enough of the child in himself to relate well towards them. Perhaps the childlike capacity that Louis and Fanny had noted in Adelaide enabled Stevenson to better understand her too. While she may have had her faults, she was clearly imaginative, sincere, and direct. She was also strong-willed and determined enough to eventually leave the comparative safety and security of her family, friends, and the Anglican communion in Bournemouth in order to embrace the "greatness" and the "roughness" of the world as Stevenson had described it [Booth and Mehew 7: 73].

In July 1894, Stevenson wrote to Adelaide. Speaking of her decision to become a missionary,[4] he tellingly comments that it is "where I think your heart always was" (Booth and Mehew 8: 325). He then proceeded to give her some advice based upon what he had learned from his own life experiences:

> Forget wholly and forever all small pruderies, and remember that *you cannot change ancestral feelings of right and wrong, without what is practically soul murder.* Barbarous as the customs may seem, always hear them with patience, always judge them with gentleness, always find in them some seed of good; see that you always develop them; remember that all you can do is to civilize the man in the line of his own civilization, such as it is [*RLS and His Sine Qua Non* 164–165].

As David Daiches has observed, "Anthropologists today recognize the wisdom of [Stevenson's] advice [the gist of which was] ignored by so many nineteenth-century missionaries with unhappy social and cultural consequences" (Daiches 94). Stevenson did not believe in "thaumaturgic conversions." He felt that one had to "teach the parents in the interests of their great-grandchildren" (*RLS and His Sine Qua Non* 165), and perhaps he was right. In spite of theories to the contrary, history has shown that customs, habits, and systems of belief cannot simply be imposed by force because change must occur gradually over a period of time both in the natural world and in terms of human existence. Describing the theory of evolution as "A new doctrine, received with screams a little while ago by canting moralists, and still not properly worked into the body of our thoughts," Stevenson nonetheless seemed to feel that it "lights us a step further into the heart of this rough but noble universe" ("Pulvis et Umbra" 321–322).

Adelaide, like the majority of Victorian men and women, was capable of "small pruderies." In declining Louis and Fanny's invitation to visit them in Samoa, she had bowed to social convention. However, after the death of her mother in 1894, she finally "[got] clear of that amusing artificial scene"—the Victorian drawing room and its stifling conventions—and left the country to follow her vocation. Stephen Arata has argued that for Stevenson any capitulation to the conventional and bourgeois "was to embrace the very blindnesses, evasions, and immoralities delineated in *Jekyll and Hyde*"(1886)—a novel that was written during "Stevenson's three-year 'imprisonment' at Skerryvore" (Arata 44). Upon his father's death in 1887, Stevenson left the British Isles and never returned. He wrote of his own calling that "There are two just reasons for the choice of any way of life: the first is inbred taste in the chooser; the second some high utility in the industry selected" ("The Morality of the Profession of Letters" 73). In terms of utility, Stevenson believed that "like the missionary, the patriot, or the philosopher, we should all choose that poor and brave career in which we can do the most and best for mankind" ("The Morality of the Profession of Letters" 74). Both he and Adelaide Boodle chose careers in which they could do "the most and best for mankind;" she devoted much of her life to missionary work and he devoted his to writing literature.

Stevenson believed that "There is not a life in all the records of the past but, properly studied, might lend a hint and a help to some contemporary" ("The Morality of the Profession of Letters" 79). Art does not 'compete with life' because it competes on its own terms, namely as art. Interesting though it is to read in retrospect, Adelaide Boodle's memoir of life at Skerryvore is not a work of art because Adelaide was not a writer. However, there is a "significant simplicity" in Stevenson's letters to her and "the Children in the Cellar" which not only demonstrates his sympathy for Adelaide and for all women, but which also shows him to have been engaged in a struggle to fathom some of life's complexities in such a way that he "lights us a step further" on the path to human understanding.

NOTES

1. The house that Louis and Fanny Stevenson occupied at Skerryvore, Bournemouth, in England no longer exists because it was completely destroyed by a bomb during the Second World War.

2. See *The Letters of Robert Louis Stevenson* (8 volumes). Edited by Bradford A. Booth and Ernest Mehew (New Haven & London: Yale University Press, 1994 and 1995), particularly Volumes 5–8.

3. The "Letters to Young People" appear, for example, in *Letters and Miscellanies of Robert Louis Stevenson: Sketches, Criticisms, Etc.*, Volume 22 of *The Works of Robert Louis Stevenson* (New York: Charles Scribner's Sons, 1902), pp. 501–527.

4. One can but surmise from Stevenson's reference to Andaman islanders that Adelaide's missionary work took her to those islands situated in the eastern part of the Bay of Bengal and south of the territory that used to be known as Burma (Myanmar).

BIBLIOGRAPHY

Arata, Stephen. *Fictions of Loss in the Victorian Fin De Siecle*. Cambridge: Cambridge University Press, 1996.

Bell, Ian. *Dreams of Exile: Robert Louis Stevenson: A Biography*. New York: Henry Holt and Company, 1992.

Boodle, Adelaide. *RLS and His Sine Qua Non: Flashlights from Skerryvore*. New York: Charles Scribner's Sons, 1926.

Booth, Bradford A. and Ernest Mehew, eds. *The Letters of Robert Louis Stevenson* (8 vols.). New Haven & London: Yale University Press, 1994 and 1995.

Calder, Jenni. *Robert Louis Stevenson: A Life Study*. New York & Toronto: Oxford University Press, 1980.

Cunningham, Gail. *The New Woman and the Victorian Novel*. New York: Harper & Row Publishers, Inc., 1978.

Daiches, David. *Robert Louis Stevenson and His World*. London: Thames & Hudson, 1973.

Furnas, J. C. *Voyage to Windward: The Life of Robert Louis Stevenson*. New York: William Sloane Associates, 1951.

Hennessy, James Pope. *Robert Louis Stevenson*. With an Introduction by Nigel Nicholson. London: Jonathan Cape, 1974.

Linehan, Katherine. "Revaluing Women and Marriage in Robert Louis Stevenson's Short Fiction." *ELT* 40:1 (1997): 34–59.

Menikoff, Barry, ed. *Kidnapped; or the Lad with the Silver Button* by Robert Louis Stevenson. San Merino, California: Huntington Library, 1999.

Pinney, Thomas, ed. *Essays of George Eliot*. London: Routledge & Kegan Paul, 1963.

Stanton, Elizabeth Cady. *Eighty Years and More: Reminiscences, 1815–1897*. Boston: Massachusetts: North Eastern University Press, 1993.

Stevenson, Robert Louis. "A Humble Remonstrance" in *Memories and Portraits/Other Essays and Reminiscences* (The Skerryvore Edition). London: William Heinemann Ltd., 1925.

_____. "Crabbed Age and Youth" in *Essays by Robert Louis Stevenson*. With an Introduction by William Lyon Phelps. New York, Chicago & Boston: Charles Scribner's Sons, 1918.

_____. *Kidnapped; or, the Lad with the Silver Button*. Edited with an Introduction and Notes by Barry Menikoff. San Merino, California: Huntington Library Press, 1999.

_____. "Letters to Young People" in *Letters and Miscellanies of Robert Louis Stevenson: Sketches, Criticisms, Etc.* (*Works*, Volume 22). New York: Charles Scribner's Sons, 1902.

_____. "The Morality of the Profession of Letters" in *Robert Louis Stevenson: Selected Essays*. Edited and With an Introduction by George Scott-Moncrieff. Chicago: Henry Regnery Company, 1959.

_____. "Notes on the Movements of Young Children" in *Memories and Portraits/Other Essays and Reminiscences* (The Skerryvore Edition). London: William Heinemann Ltd., 1925.

_____. "Pulvis et Umbra" in *Essays by Robert Louis Stevenson*. With an Introduction by William Lyon Phelps. New York, Chicago & Boston: Charles Scribner's Sons, 1918.

_____. "Talk and Talkers: Second Paper" in *Memories and Portraits/Other Essays and Reminiscences* (The Skerryvore Edition). London: William Heinemann Ltd., 1925.

Forty-Eight Pages
and Speech Balloons:
Robert Louis Stevenson
in *Classics Illustrated*

William B. Jones, Jr.

From the Sunday morning when the names Jekyll and Hyde first sounded from a pulpit, the works of Robert Louis Stevenson have been at home in popular culture. Stage, film, radio, and television have proved hospitable—if not always solid—ground for much of the author's fiction. During the twentieth century, two related sequential-art forms, comic strips and comic books, introduced generations of youngsters to Stevenson's novels, stories, and poems.

In 1925, colorful entrepreneur Major Malcolm Wheeler-Nicholson produced a daily newspaper adaptation of *Treasure Island*. Ten years later, Wheeler-Nicholson serialized the pirate yarn in his publication, *New Fun*, thus marking Stevenson's comic-book debut.[1] The popular tale, drawn by Harold deLay, began a four-issue run in the *Doc Savage* series in 1940, and another rendition appeared in *Target Comics* in 1941–42. A handsome sixty-four-page version illustrated by Robert Bugg inaugurated Dell's short-lived *Famous Stories* in 1942 and was the first single-issue abridgment of a Stevenson text.

In the meantime, Albert L. Kanter, a Russian Jewish immigrant and New York businessman who loved literature and had once made a living selling sets of works by Jack London and other authors, dreamed of a means of elevating the literary taste of young Americans who subsisted on the superhero fare of Golden Age comic books. In October 1941, employing the same medium but substituting d'Artagnan for Superman, he launched *Classic Comics* with a sixty-four-page adaptation of Alexandre Dumas's *The Three Musketeers*. Like the first number, each successive issue was devoted to a single abridged work, a novel concept at the time, and most titles were reprinted numerous times.

Renamed *Classics Illustrated* in 1947 as part of an effort to enhance the publication's reputation with parents and teachers, the 169-title series featured during the thirty years of its existence comics-style retellings of *Ivanhoe*, *Moby Dick*, *A Tale of Two Cities*, *Les Miserables*, *Don Quixote*, *Huckleberry Finn*, *Hamlet*, *Faust*, and other canonical texts (as well as some decidedly non-canonical works, *e.g.*, *Under Two Flags*, *Bring 'Em Back Alive*, *King–of the Khyber Rifles*, and *The Covered Wagon*). Although the page count dropped from sixty-four to fifty-six to forty-eight, both artwork and adaptations steadily improved, and by the late 1950s *Classics Illustrated* was the most successful juvenile publication of its kind in the world, with editions printed in twenty-six languages in thirty-six countries.

No other comic-book series devoted greater attention to the fiction of Robert Louis Stevenson.[2] Between 1943 and 1954, Kanter's Gilberton Company produced, under the yellow *Classics* banner, seven issues containing eight works by the author: No. 13, *Dr. Jekyll and Mr. Hyde* (first edition, August 1943, eight printings; revised edition, October 1953, nine printings); No. 31, *The Black Arrow* (October 1946, fourteen printings); No. 46, *Kidnapped* (April 1948, sixteen printings); No. 64, *Treasure Island* (October 1949, thirteen printings); No. 82, *The Master of Ballantrae* (April 1951, three printings); No. 94, *David Balfour* (April 1952, three printings); No. 116, *The Bottle Imp* ["The Bottle Imp" and "The Beach of Falesá"] (February 1954, two printings). Only Jules Verne (ten titles), Alexandre Dumas (nine titles), and James Fenimore Cooper (eight titles) were represented more often in *Classics Illustrated*. A revived *Classics Illustrated* series in 1990–91 featured new covers and contemporary interiors of two Stevenson titles: No. 8, *Dr. Jekyll and Mr. Hyde* (April 1990, one printing); and No. 17, *Treasure Island* (January 1991, one printing).

The earliest of the Stevensonian abridgments, *Dr. Jekyll and Mr. Hyde*, has some significance as the first example of what would become a major subliterary genre—horror comics.[3] Despite its pop-culture credentials, however, the 1943 issue was an overstated clunker, with a howler of a script by Evelyn Goodman, an adapter known for her free hand in literary "treatments," and crude drawings by Arnold L. Hicks, an otherwise reliable comics artist who acquitted himself well in *Classic Comics* and

Illustrations by Arnold L. Hicks for *Dr. Jekyll and Mr. Hyde, Classic Comics* No. 13 (New York: Gilberton Co., Inc., August 1943).

Classics Illustrated editions of *Oliver Twist, Michael Strogoff*, and *The Spy.*

Where, in Stevenson's story, the doctor describes the projection of the "evil side of my nature" as "smaller, slighter, and younger than Henry Jekyll," and elsewhere Hyde is said to be "pale and dwarfish," giving "an impression of deformity without any namable malformation,"[4] Hicks's stocky, "unbridled, monster-like" double came equipped with fangs, claws, and olive-green skin, the better to scare you with. Hyde is shown snarling over his shoulder as he makes his way down a dark street or leering at a young woman he attempts to strangle ("Vulture-like fingers smother her cry...").

In a probable act of pop-culture homage, Goodman and Hicks appear to have relied upon the 1931 Fredric March film to flesh out their conceptions of the tale. As in the movie versions, a love interest, Jekyll's fiancée Lorraine, is interpolated. Goodman begins the *Classic Comics* adaptation with a party scene in which a fun-loving, debonair Jekyll, costumed as a matador, improbably exclaims, "To life! To laughter! To a gay evening!" On the next page, our hero explains his new line of inquiry to his friend Dr. Lanyon: "We have two sides to us.... But we can't forget the character we have been all our lives. Suppose ... suppose those two sides could be separated!"

A few pages later, he does the deed and finds himself staring at a startling, animalistic face. "This ugly creature fascinates me!" Jekyll (or Hyde) exclaims. After a series of assaults and murders, Hyde is pursued by the police, who shoot and kill him, only to discover Jekyll's face when they turn the body over. The comic book ends with another example of the unintentional humor that Goodman excelled in providing. Commenting on Jekyll's fate, Dr. Lanyon (who survives his former friend in this rendering) sagely counsels, "[E]vil becomes a habit forming drug. My advice is to stay away from that first taste!" In case the reader missed the point, Hicks helpfully drew a devil's head and pitchfork beneath the speech balloon.

Dr. Jekyll and Mr. Hyde proved problematic for Gilberton as the publisher endeavored to distance itself from the perceived excesses and general disrepute of the comics industry. In 1949, two years after the name of the series had been changed to the more respectable *Classics Illustrated*, Hicks's original *Classic Comics* cover, which depicted a rampaging Hyde scattering panic-stricken Londoners, was suppressed. A somewhat tamer line-drawing cover by Henry C. Kiefer, showing Jekyll in his laboratory conjuring a still-fanged Hyde, was substituted. The truly offensive portion of the issue—the laughable interior—remained unchanged.

During the late 1940s and early 1950s, a widespread anti-comics campaign was underway in the United States. Politicians, psychiatrists, and cultural critics joined forces in the attack on comic books, which were held responsible for promoting juvenile delinquency and all manner of deviancy.[5] Dr. Frederic Wertham fed public fears of comic-book degeneracy in his overheated jeremiad, *Seduction of the Innocent* (1954), and included *Classics Illustrated* in his indictment. In the meantime, as the Gilberton series gained prestige through educational endorsements and an international readership, some of the badly drawn, poorly adapted earlier issues seemed embarrassing anachronisms. Hence, in 1953, managing editor Meyer A. Kaplan, who two years earlier had delivered an eloquent defense of the Gilberton series before the New York Joint Legislative Committee to Study the Publication of Comics, ordered a new adaptation, new interior art, and a new painted cover for *Dr. Jekyll and Mr. Hyde*.

The revised adaptation cast the different narrative voices of the *Strange Case* in the third person and shifted their sequence to allow for linear plot development. Otherwise, the 1953 *Classics Illustrated* edition adhered fairly faithfully to the letter and spirit of Stevenson's story. An anonymous cover artist painted a rather contemplative, fangless Hyde rising from Jekyll's green formula. For the interior, Lou Cameron, an artist with horror-comics credits who later became an award-winning Western writer, emphasized the moral desperation in the physician and his alter ego through dramatic shading and striking angles. Jekyll's park-bench discovery of his involuntary transformation into Hyde is a striking sequence of panels shown from different perspectives.

Decades later, in 1990–91, an attempt was made to revive the *Classics Illustrated* line by First Publishing, a Chicago comics company. A new logo was supplied and new scripts and art were commissioned in an effort to make the series more appealing to a generation of young readers accustomed to the more sophisticated visual style of "graphic novels." *Dr. Jekyll and Mr. Hyde*, No. 8 (April 1990), adapted and illustrated by John K. Snyder III, represented an emphatic break with the Gilberton past. The artist's work owed an obvious debt to German Expressionism in general and, with its menacing buildings and distorted faces, *The Cabinet of Dr. Caligari* in particular. Snyder's treatment of the text was the closest to the original of all *Classics Illustrated* editions.

For the second Stevenson *Classic Comics* title, *The Black Arrow*, scriptwriters Ruth A. Roche and Thomas T. Scott offered a fluid, reasonably faithful adaptation of the author's exercise in Lancastrian-Yorkist "tushery." Much of the dialogue in the 1946 issue was simplified (contrary to later Gilberton editorial practice), and Lord Risingham was reduced to "Sir Risingham," while Catesby became "Gatesby." Still, the abridgment retained some of the novel's ethical ambiguity, especially in the fifty-six-page original edition, which includes the episode of Richard Shelton killing the spy. At the same time, Gilberton's *Black Arrow* never sacrificed its visual energy or comic-book identity.

Arnold L. Hicks showed dramatic improvement in his second Stevensonian effort. He created a strong heroine in his Joanna Sedley and a troubled villain in his Sir Daniel Brackley. Dick Shelton, Bennet Hatch, Sir Oliver Oates, and Lawless are all vividly realized. But the artist missed the point of the character of Richard Crookback, who is given the sturdy jaw and musclebound frame of a 1940s comic-book superhero. Hicks apparently spent a fair amount of time in period research and paid some attention to N.C. Wyeth's paintings for the 1916 Scribner's edition of the book.

Kidnapped appeared in the *Classics Illustrated* series in 1948, one year after it had been serialized in a weekly newspaper format. The length was reduced from sixty-four to forty-eight pages, but the further abridgment mattered little to the young readers who made it the second-most-popular Stevenson title in the series. Robert Hayward Webb, who specialized in drawing rugged seafaring tales for Gilberton (*Two Years Before the Mast, The Dark Frigate*), obviously enjoyed swashing buckles with Alan Breck Stewart in the siege of the Round-House — no other Stevenson adaptation was rendered with such *brio*. He also caught something of the dark, mythic overtones in the first sections of the story, producing a memorable sequence of panels tracing David Balfour's ascent of the unfinished tower in the House of Shaws. The only disappointing aspect of the issue was John O'Rourke's script, which, though faithful to the novel's dialogue, muted an entire layer of meaning in its abandonment of the first-person narrative voice.

Webb's heroic rendering of Alan Breck was somewhat off the mark. He was not helped by the anonymous colorist who turned the Jacobite's blue coat into one of Hanoverian red. But the artist himself was responsible for drawing the compact "wild Hielandman" as if a composite 1940s matinee idol had sat for the portrait. Nowhere is there a hint of Alan Breck's "smallish" stature or the face that was "sunburnt very dark, heavily-freckled, and pitted with the small-pox."[6]

Eight years after Albert Kanter began publishing his *Classics*, the most popular work by Stevenson had yet to appear in the series. In 1949, however, Walt Disney was soon to release a film version of *Treasure Island*, and Gilberton issued an adaptation, taking advantage of the timing and the recent expiration of copyright. The assignment was handed to future art director Alex A. Blum, an award-winning etcher whose fine linework was not ideally suited to the robust boyhood favorite. It is likely that Robert Hayward Webb would have infused the adventure tale with greater swagger, but Blum's interpretation held its own through thirteen printings and achieved a kind of iconic status with young readers.

The artist's Long John Silver is a leaner model of the buccaneer than N.C. Wyeth's or Norman Price's familiar depictions, to say nothing of Wallace Beery's or Robert Newton's cinematic impersonations. Stevenson described the sea cook as "very tall and strong, with a face as big as a ham—plain and pale, but intelligent and smiling."[7] Blum's Long John may be tall, strong, intelligent, and smiling, but he has the lean and hungry look of a feral Cassius. Even so, the artist captured a measure of the character's ambivalent charm.

Jim Hawkins, sporting a page-boy bob in the *Classics Illustrated* version, looks like a startled Vassar undergraduate, *circa* 1925. The artist may have had at hand stills from the 1920 Maurice Tourneur film, in which actress Shirley Mason appeared as the boy hero. The waistcoat, blouse, and knee breeches in which the artist outfitted Jim from start to finish in the comic book resemble the costume Mason wore in the silent movie.[8]

Blum had better success with secondary characters. The artist effectively conveyed the hollow bluster of Billy Bones, the embittered malice of Blind Pew, and the dull-witted menace of Israel Hands. Squire Trelawney is sufficiently stout and obtuse, and Captain Smollett appears abrasively forthright and resolute. The best of the lot, perhaps, is Ben Gunn. Avoiding the common pitfall of turning the marooned seaman into a cartoon version of Robinson Crusoe, Blum drew a wiry man with haunted eyes—a figure resembling someone who might have spent three years alone, dreaming of toasted cheese.

Throughout the comic book, Blum makes creative use of panel shapes to enhance visual interest and to speed the action along. Many of the crucial episodes are dramatically potent: Black Dog's cutlass battle with Billy Bones; the pirates' search of the Admiral Benbow Inn; Silver's parley with Captain Smollett; Jim's shipboard showdown with Israel Hands, and the treasure hunt itself. Other scenes, however, such as Jim hiding in the apple barrel (never shown from his perspective) or the mutineers storming the stockade (weakly derivative of Wyeth), are disappointingly unimaginative in composition or point of view.

A January 1991 First Publishing revision of *Treasure Island* by artist and adapter Pat Boyette was packed with a rough vigor. Textually faithful to the original, the book exhibited, however, a certain pictorial indifference to period details, such as the appearance of Captain Smollett, whose facial hair seemed to have sprouted in the wrong century. Jim Hawkins was rather stocky, but Boyette's Long John Silver was a decided improvement on Blum's model.

In the 1951 adaptation of *The Master of Ballantrae*, Lawrence Dresser, an artist primarily known for his work in juvenile books, based some of his panels on William Hole's illustrations. The title-page splash of the brothers' duel by candlelight and the depiction of Mackellar's unsuccessful attempt to boot the Master overboard are instantly recognizable visual allusions—or, as comics artists more honestly put it, "steals."

Without adhering strictly to the Stevensonian letter, scriptwriter Kenneth W. Fitch distilled the murky moral atmosphere of Stevenson's tale of fratricidal hatred, while the contrasts between Dresser's light linework and heavy shading underscored the thematic point. As much illustrated text as comic book, the Gilberton abridgment of *The Master of Ballantrae* provided more than a hint of the complex psychological dimensions of the principal characters—the manipulative charm of James, the thwarted decency of Henry. All in all, it was a notable achievement, marred only by Fitch's insertion of a spoken line ("Hello, Mackellar") delivered by the revived James.

The next year, *Catriona*, the sequel to *Kidnapped*, was added to the *Classics Illustrated* list under the American title *David Balfour*. In some ways, the issue is visually the most interesting of Gilberton's Stevensonian adaptations, thanks to artist Rudolph Palais, an eccentric stylist whose figures were either springing into action or suffering agonies of suspense, with muscles tensed, knuckles tightened, and sweat pouring. At his best, the artist, who had designed movie posters for Warner Brothers and Columbia Pictures before entering the comics field, brought a cinematic sensibility to the expressionistic panels he drew.

In *David Balfour*, Palais skillfully exploited the comic-book panel's adaptability, deploying variously shaped frames and occasionally pushing characters outside them to achieve the desired effect. David's encounters with the fortune-telling "weird old wife" and the cynical representatives of the Scottish judicial system are given an ominous edge through the constant relocation of the viewer's position and the prominence accorded the figures' hands, a recurring motif elsewhere in the artist's work, notably in his illustrations for the Gilberton abridgment of *Crime and Punishment* (1951).

As was the case with *Kidnapped*, the scriptwriter (most likely Fitch) opted for third-person narrative links, some of them of telegraphic brevity ("A little later..."; "Suddenly..."; "Soon..."), which had the effect of entirely removing David's often-wry commentary from the adaptation. The principal characters—David, Catriona, Prestongrange, Alan Breck, and James More—are well delineated. On the other hand, Barbara Grant was a missed opportunity for both adapter and artist; she appears to serve merely expository functions.

After supplying illustrations for the revised *Dr. Jekyll and Mr. Hyde*, Lou Cameron tackled a pair of Stevenson's South Seas tales, "The Bottle Imp" and "The Beach of Falesá," issued together in 1954 under the title *The Bottle Imp*. Instead of inking his drawings, the artist experimented with a Wolff carbon pencil, a technique that resulted in impressively textured panels and splashes, particularly in "Falesá," with its full-page illustrations of Wiltshire knocking Case to the ground and flattening himself during the explosion.

The treatment of "The Bottle Imp" by adapter Richard E. Davis retained a good bit of the charm of the original, though Keawe, as drawn by Cameron, looked more European than Hawaiian. (Actually, he looked more like a typical Cameron hero than anything else—the artist tended to give characters as different as Edmond Dantes, Davy Crockett, and the Time Traveller the same broad smile and masculine features.)

Harry Miller's script of "The Beach of Falesá" softened the sexual and racial themes to some degree and dispensed altogether with the distinctive first-person voice of the narrator, Wiltshire, and thus much of the author's carefully crafted irony. However, the bogus marriage was treated in a matter-of-fact manner ("Black Jack here will perform the ceremony"), and colonial and sexual exploitation blend in Case's leering admonition to Uma, "I hope you will tend to his wants as is befittin' the wife of a white trader." Case's line, and the leering smile Cameron supplied, conveyed to the perceptive young reader the gist of the contents of the certificate he hands to Uma in the panel.

Forceful arguments have been advanced concerning the corruption or vulgarization of literary texts through the inherent reductionism of comic books. Bart Beaty, in a perceptive analysis of the cultural context in which *Classics Illustrated* thrived, notes that in the mid–20th century an intellectual elite, in its efforts to promote a modernist sensibility, insisted on an approved way to read literary texts.[9] Poet and critic Delmore Schwartz, among others, disparaged "middlebrow" attempts to popularize canonical authors.

Classics Illustrated was a particular target of the mandarins, who viewed it as a vehicle for diluting the proper response to Shakespeare, Hawthorne, and Dostoevsky. But comic-book adaptations of literature, like motion-picture versions, are part of the popular reception of works of art. They affect the public response and become cultural artifacts in their own right.

The fact remains that many readers from 1941 to 1971 first had their interest sparked in the works of Robert Louis Stevenson and other authors through their early encounters with *Classics Illustrated*. Many continued to return to those writers throughout adolescence and as adults, having taken to heart the injunction that appeared at the end of most issues: "Now that you have read the *Classics Illustrated* edition, don't miss the added enjoyment of reading the original, obtainable at your school or public library."

This article is adapted in part from the author's Classics Illustrated: A Cultural History *(Jefferson, N.C.: McFarland & Co., Inc., Publishers, 2002). A substantially shorter version of it first appeared in* Robert Louis Stevenson: 150th Anniversary Book, *ed. Karen Steele (Edinburgh: RLS Club, 2001), and is reprinted in expanded form with permission.*

NOTES

1. Ron Goulart, *Ron Goulart's Great History of Comic Books* (Chicago: Contemporary Books, 1986), pp. 56, 58.

2. Marvel, in the 1970s, came closest with three titles by the author: *Dr. Jekyll and Mr. Hyde*; *Treasure Island*; *Kidnapped* (*Marvel Classics Comics* Nos. 1, 15, 26).

3. Mike Benton, *Horror Comics: The Illustrated History* (Dallas: Taylor Publishing Company, 1991), p. 10.

4. Robert Louis Stevenson, "The Strange Case of Dr Jekyll and Mr Hyde" in *Dr Jekyll and Mr Hyde and Other Stories*, ed. Jenni Calder (Harmondsworth: Penguin Books, 1979), pp. 84, 40.

5. See, for background, Amy Kiste Nyberg, *Seal of Approval: The History of the Comics Code* (Jackson: University Press of Mississippi, 1998).

6. Robert Louis Stevenson, *Kidnapped; or, The Lad with the Silver Button: The Original Text*, ed. Barry Menikoff (San Marino, Calif.: Huntington Library Press, 1999), p. 73.

7. Robert Louis Stevenson, *Treasure Island* (New York: Charles Scribner's Sons, 1911), p. 60.

8. See, for a discussion of the Tourneur film and a photograph of Mason as Hawkins, Scott Allen Nollen, *Robert Louis Stevenson: Life, Literature and the Silver Screen* (Jefferson, N.C.: McFarland & Company, Inc., Publishers, 1994), pp. 93–94, 96.

9. Bart Beaty, "Featuring Stories by the World's Greatest Authors: *Classics Illustrated* and the 'Middlebrow Problem' in the Postwar Era," *International Journal of Comic Art*, 1:1 (Spring/Summer 1999), 122–139.

Discovering Mr. Stevenson: A Personal Chronicle

Karen Steele

The question asked by anyone when I tell them who I have studied for the past ten years is, "Why Robert Louis Stevenson?" My answer can only be, "How long have you got?" As a non-academic, I cannot delve into the depths of his writing with alacrity; the intense analysis needed to do so is a learned process, and my own conclusions have a much more subjective approach. I came upon RLS in an accidental and very personal manner and began to know him as a person when there was a gateway in my life for serious changes, before I ever began to read his writings.

The time was February 1991, and I was starting a six-month trip around the islands of the South Pacific. In the preceding months I had read all kinds of literature about the area, factual and fictional, trying to impose a pattern on my journey. On the plane, I opened a package a friend had given me at the airport. It was a book, a book that would at first divert and delight me and finally redirect my life. It was *In the South Seas* by Robert Louis Stevenson.

The author meant little to me; I think I recalled that he wrote *Treasure Island* but was not even aware that one of my favorite childhood books, *A Child's Garden of Verses*, was from his pen. I had a long flight ahead of me, so I settled in and started reading. Stevenson says, at the beginning of *In the South Seas*, that his intention was "to communicate to fireside travelers some sense of its [the South Seas'] seduction." I was one step ahead of the armchair; I was being carried mile upon mile towards his journey, and as the flight progressed and I read eagerly, it was long before my destination that I was inspired to follow directly in his foot-steps. I had found a purpose to my own journey. The ten-hour flight to Los Angeles passed easily. I made notes as I read, highlighting particular places in the book, listing names of islands in my notepad. From California my first stop was to be Tahiti, where I spent several weeks acclimatizing and making plans.

Following in the footsteps of a famous person is a journey, almost a pilgrimage, undertaken by many people, but to follow someone you know nothing about is possibly a rarer event. For five months I moved amongst the magical islands, experiencing those first moments that can never be repeated. I traveled by cargo boats and small planes, visiting islands from the Marquesas to Makin in the old Gilbert Islands, Makin the island where dead souls congregate; encompassing as many of the pages of *In the South Seas* as was possible; sifting down at each stopover to the smallest detail described, bays and trees, houses and people, lifestyle and environment, finding little caches of resemblance that gave evidence of Stevenson's footsteps. Although not written about in the book, I discovered on my journey that Samoa had been his final home, and it was here that I ended my voyaging. By this time my curiosity was bursting at the seams; the time had come for me to learn some facts about the man I had so faithfully followed for so long.

I was delighted to discover that the library in Apia, the small capital town of Samoa, had a well-stocked room of South Pacific literature and shelves of volumes about Robert Louis Stevenson. The room itself was air-conditioned, but I was not allowed to sit and read, so day in and day out I sat with the perspiration running down my back, the weak ceiling fan doing little but help it on its way, my hair clinging to my face and neck and my lava becoming a limp rag. For obvious reasons I worked backwards, starting with his life in Samoa, and as I read his Vailima letters I warmed to a living person; I laughed at the ordeals he and Fanny went through whilst starting their little estate, admired their determination, but still knew little of his past ill health and ultimate death. It was time for a biography, and the first one I read was by James Pope Hennessy, a gentle guide for a first-timer. And then I found J.C. Furnas's extraordinary *Voyage to Windward*.

It was very easy to get drawn into the romantic life Stevenson lived, which by chance of ill health was perhaps thrust upon him, and for a while this held precedence for me over his writing. Now, that will no doubt sound a little strange to serious students, but, dreamer that I am, those early discoveries in the romantic surroundings of Samoa made me feel that way. Make no mistake, I was to become a serious student. But I was excited and full of anticipation concerning everything I had yet to learn about

Robert Louis Stevenson—not only his life but his writing, which I was amazed to discover was so varied and prolific.

A question I later asked myself was whether his life would have attracted attention if he had never written a word? I doubt it. He would have been anonymous amongst the many other adventure seekers of the 19th century. I for one would never have discovered him had it not been for *In the South Seas*. Therefore, this helps answer the question of what came first: the man or his work? Each is unconditionally linked; one cannot be viewed without the other.

After spending a month in Samoa reading, going to Vailima (a permit from the government had to be applied for then), and climbing Mount Vaea to visit the tomb, I returned home to England feeling isolated. Strangely, I did not share my delight in my newfound knowledge with anyone. I had yet to come to terms with an interest that exceeded any I had ever had before, thinking I had discovered something unique. I could not know that there were many others who felt the way I did. Indeed, it took me six months to discover the whereabouts of the Robert Louis Stevenson Club, in Edinburgh. The following year I went to California, to Monterey and Silverado, where I began to meet with people who had the same affinity with RLS. All this could not have happened at a more opportune time. The centenary of Stevenson's death, 1994, began to loom on the horizon, and I was able to involve myself with events that would occur in Edinburgh.

Wherever I went, the name of Stevenson prompted immediate friendships, a kinship almost. Stevensonians are many and varied, scattered across the globe in countries far and wide, from the USA to Australia, from Edinburgh to France and beyond. They seem to come in two completely different camps. One consists of people who can and will happily talk endlessly about their favorite subject, discussing opinions, anecdotes and knowledge; amicably fighting over a discovered old edition on a secondhand bookshop shelf that both have coveted; exchanging duplicated copy of interest to the other; encompassing the generosity and pleasure of sharing that was such an integral part of Stevenson's character. Above all, they are never backward in acknowledging that differences in judgment of any of Stevenson's life or writing is open to discussion.

The second group are fiercely protective of their own knowledge and the unique relationship they believe they have with RLS. They put him on a pedestal and hug him to themselves, hoping beyond hope that they know something nobody else knows, whilst questioning you closely in an endeavor to find out if you know something they do not. If this be the case, the fact will be assimilated and stored at the same time as they pronounce, "I knew that." What they know is the truth, and nothing is open for discussion. It is as if RLS has appeared to them personally, and they have been designated a chosen one and therefore a person apart.

So what is it that draws people from all lands and all languages to be devotees of Robert Louis Stevenson? Japan, Italy, France, and the United States are just some of the countries where he is held in high regard. France is understandable; RLS was a francophile, spoke the language fluently, and spent a great deal of time there. He met his American wife in France, and they then made their mark in the United States. Of the many places they stayed in America, never longer than months in any one spot, plaques have been mounted, museums have sprung up, societies have been founded, a devoted following has been launched. The majority of his memorabilia and manuscripts are found in university libraries in the United States.

The saddest aspect to be contemplated regarding Stevenson's popularity is England, my own native country. Vastly underrated, little known, and even less cared about, he holds small standing there. In Bournemouth, where he and Fanny lived for three years and where he wrote *Dr. Jekyll and Mr. Hyde*, only a small plaque set in a small public garden marks the spot where Skerryvore stood, the house unfortunately having been destroyed by a stray bomb in World War Two. In the memories of the people of Bournemouth it also erased RLS. As to remembering his stay, when I inquired about the town's plans for a 1994 commemorative event, the powers that be saw no reason to do anything.

The study of RLS's life before his works was a fascination I had little control over. I love to travel, and here I had in my hand an excuse to take me to places I might otherwise never have visited. It is often said that the best way to explore a town or a region is in the company of somebody who lives there; they take you to places a stranger would not find. Thus RLS became my companion, leading me through his life and writing, spinning the tales off the page in what was his own eloquence, fanciful or factual: from the fairyland of Tautira to the wars of Samoa; to unfamiliar haunts of Scotland and other parts of the globe that are now part of my vocabulary. "It is this sense of kinship that the traveler must rouse and share," wrote Stevenson (the quote is slightly out of context but nevertheless true).

Nearest to home was Edinburgh, a city that meant nothing to me before, where I had the good fortune of making a friend, Jean Leslie, whose grandfather was RLS's cousin David. She has shown me every nook and cranny where he may have walked, including the little wooded hill behind the beach in North Berwick where as a young boy he sampled his first cigarette, a mistake as we all know, for he became an inveterate smoker for the rest of his life.

One delightful story I have to tell here. When I visited the cottage in Braemar where *Treasure Island* was conceived as an amusement for Stevenson's stepson Lloyd Osbourne, I chatted for a while in the garden with the young woman who lived there and her five-year-old son. When it was time to say goodbye, she moved towards the door and called, "Come on in now, Lloyd." I stopped in my tracks, turned, and asked how long they had lived in the cottage, thinking perhaps the child had been born there and that she had given him the associated name. "Two years," was her reply, "and we didn't know about the Stevenson family until we moved in."

Once I could visualize as many places as possible that could be the backdrop to where and possibly why he wrote what he did, it was time to start exploring his works. I hoped I had reached an understanding of his frame of mind, health and happiness in each residential locale, both before and after he was married, and with this in my mind I approached my now-growing collection of books. I found the Tusitala edition initially the best, they were small enough to slip into my pocket or bag and take anywhere. The *Letters*, edited by Ernest Mehew, have been unlimited nourishment for my own endeavors to reach between the lines of the day-to-day living man, writer, lover, husband, father, and friend in sickness and in health.

Can we read his works at random? Pick up a poem, choose a novel or a short story, peruse his essays, read the letters. Well, of course we can. But with the reading come questions. Where did his ideas or inspiration come from? We know that Dickens's tales reflect the society of his day, his abhorrence of the state of the poor, his wish to right wrongs. All these are apparent in his stories, we don't have to know about his own life to discover this. You need to know nothing of the life of Jane Austen; her novels reflect the world she observed. Thomas Hardy writes romances set in the environment in which he lived; Scott reveals nothing of himself. Their books do not make demands on you to explore the author's life. Yet those of RLS are so varied; they encompass so many different periods of time set in numerous landscapes, and all of them reveal little aspects of his personality. His life and his work are so intertwined that, unlike with other writers, it becomes a compulsion to link the two together. RLS himself said in the dedication of *Travels with a Donkey* that "Every book is, in an intimate sense, a circular letter to the friends of him who writes it."

His essays pass from frivolous umbrellas to the meaning of marriage but they leave you wondering what motivated the subject. Without connecting with the time of writing it is difficult to recognize, for example, the earnestness with which he wrote about love and marriage during his own personal process of discovering these states.

Stevenson seems to have written many of his shorter poems as I remember doing as a teenager, albeit with much less craft. Every important moment in my life had to carry a verse. Some of his verses are like bursts of song, whether to lighten the tone a letter or to express his feelings on somebody's birthday. The thrumming of tropical rain on an iron roof makes him pick up his pen and write to its tune; the sight of someone dear to him glimpsed through the window, working in the garden; memories that intrude perhaps on a day's work and inspire a moment set aside to put them into verse. From the light verses to the *Child's Garden of Verses*, written in his thirties, and the ballads *Ticonderoga* or *The Song of Rahero* stretches an immense contrast. It is always clear to me when his poems leave the impromptu and take on a deeper thought inspired by environments or memories.

So where do we begin? Do we learn about his life or read his words? That is down to chance for each individual. The approach to becoming an RLS devotee is a two-forked path. For me it was via his life, and after ten years of speaking to different Stevensonians, I realize I may be in the minority. His life is a tale in itself from his familiarly rebellious student days through romance, adventure, travel, friends, good times and bad— and yet a life like anyone who is striving to make the best of the time given to him. To work at his chosen profession, to love and be responsible for his family, to enjoy his friends, and at the same time wanting to squeeze every beauteous moment out of each precious day he had.

Many profess that it all started in their youth with *Treasure Island* and *Kidnapped*. In retrospect, we probably all read them, but did we really go on to seek out his other works at that time? Or is the memory of a later date, when by some chance he crossed our paths again, really the starting point. Had my teacher explained that the author of *Travels with a Donkey* was walking to cure himself of a broken heart at the loss of a lover, would I not have leaned more sympathetically towards my examination studies? But then she probably did not know that herself, and I would perhaps have started too early on my quest.

As mentioned earlier in this passage, I began at the end and worked backwards. Samoa came foremost in my heart. I loved the island and its people and returned to it on five occasions for long stays so it seemed natural to me to go on this course. It was therefore very fitting that on my homeward-bound journey from the first visit to Samoa I bought, in a second-hand book shop in Auckland, my first RLS book. It was, of course, the *Vailima Letters*, mine to study at my leisure. These were followed by more biographies, and incidental biographies such as *Stevenson in Samoa*, until in my own mind I had firmly fixed as many facts as it could contain for a while. It was time to be entertained, time to read the words from the man himself.

"It bored me hellishly to write *The [Amateur] Emigrant*; well it's going to bore others to read it, that's only fair," wrote RLS to Colvin. Well, sorry to disappoint him, but I enjoyed it immensely and followed it swiftly with *The Silverado Squatters*. His piercing and humorous observation of people in general captured me and his willingness to turn this on himself at times with pure honesty made me giggle. It is perhaps significant to note here that my reading directed itself in the first place to those writings that reported his own experiences, they seemed of a necessity to fill out the facts I had been so busy imbibing.

I do not believe in the "barley sugar effigy," which still exists in certain quarters; his fight against his ill-health seems to be an excuse to exclude him from the frailties of behaving in a human fashion whether in youth or older. The censoring by friends and family after his death lingers on. I believe his student days were those of any student of any age, rebellious, adventurous, and full of drunken maudlin; the years brought maturity because of his escapades, and so to ignore them is to ignore the growth of a person and his writing. Confines of bed we can sometimes forget when faced with his exuberance between times. For such a mentally and physically energetic person to be literally bound down to restrain him from writing, or to be too weak to talk must have contributed to his need in healthy times to have fun, sometimes in excess, with his friends, and also to his moods, his flares of temper or irrational shortness of tolerance that are often criticized.

"For I always feel sure that you can read between the lines with me, and see the whole struggle of motives and considerations that has moved me to say anything." These words written to Fanny Sitwell, when he was twenty-three, encouraged me to try and do likewise, whether in his letters, travel books, essays, and poetry before I moved on to the novels and short stories. If allowed the privilege, RLS builds a personal relationship with his readers, which leads you on to another book and another. He is a universal writer who has something to say to everyone. This is no accident, despite the fact that he wrote to Edmund Gosse: "I know that good work sometimes hits; but with my hand on my heart, I think it is by accident." He did not write words "a little loosely executed," as he also professed the public liked; he set high standards for himself which in his own opinion were not always reached. But the striving and the intention reaches out and knocks on the doors of the readers' hearts, to misquote from *A Retrospect*.

I can read his short stories again and again, their intensity never spoiled by knowing the outcome. These I will recommend eagerly to somebody wanting to read Stevenson for the first time. The novels are the last suggestion, for the pen with which they are written needs to be a familiar one. I find they cannot be read lightly and I have to hear them aloud in my head so that the nuances and colors come to life and the characters speak with their own voices. I am quite sure that many people will disagree with me on this, but as I have stressed from the beginning, this is my own personal response to all things Stevenson. Occasionally, I find parts of them hard work, but then suddenly, as if he knows your mood, a paragraph, a character will leap out at you and pull you back into the tale.

He peoples his work with personalities observed from life, and it is intriguing to sidetrack and research a particular person who has inspired or amused him enough to use in one of his tales—or to read the letters sent at the time of composing a particular work revealing some of his thought processes during the writing of a story. Research alone can take you into realms of his life that could easily be passed by; to the finding of a map to place visually his scenery; or a photograph to bear in mind the image of a person to whom to he is writing. His life is littered with faces and brief relationships we know little or nothing about: the nuns that so impressed him aboard the boat to Molokai; Tin Jack on the *Janet Nicholl*, Captain Otis and his seafaring; Ori of Tautira. These are characters that could tempt any writer to weave a tale around.

I would like to say at this point that, since "discovering" RLS, I have applied myself to the writing I had always dreamed of doing. His advice and example is inspirational, and I have had several pieces published about my travels; a beginning only I hope for other work in progress, as it was for him. I am now also a creative-writing teacher, and I frequently quote to my students from his essays and letters or read a description of a character from a story they do not know to get their imaginations fired to fitting it into a tale of their own.

One of the problems of traveling afar is absence from friends and the desire to share one's experiences with them. RLS craved the company of his friends when away from them, and his only contact being by letter he would often write spontaneously in an informal manner and dependent on his mood, releasing his problems on the page. With no interaction of conversation, what else does one write about but what's happening in one's life at the moment?

This self-disclosure, I read, became reason enough for criticism, especially after his death. G.K. Chesterton talks of the critics' attitude towards his letters, for example, as a "thin stream of selfish soliloquy devoid of feeling for anybody but himself." My enjoyment of all of his letters has to argue against this viewpoint. What does anyone write letters for when absent from the society of friends? They are the lifeline of chat taking the place of a much-needed conversation with someone you trust over a glass or two of wine. He was not out to impress; his letters were a commentary on his life and state of mind. He said at one time that the trouble with writing a letter is that the mood it was written in has dissipated by the time the answer arrives. How familiar that is when one's mood point can change overnight, and you yourself wonder what the worry was all about. Digging into a person's life can have connotations of intrusion. The adage of today is that we want to know too much about public persons' private lives; but when a man of letters reveals himself in and between the lines of so much of his work, the bait is laid and the temptation is to follow it up.

How many times can his life be told, his biography varied, except in the light of occasional new information and different viewpoints of the biographer? It can become monotonous, chapter after predictable chapter; therefore it becomes necessary to relate his writing to the hard work and dedication he put into his creativity because of the life he led, rather than the life itself being the inspiration.

How deeply his family and friends must have grieved his passing; but those familiar in the present time with his literature know only too well that he can still perhaps be mourned in the knowledge that by his early death he had not reached the top of the ladder on his way to even greater achievements, a fact he knew himself when he believed *Weir of Hermiston* would be his greatest yet, his masterpiece.

I am asked sometimes who I am going to study next, and I watch a bewildered face as I reply that the study of RLS is a lifetime's job for me. There is always something new revealed that I have not examined before, and this leads to others, making the search an endless one. I am happy to have fortuitously fallen into his path "life first," but equally happy for the fact that this was not sufficient. I have a long way to go within his books. Above all, for as long as I continue to meet new people and make new friends on uttering the password "Stevenson," I cannot see that my enjoyment of this particular man and his work will end in the near future.

Index